THE
FIGHT
of
FAITH

THE
FIGHT
of
FAITH

Studies in the Pastoral Letters of Paul
I AND II TIMOTHY AND TITUS

RAY C. STEDMAN

DISCOVERY HOUSE
PUBLISHERS®

Feeding the Soul with the Word of God

The Fight of Faith

© 2009 by Elaine Stedman

All rights reserved.

Discovery House Publishers is affiliated with RBC Ministries,
Grand Rapids, Michigan.

Discovery House books are distributed to the trade exclusively by
Barbour Publishing, Inc., Uhrichsville, Ohio.

Requests for permission to quote from this book should be directed to:
Permissions Department, Discovery House Publishers, P.O. Box 3566,
Grand Rapids, MI 49501.

All Scripture quotations, unless otherwise indicated, are taken from the
Holy Bible: New International Version®. *NIV*®. Copyright © 1973, 1978, 1984 by
International Bible Society. Used by permission of Zondervan.
All rights reserved.

Interior design by Sherri L. Hoffman

Library of Congress Cataloging-in-Publication Data
Stedman, Ray C.
    The fight of faith : studies in the pastoral letters of Paul
(1 and 2 Timothy and Titus) / Ray C. Stedman.
        p.   cm.
    Includes bibliographical references.
    ISBN 978-1-57293-266-1
    1. Bible. N.T. Pastoral Epistles—Sermons.   I. Title.
BS2735.54.S74 2009
227'.83077—dc22   2009045388

Printed in the United States of America

09 10 11 12 / / 10 9 8 7 6 5 4 3 2 1

Contents

PART III
Fighting Falsehood with Truth—*Titus*

Publisher's Preface

Ray Stedman (1917–1992) served as pastor of the Peninsula Bible Church from 1950 to 1990, where he was known and loved as a man of outstanding Bible knowledge, Christian integrity, and humility. Born in Temvik, North Dakota, Ray grew up on the rugged landscape of Montana. When he was a small child, his mother became ill and his father, a railroad man, abandoned the family. Ray grew up on his aunt's Montana farm from the time he was six. He came to know the Lord at age ten.

As a young man he lived in Chicago, Denver, Hawaii, and elsewhere. He enlisted in the Navy during World War II and often led Bible studies for civilians and Navy personnel. He sometimes preached on the radio in Hawaii. At the close of the war, Ray was married in Honolulu. (He and his wife, Elaine, had first met in Great Falls, Montana.) They returned to the mainland in 1946, and Ray graduated from Dallas Theological Seminary in 1950. After two summers interning with Dr. J. Vernon McGee, Ray traveled for several months with Dr. H. A. Ironside, pastor of Moody Church in Chicago.

In 1950, Ray was called by the two-year-old Peninsula Bible Fellowship in Palo Alto, California, to serve as its first pastor. Peninsula Bible Fellowship became Peninsula Bible Church, and Ray served for forty years, retiring on April 30, 1990. During those years, Ray Stedman authored a number of life-changing Christian books, including the classic work on the meaning and mission of the church, *Body Life*. He went into the presence of his Lord on October 7, 1992.

This book contains Ray Stedman's insightful studies in Paul's three pastoral epistles, 1 and 2 Timothy and Titus. These studies have never before been published in book form. This important work was edited from several sermon series and individual sermons that Ray Stedman preached from the 1960s through the 1980s. Over the years, his views on some aspects of these letters changed. This book reflects the most complete and definitive form of Stedman's insights into the three Pastoral Epistles.

In these pages you will come to know the apostle Paul in a new and more intimate way as you explore his letters to Timothy and Titus. Pastor Stedman leads you on a grand tour of Paul's Christian experience, from his dramatic conversion on the Damascus Road to his execution on the Ostian Way, outside of Rome. The great apostle's life, intellect, and unconquerable spirit will come alive in your mind as never before.

These letters are the most intimate and personal of all of Paul's letters, yet they also contain some of the most profound theological insights to be found in Scripture. In these letters, Paul flings back the curtain of time and space to reveal the unseen realities of God's eternal plan for the human race. We believe that as you explore the truths of these three letters of Paul, you'll discover new depths of appreciation for God's Word—and new encouragement and inspiration for your daily walk with Christ.

—Discovery House Publishers

Part I

Fight the Good Fight

1 Timothy

CHAPTER 1

Letter to a Young Leader

Overview of 1 Timothy

D r. Harry A. Ironside committed his life to Christ at an early age. When he was eleven years old, his family moved to California. The church they attended had no Sunday school, so young Harry enlisted some friends to help him stitch burlap bags together to make a tent big enough to hold one hundred people. In this burlap tent, the eleven-year-old boy taught Sunday school classes to children and adults.

As a teenager, Harry Ironside was active in the Salvation Army and became known as "The Boy Preacher," preaching more than five hundred sermons a year. In his adult years, he preached to well over a million people. In 1929, he became senior pastor of Moody Memorial Church in Chicago. He resigned in 1948, shortly after the death of his wife. By 1950, he suffered from cataracts in both eyes and was nearly blind.

For three months in 1950, I had the privilege of living and traveling with Dr. Ironside, serving as his chauffeur, secretary, and companion. I had just graduated from Dallas Theological Seminary and had not yet served in the pastorate. So, during those three months, Dr. Ironside became my mentor in the ministry.

Though I often took dictation for Dr. Ironside, he would sometimes write short handwritten notes, writing in a very large script. Whenever I saw Dr. Ironside's handwriting, I was reminded of the apostle Paul's words: "See what large letters I use as I write to you with my own hand!" (Galatians 6:11).

Dr. Ironside reminded me of the apostle Paul in many other ways. During those three months, we spent almost all of our time together. I listened carefully to every word he said. I studied his example as a Bible teacher and a man of God. He influenced my life in unforgettable ways. I think that my three-month journey with Dr. Ironside must have been a lot like the relationship between the apostle Paul and two young men he discipled, Timothy and Titus.

Who were Timothy and Titus?

Paul's letters to Timothy and Titus are often called the Pastoral Letters. This is because they were written not to churches, as most of his letters were, but to two young pastors, Timothy and Titus. So much of what Paul writes about in these three letters could be viewed as a handbook for pastors.

Paul views these two young men as his sons in the faith. He led them both to Christ, and they had shared many hardships with him on his journeys. They were as dear to him as sons. In these letters we find wise, caring counsel for young people in all walks of life. Moreover, we see in Paul a wonderful example of how Christian teachers and mentors should relate to their students and disciples and how older, more experienced Christians should pass on their faith and wisdom to the next generation.

Let's look at the background and setting of these letters and take a look at the lives of the two men to whom Paul is writing.

First, who was Timothy? He was the son of a Jewish-Christian mother, Eunice, and a Greek father. Paul had led this young man to Christ years before while preaching in Timothy's home town of Lystra. Timothy responded to the gospel when he was probably no more than sixteen. By the time Paul wrote this letter, Timothy was likely in his late twenties or early thirties.

Timothy accompanied Paul on his second missionary journey. Now, because of Paul's great confidence in this young teacher-preacher, he has left Timothy in charge of the church at Ephesus. That city, a major Mediterranean seaport and pleasure resort in western Asia Minor, was also a hotbed of pagan goddess worship and immorality.

Paul's letters to Timothy indicate that this young pastor faced pressures and crises in his ministry. He faced criticism from the people in Ephesus, who looked down on him because he was young. That's why Paul wrote, "Don't let anyone look down on you because you are young, but set an example for the believers in speech, in life, in love, in faith and in purity" (1 Timothy 4:12).

To complicate matters, some strong personalities apparently tried to manipulate or bully Timothy because of his shy and insecure demeanor. So Paul had to encourage Timothy to stand firm and remember that "God did not give us a spirit of timidity, but a spirit of power, of love and of self-discipline" (see 2 Timothy 1:6–7).

So, in his letters to Timothy, Paul offered practical guidance on how this young leader should govern the church in Ephesus. Most evangelical scholars agree that Paul's second letter to Timothy is probably the last surviving letter from the hand of the great apostle.

Next, who was Titus? We find this young man mentioned in several of Paul's letters. He was a Gentile Christian who served with Paul and Barnabas at Antioch and whom Paul trusted with the task of taking a collection in Corinth for the famine-stricken Christians in Jerusalem. Titus was with Paul at Rome during his second imprisonment; Paul apparently sent Titus from Rome to Dalmatia (part of modern Croatia) on a missionary errand. Ancient tradition suggests that Paul ordained Titus as bishop of the church at Gortyn, a major city on the island of Crete.

So in Timothy and Titus we find two young leaders who were more than mere colleagues or students of the ministry. To Paul, they were like sons—and in these letters, we can readily sense the fatherly love and pride Paul felt for them.

How do these three letters fit into the chronology of Paul's life? The book of Acts closes with Paul under house arrest, living under guard in a hired house in Rome, where he stayed for two years. Luke suggests that Paul was later released, and many scholars feel that after his release from his first imprisonment, Paul traveled with Timothy and Titus around the Roman Empire. He left Titus on the island of Crete to oversee and guide the young church there. And he took Timothy along to Ephesus, where a church was already established, and left Timothy in charge there.

Paul then continued to Macedonia. Many Bible scholars believe Paul went from there to Spain, and perhaps even to Britain. During these travels, Paul probably wrote the letters of 1 Timothy and Titus.

At some point, Paul returned to the Mediterranean region and—probably in Troas in western Asia minor (modern Turkey)—he was arrested again and taken to Rome. Instead of being kept under house arrest this time, he was probably kept in Rome's Mamertine Prison—a cold, dark dungeon, the most miserable and infamous prison of the first-century world. There, Paul wrote 2 Timothy—and the gloom of Mamertine Prison can be felt in its pages.

It wasn't long after Paul wrote 2 Timothy that, tradition tells us, Paul was beheaded on the Ostian Way, outside of Rome.

Two interwoven themes

The two letters to Timothy reflect more than just a father-son relationship. Though Paul's overall tone is intimate, both letters begin with a rather formal greeting:

Paul, an apostle of Christ Jesus by the command of God our Savior and of Christ Jesus our hope. (1 Timothy 1:1)

Paul, an apostle of Christ Jesus by the will of God, according to the promise of life that is in Christ Jesus. (2 Timothy 1:1)

The apostle felt it necessary, even when writing to his son in the faith, to assert his apostleship. Timothy surely didn't need such a reminder. He knew Paul's position and authority well. But Paul probably knew that these letters would have a wider readership than Timothy alone, because his previous letters had already been circulated among the churches. By opening these letters with a statement of his apostolic authority, Paul makes it clear that these letters have authority over all the churches in Christendom. They spoke with apostolic authority then, and they still do today.

Christians often forget what it meant for Paul to be an apostle. Every now and then someone will refer to Paul in a disparaging way: "Well, Paul wrote some things that we can't take as authoritative." And those who make such statements forget that the apostles had a unique, God-given ministry. They had received the apostolic authority and commissioning from the Lord Jesus. God gave them the role of speaking authoritatively in every area of doctrine or practice.

This first letter, 1 Timothy, focuses on the nature, ministry, and function of the church in the world. Paul's second letter, 2 Timothy, focuses on the message that the church is called to convey to the world—that is, the gospel of Jesus Christ.

Throughout 1 Timothy, we see two themes interwoven. Paul summarizes the first of these two themes in 1 Timothy 3:

Although I hope to come to you soon, I am writing you these instructions so that, if I am delayed, you will know how people ought to conduct themselves in God's household, which is the church of the living God, the pillar and foundation of the truth. (1 Timothy 3:14–15)

When Paul talks about "how people ought to conduct themselves in God's household," the church, he is not talking about how we should behave while we are in the church building. Rather, he is talking about how we, as members of the church, the household of God, ought to behave when we are in the world.

One of the great flaws in evangelical thinking today is the view of the church as a building. Such a thought never entered Paul's mind. Whenever he writes of the church, he is writing about people, not buildings. So, in this letter, Paul wanted to instruct young Timothy in how he should conduct himself—not as the leader of an organization housed in a building but as a minister in a network of relationships within the body of Christ, the living church of the living God.

The first theme is Christian conduct—the conduct of leaders and members of the living church.

The second theme is embodied in a statement in 1 Timothy 1, where Paul writes, "The goal of this command is love, which comes from a pure heart and a good conscience and a sincere faith" (1 Timothy 1:5).

This second theme is a more personal issue. While the first theme, Christian conduct, deals with the church and its ministry, the second issue involves the individual's relationship to the world and to God. That issue is Christian love—or, as Paul states it, "love, which comes from a pure heart and a good conscience and a sincere faith."

We come into the Christian life by means of a sincere faith, by believing and living out the Word of God. A life of obedient faith leads us to a good conscience. And sincere faith and a good conscience produce a pure heart—a heart that has been purified by the washing of the Word of God and the cleansing of the blood of Christ. And the result of a purified heart is an unceasing flow of love.

So these are the two main themes that are woven throughout 1 Timothy: Christian conduct and Christian love.

Part 1: God's grace (1 Timothy 1)

The letter of 1 Timothy falls into two major divisions—the first chapter and the last five chapters. In the first division, Paul gives us the background of his instruction to his spiritual son Timothy. Paul had left Timothy in charge of the church in Ephesus, a city given over largely to the worship of the heathen goddess Diana (also called Artemis). Timothy faced the formidable challenge of leading and ministering to a church that was surrounded by pagan idolatry, superstition, and immorality.

Paul begins by instructing Timothy to oppose false teaching. This tells us that the church had already been infiltrated by false teachers, just as the church today is under assault from without and within by heresies. Paul says:

> As I urged you when I went into Macedonia, stay there in Ephesus so that you may command certain men not to teach false doctrines any longer nor to devote themselves to myths and endless genealogies. These

promote controversies rather than God's work—which is by faith. (1 Timothy 1:3–4)

Some in the church are trying to regulate people's conduct by imposing rigid rules and regulations. Paul wants Timothy—and us—to understand that true Christian conduct is not motivated by external rules and laws. True Christian conduct can be motivated only by the indwelling life and grace of the Lord Jesus Christ.

The law, Paul says, was given "for lawbreakers and rebels" (1 Timothy 1:9b). He goes on to list the sort of "lawbreakers and rebels" he is talking about: "the ungodly and sinful, the unholy and irreligious; for those who kill their fathers or mothers, for murderers, for adulterers and perverts, for slave traders and liars and perjurers—and for whatever else is contrary to the sound doctrine" (1 Timothy 1:9c–10). The law and its penalties exist to curb the destructive impulses of sinners.

But if you love the Lord, you want to please Him. You don't need a law to keep you from doing evil; your conduct will be controlled by love alone.

This does not mean that we dispense with the law. Christian love and Christian conduct are defined by the terms of the law. When the law tells us not to commit adultery, not to kill, not to bear false witness, and not to covet or steal, it is describing how authentic Christian love conducts itself. Love is always consistent with the law.

Some people will say, "I'm a Christian, and I live by Christian love and grace. Therefore I am free to disregard the law." In this passage, Paul makes it clear that this is false, heretical thinking. While it's true that our conduct is not to be motivated by fear of the law, Christian conduct should be lawful conduct, motivated by love for God.

Paul's own love was motivated by gratitude. He never forgot that he had once been a blasphemer and a persecutor of Christ—and he never ceased being amazed at the wondrous fact that God had forgiven him and delivered him from guilt and sin. From time to time in Paul's letters, including 1 Timothy, he breaks into lyrical passages, expressing his love and thankfulness for God's grace in his life.

So the background of Paul's instruction to Timothy in this letter, as expressed in 1 Timothy 1, is grace. He urges Timothy to resist false teachers who undermine the gospel of grace—and he reminds Timothy of the vast riches of grace that he, Paul, "the worst of sinners," has received through Jesus Christ (see 1 Timothy 1:16).

Part 2: Paul's fivefold charge to Timothy (1 Timothy 2–6)

The second division of the letter, 1 Timothy 2–6, contains Paul's charge (that is, Paul's command or instruction) to his young son in the faith. Paul's charge to Timothy consists of five elements:

1. Instructions for public worship   1 Timothy 2
2. Qualifications for church leaders   1 Timothy 3
3. Resisting error; holding fast to truth   1 Timothy 4
4. Dealing with problems and controversies   1 Timothy 5
5. Issues of class, wealth, and knowledge   1 Timothy 6

In 1 Timothy 2, Paul instructs Timothy in the proper conduct of public worship. He addresses the roles of men and women in public prayer and worship. This section of 1 Timothy has often been misunderstood, so we will examine this passage and see that women have the right to minister and pray in public, just as men do.

Next, in 1 Timothy 3, Paul charges Timothy concerning the qualifications for church leaders. He deals first with the qualifications for bishops (or elders) in the church. Then he deals with the qualifications for deacons and deaconesses.

Then, in 1 Timothy 4, Paul turns to the subject of apostasy. People often use the words *apostate* and *heretic* interchangeably, but they are not the same. A heretic is a Christian who knows the Lord Jesus Christ but has fallen into error regarding a doctrinal issue. An apostate is a much more serious matter, because an apostate is a person who claims to be a Christian but is not. The apostle John spoke of apostates when he wrote, "They went out from us, but they did not really belong to us. For if they had belonged to us, they would have remained with us; but their going showed that none of them belonged to us" (1 John 2:19).

The Lord Jesus spoke of apostates in His parable of the wheat and weeds in Matthew 13. In that parable, a farmer planted a field of wheat, but enemies came in and planted weeds among the wheat. The weeds represent apostates, counterfeit Christians who operate within the church. Jesus said that the weeds and wheat would grow up together until the harvest, which is why we are never able to get rid of apostates within the church. The apostates have false beliefs because they follow doctrines of demons and deceitful spirits, not merely the twisted ideas of other people—and they lead others astray. In 1 Timothy 4, Paul tells Timothy how to respond to apostates in the church.

Then, in 1 Timothy 5, Paul deals with a number of specific problems and controversies in the church. For example, he instructs Timothy in how to treat older and younger people in the church, how to handle accusations against elders, and so forth. He also prepares Timothy for certain personal challenges he will encounter as a minister of the gospel.

In 1 Timothy 6, Paul deals with matters of class, status, and knowledge in the church. He instructs Timothy about meeting the needs of people who are downtrodden and marginalized in society—specifically slaves. Though we no longer have slaves in our society, these principles are still valid as the church seeks to reach out to the poor, oppressed, and marginalized people in our society.

Paul also deals with issues of wealth and privilege in society and the church. What is the biblical Christian view of money? What is the responsibility of wealthy Christians to the poor? Paul charges Timothy to warn the people in the Ephesian church not to put their trust in either money or knowledge.

This letter clearly speaks to the church in our time, just as it spoke to the Christians of the first century. Now that we have gained an overview of Paul's first letter to his spiritual son Timothy, let's plunge into this marvelous letter and discover how to apply its rich truths to our lives.

CHAPTER 2

Guard the Truth

1 Timothy 1:1–7

The church of Jesus Christ is a spiritual family. Like any family, it is made up of fathers and mothers, brothers and sisters, sons and daughters. Paul was a father in the early church—an authority figure, a role model, and a progenitor, founder, and establisher of churches in many cities. He had Christian brothers—men like Barnabas and the apostle Peter. And he had Christian sons—younger men like Timothy.

As we study this letter from a father to a beloved spiritual son, we should ask ourselves, "What is my place in the family of faith? Who is my spiritual father or mother? Who are my spiritual brothers and sisters? And most importantly, who are my spiritual children? Who are the young people I'm mentoring and discipling, so that a new generation can come behind me and carry on the work of the faith?"

As 1 Timothy opens, we find Paul's spiritual son Timothy undertaking a demanding work as the leader of the church in Ephesus. Paul writes:

> Paul, an apostle of Christ Jesus by the command of God our Savior and of Christ Jesus our hope,
>
> To Timothy my true son in the faith: Grace, mercy and peace from God the Father and Christ Jesus our Lord.
>
> As I urged you when I went into Macedonia, stay there in Ephesus so that you may command certain men not to teach false doctrines any longer. (1 Timothy 1:1–3)

Verse 1 sounds surprisingly formal for a fatherly letter. But when you consider the situation in the church at Ephesus, you can better understand Paul's formality.

Paul underscores his authority—and fatherly affection

The Ephesian church was under severe attack. Paul had said this would happen. In Acts 20, we read that Paul, at the port of Miletus, called together the elders of the church at Ephesus for a word of farewell. In his farewell message, he told them: "I know that after I leave, savage wolves will come in among you and will not spare the flock. Even from your own number men will arise and distort the truth in order to draw away disciples after them" (Acts 20:29–30).

Paul spoke these words years before he placed Timothy in charge of the church at Ephesus. By the time Timothy was at Ephesus, the conditions Paul predicted had already come to pass. The church was under attack from savage wolves without and false teachers within. So, Paul, who was writing not only to Timothy but also to the Ephesian church and by extension to all churches, underscored his apostolic authority because Timothy faced a crisis that could be resolved only by the authority of an apostle.

Timothy was not sent to Ephesus as an elder. There were already elders in the Ephesian church. As we just saw, these were the men Paul addressed in Acts 20. Timothy was sent as an apostolic representative, that is, as Paul's surrogate. Timothy served as a bridge from the early days of the church, when it was ruled by apostolic leaders, to a more permanent phase in which the church would be overseen by elders, relying upon the guidance of Scripture. At the time of this letter, of course, much of the New Testament canon was not yet written. So Timothy, as Paul's representative, was to convey apostolic truth to the church at Ephesus, just as the apostle Paul had done. Today, we are guided by the written Word of God, not by apostles. The apostles have already recorded their witness to us in the Scriptures, and we rely upon those Scriptures as our authority.

Following this formal opening, Paul reveals his warm and human side. He writes, "To Timothy my true son in the faith." Here we find a reminder of Paul's fatherly affection toward his spiritual son Timothy.

These words are followed by a word of blessing that gives us an insight into the heart of the apostle Paul: "Grace, mercy and peace from God the Father and Christ Jesus our Lord." Paul's usual salutation was the simple phrase "grace and peace." But here (and in the opening lines of 2 Timothy) he adds the word *mercy*. Why is this significant?

I believe Paul chose this word *mercy* because of Timothy's fears. What is mercy? It is God's grace exercised in deliverance from painful or perilous circumstances. That is what Timothy needed. He was a timid, shy young man—an introvert. He faced tough challenges and exciting opportunities. Paul knew Timothy needed assurance that God would deliver him from his trials and make him victorious. Paul encouraged him, saying in effect, "May you receive mercy from God the Father."

Timothy's two primary duties

Next, Paul tells Timothy what his work in Ephesus will involve. It will consist of two essential duties. First, Timothy will need to confront an attack of false teaching that has infected the church. Second, Timothy will need to teach the Ephesian Christians how the Old Testament law of Moses fits into the life of the New Testament believer.

Paul's instruction of Timothy in these two duties has enduring relevance for our lives. The church is as prone to false teaching now as it was then. And the church today is often confused about the role of God's law in the life of believers. The apostle instructs Timothy to challenge certain teachers who have come into the church:

> As I urged you when I went into Macedonia, stay there in Ephesus so that you may command certain men not to teach false doctrines any longer nor to devote themselves to myths and endless genealogies. These promote controversies rather than God's work—which is by faith. The goal of this command is love, which comes from a pure heart and a good conscience and a sincere faith. Some have wandered away from these and turned to meaningless talk. They want to be teachers of the law, but they do not know what they are talking about or what they so confidently affirm. (1 Timothy 1:3–7)

It's significant that Paul begins by instructing Timothy to guard the teaching of the church. He says, "Command certain men not to teach false doctrines any longer." In this way, Paul makes it clear that teaching is a critically important ministry of the church. The church's teaching must be kept pure and undefiled.

What is the teaching Paul speaks of? Later, in verses 10–11, Paul tells us that "sound doctrine" is doctrine "that conforms to the glorious gospel of the blessed God, which he entrusted to me." In other words, the pure and undefiled teaching of the church is that which was entrusted to Paul and the other apostles.

It's good for believers to have a thorough and well-rounded understanding of many subjects, including mathematics, literature, art, history, science, and more. But when you examine the question of what the church should proclaim, there is one body of teaching, and only one. The church exists to declare this unique body of truth. Anything that departs from this body of truth is not to be taught in church.

This is not to say that we will not struggle with different details and dimensions of this body of truth. We will sometimes disagree about secondary issues. But when it comes to the essence of our faith, we must be true to the apostolic witness. The first duty Paul charges Timothy to carry out is this: Confront those who teach doctrines that contradict the apostolic faith. Defend the purity of the teaching of the church.

Who were these teachers of false doctrine? Were they blatant apostates and heretics? I don't believe so. I think they were probably men from the congregation who, in many ways, were good teachers. But they had begun to introduce ideas derived primarily from human philosophy.

Paul doesn't state whether the philosophy in question was Greek or Jewish philosophy. We do know that Greek philosophy invaded the church and became known as the heresy of Gnosticism. However, I believe the philosophy Paul referred to came from Jewish sources. In these verses, Paul refers to "false doctrines" that are related to "myths and endless genealogies" taught by people who "want to be teachers of the law." This suggests that people who wanted to be thought of as experts in the Old Testament law spread concepts based on Jewish traditions, myths, and genealogies and that these teachings infected the church at Ephesus.

Teachings that promote controversies

God's Word is the most powerful weapon in the church's arsenal against error and false teaching. If we hope to deliver people from bondage to sin, we must begin with the revealed truth of Scripture. The purity of God's truth is central to the ministry of the church. Whenever there is weakness in the church, we invariably find biblical illiteracy—that is, we find that people in the church do not know God's Word. They do not live according to God's truth.

Timothy was sent to Ephesus to correct that situation. Paul charged him to confront false concepts being taught at Ephesus. Furthermore, Paul told Timothy to expose the faulty sources of information these teachers relied on: philosophies, traditions, fables, and genealogies from outside the teachings of the apostles.

If these sources were Jewish myths, as I suspect they were, you can find examples of these concepts in books of pseudo-scripture known as the

Apocrypha. The Apocrypha can be found in Catholic translations of the Bible. It consists of fourteen ancient books that are not included in Protestant Bibles.

The word *apocrypha* comes from the Greek word *apókryphos,* meaning "hidden, unknown, spurious, or of questionable origin." These fourteen books were never accepted by the Jews as part of their Scripture but were widely circulated in early centuries. When you read these books, it's easy to see why they were not accepted as Scripture by either Jewish scholars or Protestant church leaders. Many of these books are clearly fabulous accounts of imagined events, usually involving wise men who had strange teachings. Some contained genealogies that attempted to connect the apocryphal tales to the narrative of Scripture.

Evidently, some of the teachers at Ephesus were taking these apocryphal concepts and presenting them as Christian truths, even though they conflicted with the apostolic teachings. The teaching of the church was becoming corrupted.

The fruit of false teachings

Jesus told us how to tell a true teacher from a false teacher: "Thus, by their fruit you will recognize them" (Matthew 7:20). Paul tells us plainly that the fruit of these teachings in Ephesus was destructive: "These [teachings] promote controversies rather than God's work." Teachings that produce endless debate and specious reasoning are harmful to the work of God and the work of the church.

The Bible is a wonderful book, containing intriguing themes and events that fire the imagination. There's nothing wrong with reflecting on Scripture by means of our imagination. It's fascinating to think about such questions as, "What did Jesus write in the dust with his finger in John 8:6?" Or, "How will we spend our time in heaven?"

However, some Christians occupy much of their time with matters of sheer speculation. In the process, they neglect to ground themselves in the great revealed truths of the Word of God. Paul told Timothy that he needed to turn these Ephesian teachers away from unprofitable speculation and back to God's Word. Paul explained how Timothy should guard God's truth by contrasting those who "devote themselves to myths and endless genealogies" with those who engage in "God's work—which is by faith." This latter phrase should be translated "the stewardship from God which is by faith."

This stewardship is referred to throughout the writings of Paul. It is the stewardship God entrusted to Paul and that, in verses 10–11, he refers to as "the sound doctrine that conforms to the glorious gospel of the blessed God, which he entrusted to me." Paul is saying that these teachers in Ephesus ought to have been teaching the deposit of truth given by God to the apostles, including Paul—the deposit of truth that is appropriated by faith.

Now, faith is not merely belief. Many people say they have faith when all they have is an opinion or a mindset. Authentic biblical faith is acting on the basis of the truth that God has revealed. If faith does not radically change the way we live, then it is not truly faith.

There are two essential ingredients in the gospel, and these two ingredients demand that our lives be transformed. The first ingredient of the gospel is the death of Christ on the cross. The crucifixion declares the end of the old life. By His death, Jesus demonstrates that we must die to sin and self. The people we once were must be nailed to the cross.

The second ingredient of the gospel is the resurrection of the Lord Jesus from the dead. When Jesus was raised from the tomb, He demonstrated a new life. His resurrection brings us new life. We become new people, delivered from bondage to our old lives. That is the good news!

The essence of Christianity is life. We are freed from our old life. We have been given a new life, a new way to live. The apostle John put it this way: "He who has the Son has life; he who does not have the Son of God does not have life" (1 John 5:12).

Though I am grateful for the Protestant Reformation, I believe the Reformers went astray on this very point. Martin Luther, John Calvin, and the other Reformers viewed justification by faith as the decision of God the Judge that we are forgiven for our sins. Certainly, the biblical concept of justification does include forgiveness of sin—but it means so much more than that. We are forgiven because we share the life of Jesus Christ. What He is, we are. That is the central truth of the Christian faith.

Throughout his letters, Paul drives home the truth that we share in the life of our Lord: "When Christ, who is your life, appears, then you also will appear with him in glory" (Colossians 3:4). He tells the Corinthians, "Therefore, if anyone is in Christ, he is a new creation; the old has gone, the new has come!" (2 Corinthians 5:17). He tells us to put off the old self and put on the new self, which is being reshaped in the image of Jesus Christ (see Ephesians 4:22–24 and Colossians 3:9–10), and to consider ourselves dead to sin but alive to God (see Romans 6:11). That's the good news of the Christian gospel—not merely that we are forgiven, but that we have new life.

The erroneous teachers at Ephesus were attacking this truth. Perhaps they didn't know they were spreading falsehood, but they were denying that the old life had truly been crucified with Christ. Through their fascination with myths and genealogies, they were suggesting that there was something of value that carried over from the old life. These teachers held that there was mystical significance to one's ancestry or to esoteric knowledge. They built false doctrines on myths that exalted hidden knowledge—and they gave these myths preeminence over the revealed truth of Scripture.

That's the problem Paul saw in the church at Ephesus. The result was controversy and conflict in the church. So Paul charged Timothy with the responsibility to confront and correct this problem.

The fruit of truth

By their fruit you will recognize them. Just as error can be detected by its destructive effects, so truth can be detected by its constructive effects. Paul tells us what truth produces in the life of the church. "The goal of this command," Paul says, "is love, which comes from a pure heart and a good conscience and a sincere faith."

Here is how you can tell, almost at a glance, what is taking place in the life of a church. If that church is giving itself to some subtle form of human philosophy, you will see controversy and endless speculation in the life of that church. But if that church is preaching God's truth, you will see a loving congregation. The goal of this command is love. The aim of the gospel is love. Speculation involves thinking, talking, and debating. Love involves action, caring, service, compassion, and involvement.

The aim and purpose of the gospel is to produce loving people. A church that is more involved in speculation and controversy than in meeting human needs is a church infected by error.

How can you know that the gospel has truly transformed your life? You know it when you see evidence that you are becoming a more loving, patient, forgiving, accepting, and tenderhearted person. You know it when others see those Christlike qualities in you, and they reflect to you that you appear to be a changed person. That is what Jesus said would happen once the gospel took root in our lives, and that is why His great commandment to us is that we should love one another.

The truth of the gospel produces love in our lives. How does this take place? Paul tells us that love "comes from a pure heart and a good conscience and a sincere faith." Let's look at each of those elements in reverse order, beginning with a sincere faith. Paul is telling us that love begins with a sincere faith that the great facts of the gospel are true—not in some grand theological sense but in an intimate and personal sense. It is a theological truth that Jesus died for the sins of the world; but for me, it is a deeply personal and life-changing truth that Jesus died for Ray Stedman and that Ray Stedman is risen again with Christ. Because I have a sincere faith in this profoundly personal truth, I love God, I am grateful to God, and I want to love others as God has loved me.

When you have a sincere faith, your actions change. You begin to see that the way you have been living is not consistent with a changed life. You now have a new life in Jesus Christ, so the old life must die. It doesn't die all at once, but for the person with a sincere faith, the old life will clearly begin to fade.

As the old way of life gives way to the new, you experience what Paul calls "a good conscience." Your conscience is the internal judge of your behavior. Your conscience monitors your daily actions, either accusing you or excusing you. As you increasingly live consistently with God's truth, your conscience afflicts you less and less. Instead of seeing yourself as riddled with sin and shame, you see yourself as forgiven, restored, and accepted. Your past has been washed away—not only your pre-Christian past but also the sins you committed as a growing Christian. Each morning, you begin anew on the basis of God's forgiveness, and this gives you a good conscience.

A good conscience produces a pure heart. Your inner attitudes and thoughts begin to change because you are no longer the same person you once were. Lustful thoughts that once gave you pleasure now disgust and repel you. Anger is replaced by forgiveness and acceptance. Resentment is replaced by understanding and love. Greed is replaced by generosity and compassion. Your heart is being purified.

As Paul wrote elsewhere, "God has poured out his love into our hearts by the Holy Spirit, whom he has given us" (see Romans 5:5). His love begins to touch you and everyone around you. That's the good news of the gospel.

A wilderness of words

Paul concludes this section by telling Timothy about the true intentions of these erroneous teachers. He wants Timothy to recognize their true state—why they teach these false concepts and what they hope to gain. He writes, "Some have wandered away from these and turned to meaningless talk. They want to be teachers of the law, but they do not know what they are talking about or what they so confidently affirm" (1 Timothy 1:6–7).

In other words, these teachers carom from one philosophical idea to another, from one theological fad to another, turning the church into a kind of doctrinal pinball machine. The result is what Paul calls "meaningless talk," or as the New English Bible puts it, "a wilderness of words." Whenever you see a church in the throes of endless debate over new doctrinal inventions and paradigms, you can be certain that the church has been invaded by these kinds of teachers.

Paul says that the motive of such teachers is a desire for position and reputation. They are not motivated by a desire for God's truth, a passion to see lives changed, or a love for God's people. Instead, they desire to be known as people of wisdom, as "teachers of the law." In short, they are motivated by ambitious, self-centered pride.

Remarkably, Paul says, these teachers do not understand what they are saying or the sources from which they take their knowledge. Though they appear to be knowledgeable, they lack true depth of understanding.

That's why these subtle doctrinal aberrations must be caught at their source and confronted as early as possible, before these false ideas have a chance to take root in the congregation. We must be careful to guard the biblical and apostolic witness of God's truth. Any teaching whose aim is anything less than love for God and for people will produce nothing but vain speculation and controversy.

So, in these first few verses, Paul has charged Timothy with a huge responsibility. The young leader's first task is to help the elders of the Ephesian church to understand that certain teachings, which are contrary to the simple gospel truth, are causing harm to the life of the church.

Next, we will look at what the apostle Paul has to say about the place of the Old Testament law of Moses in the Christian life.

CHAPTER 3

Awful Lawfulness

1 Timothy 1:8–11

Go to almost any city in the United States and you will find churches on corner after corner. At a glance, it would seem that our cities are alive with a vital Christian witness. But I submit to you that this is not the case. A multitude of church buildings does not necessarily indicate spiritual vitality. Appearances can be deceiving.

A church building may house a dynamic family of faith—or a gathering of the spiritually dead. Why are some churches so dead and lifeless? I would suggest two reasons.

First, churches (and indeed, entire denominations) often give themselves over to a rationalistic unbelief. They have set aside the light of Scripture and have gone off in pursuit of worldly philosophies, worldly goals, and worldly religion.

I once attended a conference of pastors in Nashville, Tennessee. We met on the campus of a church-affiliated university. It was a beautiful campus with ivy-covered buildings designed to accommodate huge crowds. When I was there, however, the student body consisted of thirty young people.

The school had once been a major evangelical institution. An inscription over one archway read: "Expect great things from God." Decades earlier, those words had probably inspired hundreds of students. But when I visited there, no great things were happening on that campus. Why? Because that school had drifted away from God's Word and into rationalistic unbelief.

The second reason churches often become dead is, in a sense, the opposite of the first reason. These churches depart from a dynamic faith by veering into legalism and orthodoxy. Yes, they are careful to avoid the lure of worldliness—but they become so rigid and obsessed with the law of God that there is no place in their religion for the power of God and the Spirit of God.

Later, in his second letter to Timothy, Paul warns his spiritual son about those having "a form of godliness but denying its power" (2 Timothy 3:5). In other words, such people appear deeply religious, but instead of exemplifying God's power, they are obsessed with strict obedience to the Law.

This was the problem at Ephesus. Some of the teachers there were legalists, obsessed with every fine point of the old Jewish law. So Paul sent Timothy to Ephesus to correct that problem—the problem I call the awful lawfulness of unlawful law.

The law is good

In 1 Timothy 1:8–11, Paul offers us helpful insight in how to deal with the problem of awful lawfulness. He writes:

> We know that the law is good if one uses it properly. We also know that law is made not for the righteous but for lawbreakers and rebels, the ungodly and sinful, the unholy and irreligious; for those who kill their fathers or mothers, for murderers, for adulterers and perverts, for slave traders and liars and perjurers—and for whatever else is contrary to the sound doctrine that conforms to the glorious gospel of the blessed God, which he entrusted to me.

In this passage, Paul suggests three principles regarding how Christians and churches should deal with the Old Testament law of Moses.

The first principle. The law is good and useful in the Christian life. Paul says, "We know that the law is good if one uses it properly." This squelches the mistaken claim that Christians are delivered from the law and can safely ignore it. Paul says that's not the case. The law is good, but it must be used rightly.

The law is good because God gave it. The law, as expressed in the Ten Commandments, is the only passage of Scripture written directly by the hand of God. It has been said that the Bible consists of sixty-six books composed by forty different writers but with only one author, God. Yet, even though Moses brought the stone tablets of the law down from Mount Sinai, those tablets were written by the hand of God. In fact, He wrote them twice. After the first tablets were broken, Moses returned to the mountain and God wrote the law again. Clearly, God views the law as being vitally important, and it is not to be done away with.

The Ten Commandments reflect the character and holiness of God. That's why the law never will change or pass away. The law represents God's righteous demands upon human behavior, anywhere on earth. The law is even written upon the hearts of people who have never heard of the Ten Commandments.

Paul makes this argument when he writes, "When Gentiles, who do not have the law, do by nature things required by the law, they are a law for themselves, even though they do not have the law, since they show that the requirements of the law are written on their hearts" (see Romans 2:14–15a). That is why all human law is based upon the Ten Commandments.

But what about Paul's statement that we are not under the law? It's true, Paul did say, "But now, by dying to what once bound us, we have been released from the law so that we serve in the new way of the Spirit, and not in the old way of the written code" (Romans 7:6).

When Paul writes that we have been released from the law, he is not saying that the law has no place in the Christian life. Jesus said in the Sermon on the Mount:

> "Do not think that I have come to abolish the Law or the Prophets; I have
> not come to abolish them but to fulfill them. I tell you the truth, until
> heaven and earth disappear, not the smallest letter, not the least stroke of
> a pen, will by any means disappear from the Law until everything is ac-
> complished. Anyone who breaks one of the least of these commandments
> and teaches others to do the same will be called least in the kingdom of
> heaven, but whoever practices and teaches these commands will be called
> great in the kingdom of heaven." (Matthew 5:17–19)

Jesus makes it clear that the law is not eliminated by New Testament grace. The law will endure because it is holy and good and because it reflects the character of God. The law continues to play a role in our Christian experience.

The law is for the unrighteous

The second principle. Paul says, "We also know that law is made not for the righteous but for lawbreakers and rebels." Many Christians have deduced from this statement that once you become a Christian you have no need to refer to the law of Moses any longer. But Paul corrects that notion. He wants us to understand that there is a use of the law in the Christian experience, even though the law was not made for those who are already righteous in Christ. Elsewhere, Paul wrote:

> For what the law was powerless to do in that it was weakened by the sin-
> ful nature, God did by sending his own Son in the likeness of sinful man
> to be a sin offering. And so he condemned sin in sinful man, in order that

the righteous requirements of the law might be fully met in us, who do not live according to the sinful nature but according to the Spirit.

Those who live according to the sinful nature have their minds set on what that nature desires; but those who live in accordance with the Spirit have their minds set on what the Spirit desires. (Romans 8:3–5)

The law requires something from us. It sets a righteous standard for our lives and insists that we behave in a righteous way. But we cannot meet that standard. The good news of the gospel is that when we believe in Jesus and identify with Him in His death and resurrection, we receive His righteousness as a free gift. The life of Jesus is given to us, and our spirits are joined to His. As Paul writes elsewhere, "But he who unites himself with the Lord is one with him in spirit" (1 Corinthians 6:17).

What, then, is Paul saying when he says that the law is made not for the righteous? He is saying that the law has nothing to say to Christians about fulfilling that righteous standard. Our nature is now changed. That's the good news. That's "the glorious gospel of the blessed God," which God entrusted to Paul (see 1 Timothy 1:11). We are no longer under law as a means of winning God's approval. We have His approval already through Christ.

Who, then, was the law given for? Paul says it is for "lawbreakers and rebels, the ungodly and sinful, the unholy and irreligious; for those who kill their fathers or mothers, for murderers, for adulterers and perverts, for slave traders and liars and perjurers." This list contains two groups of people for whom the law was given.

The first three pairs constitute one class of people who are identified by what they are, not by what they do. They are, Paul says, "lawbreakers and rebels, the ungodly and sinful, the unholy and irreligious." These terms describe their attitudes, their outlook on life, their fundamental nature. In other words, these people are the unregenerate.

Everyone starts life as a member of the unregenerate class of people. A baby is unregenerate. A toddler is unregenerate. We are all unregenerate—until we receive Jesus as Lord and Savior and become born again. The word *regenerate* means "generated again" or "born again." An unregenerate person is one who has never experienced the second birth of salvation through faith in Jesus Christ. The law was made for unregenerate people.

The second three pairs constitute a class of people identified by what they do. Paul says that the law is for "those who kill their fathers or mothers, for murderers"—that is, for those who wrongly take human life.

And, he says, the law is for "adulterers and perverts," for people who commit sexual sins, who indulge in sexual behavior outside of marriage, or before marriage, or in violation of their marriage vows. This includes every kind of sexual sin and perversion.

Next, Paul says that the law is for "slave traders and liars and perjurers." The Greek term that is translated "slave traders" could also be translated "kidnappers." Paul is talking about people who steal the lives of other people for money, either by selling those people into slavery or holding them for ransom. And Paul is talking about people who lie. And he is talking about people who perjure themselves, who violate an oath or affirmation to tell the truth, as in a court trial.

Finally, Paul gathers both of these classes of people together with an all-inclusive phrase, "and for whatever else is contrary to the sound doctrine." This final phrase is hard for us, as Christians, to hear, because it includes the sinful deeds not only of the unregenerate but also of the regenerate, of Christians. You and I might feel smug and self-righteous knowing that we have never murdered or kidnapped anyone. But can we self-righteously say that we have never done anything that is contrary to sound doctrine? I have certainly done such things, and I'm sure you have too.

We like to think that our own sin is insignificant; other people's sins are *really* bad. There's a clever mental game we play that enables us to maintain this double standard. We call our sins and other people's sins by different names:

You are rigid and prejudiced; I have convictions.
You lose your temper; I become righteously indignant.
You are cheap; I am thrifty.
You are tactless and abrupt; I am honest and candid.

The list goes on and on. We keep two sets of books on sins so we can convince ourselves we are not bad people. God's law is designed to show us that we all fall short of God's standard of perfect behavior.

Sometimes young people come to me and say, "I'm about to attend a Christian school that requires me to sign a pledge that says, 'I will not drink, smoke, dance, or go to movies.' Should I sign?" I say, "You may sign it if you intend to keep it—but you may want to add underneath, 'I reserve the right to indulge in malice, envy, jealousy, gossip, and other saintly sins.'" We Christians never seem to be concerned about those sins, yet these are the sins summed up under Paul's phrase "whatever else is contrary to the sound doctrine."

The law was made for the deeds of the flesh, whether the flesh is active in the unregenerate unbeliever or in the Christian believer. Paul makes this principle clear.

The law is in accordance with the gospel

The third principle. Paul says that in the Christian life, the law "conforms to the glorious gospel of the blessed God, which he entrusted to me." This principle involves four important truths.

First, the spirit in an individual who has been born again has already been made righteous. You cannot bring the law in to correct a Christian's misdeeds. You cannot make a Christian righteous by exhorting him to try harder to behave himself. That will never work. The Christian doesn't need to be made righteous but is already made righteous through Jesus Christ.

If a person is truly born again, then at the very depths of his or her being, there is a hunger to be righteous. We as Christians fall short of righteous behavior, but the desire to live a righteous life is implanted within us. When the law is used lawfully in the Christian life, it appeals to the righteous desire within us. The law is not intended to make Christians feel bad about sin but to stir within us a desire to live righteously.

The proper role of the law in the Christian life is not to say to us, "Try harder to be good." Rather, its role is to inspire us to live a lifestyle of continual renewal. When we stumble, the gospel picks us up and says, "You are already righteous in Christ. Don't feel ashamed or defeated. Rejoice, because you are forgiven and righteous in Christ."

The law no longer condemns us. It reminds us to repent, receive forgiveness, and continue on our way rejoicing. That is how the law acts in conformity with the gospel.

Second, the gospel limits the punishment Christians can receive when they transgress the law. The church is not permitted to imprison or execute people who break the law. This may seem like an odd statement to make, because you have never heard of a church that imprisoned or executed someone. But there have been times in history when the Roman Catholic Church imprisoned, tortured, and executed people for violation of the law. These practices were common during the Inquisition, a religious reign of terror that lasted from the fifteenth through the seventeenth centuries.

But the Roman Catholic Church was not the only religious hierarchy to misuse the law in this way. Some of the Protestant Reformers were similarly guilty. During the mid-1500s, a Spanish Protestant theologian named Michael Servetus was accused of heresy and condemned to death by the Protestant governing council in Geneva. The famed Reformer, John Calvin, consented to Servetus's execution but asked for "leniency"—that is, Calvin wanted Servetus to be humanely decapitated. The council rejected Calvin's wishes and ordered Servetus executed by burning at the stake. As Servetus was being burned alive, his last words were, "Jesus, Son of the eternal God, have mercy on me!"

You can search the New Testament, and you will not find any form of punishment permitted in the church except separation. In other words, if a Christian sins and remains unrepentant, the other believers in the church are to withdraw their fellowship from him—and this can take place only after the church has completed a four-step process that Jesus sets forth:

> "If your brother sins against you, go and show him his fault, just between the two of you. If he listens to you, you have won your brother over. But if he will not listen, take one or two others along, so that 'every matter may be established by the testimony of two or three witnesses.' If he refuses to listen to them, tell it to the church; and if he refuses to listen even to the church, treat him as you would a pagan or a tax collector." (Matthew 18:15–17)

Step 1 is go to the sinning brother privately and seek to win him back. If he refuses, step 2 is to go again, this time with one or two witnesses. If he still refuses, step 3 is to take the matter before the church. If even this step fails and the sinning brother resists all pleas and urgings to repent, then step 4 is to separate from that sinning brother. The Christian community is to treat the offender as if he were not a Christian.

The goal is to show the offender what his sin is costing him. When an offender is treated as "a pagan or a tax collector" by the church community, that offender often comes to his senses, repents, receives forgiveness, and is joyfully received back into the family of faith. This is the only form of punishment allowed in the church, according to God's Word.

Third, the lawful use of the law means we do not impose rigid and burdensome rules of conduct on others without their consent. We are brothers and sisters of one another. We are not to lord it over others in the church. We are not in charge of the lives of other believers.

Legalism—the misuse of the law—always sets up rules and demands for other people to follow. Legalism imposes rules on other believers and says to them, "Follow these rules or else." In a legalistic church, a few people (often self-appointed people) are the church bosses, and they use the law to boss other people around.

The church was created to be a place of spiritual freedom, where people willingly submit to one another. A healthy church does not have bosses; it has nothing but servants. The pastors, the elders, the deacons, and all the members of the congregation are servants, and they agree to live according to the law, not because they are forced to but because they want to in service to God. That is the proper place of the law in the life of the church.

Fourth, the law cannot impart vitality to the church. A vital and dynamic church is the result not of the law but of the Spirit. When Christians realize who they truly are—people born anew by the Spirit, filled with the righteousness of Christ, and living under the love of God—then the church becomes vital and energized for ministry.

The lawful use of the law is to drive us to a fresh realization of God's love for us. That is why Paul says, "Love does no harm to its neighbor. Therefore love is the fulfillment of the law" (Romans 13:10).

How do we fulfill the law? How do we achieve the righteousness that God intends for our lives? Through Christlike love.

The proper function of the law in our lives is not to set up a slate of rigid demands and say to us, "Shape up or ship out." The proper role of the law is to teach us what love looks like. We find the Ten Commandments in Exodus 20:2–17, and those commandments tell us to

1. Love God. Don't do anything that would betray your love for Him.
2. Don't make wrongful use of the name of the Lord, whom you love.
3. Keep the Sabbath day holy, out of love for God.
4. Honor your father and mother; show love to your parents.
5. Do not murder; show love to your neighbor.
6. Do not commit adultery; don't defile your love for your husband or wife.
7. Do not steal; love your neighbor by respecting his property.
8. Do not bear false witness; love your neighbor by respecting his reputation.
9. Do not covet your neighbor's property; love him by respecting his right to what he owns and has earned.

10. Do not covet your neighbor's wife; don't defile your neighbor's love relationship.

You see? The law is not about rigid demands. It's about love—love for God and love for others. The law helps us to understand how we are to relate to God and what we must and must not do in our relationships with one another.

If we love God and love one another, we will fulfill the law. That is the lawful use of the law in the Christian life. That is authentic Christianity.

CHAPTER 4

The Model Leader

1 Timothy 1:12–17

Timothy was engaged in a dangerous work in a dangerous place—the city of Ephesus. The emperor Nero had begun persecuting the church. Christians were being pressured by the Roman authorities to choose between Caesar and Jesus as Lord. Timothy was also confronted by the religious leaders of the Jewish faith—the same leaders who persecuted Paul wherever he went.

The Ephesians, among whom Timothy labored, were a volatile people, easily incited to riots and violence. Acts 19 recounts a riot led by the idol-making silversmiths of Ephesus—evidence of just how quickly a mob could be provoked to rage in that city.

So it's understandable that Timothy would be anxious about working in Ephesus. I believe that's why Paul, in the next section of this letter, offers a strong word of encouragement. Paul writes:

> I thank Christ Jesus our Lord, who has given me strength, that he considered me faithful, appointing me to his service. Even though I was once a blasphemer and a persecutor and a violent man, I was shown mercy because I acted in ignorance and unbelief. The grace of our Lord was poured out on me abundantly, along with the faith and love that are in Christ Jesus. (1 Timothy 1:12–14)

Paul tells Timothy how, from the beginning of his ministry, he has been strengthened by the Lord. We know from the accounts in Acts that Paul often faced danger, rejection, betrayal, and hardships. We tend to think of Paul as naturally fearless, but the truth is that he often experienced fear. Acts 18 tells us that Timothy was with Paul in Corinth when Paul underwent fierce opposition as he preached the gospel. Timothy saw how daunting the work of an evangelist could be.

But the Lord strengthened Paul even through time of fierce opposition. That's what Paul wants Timothy to see.

Physical strength and encouragement

Sometimes God strengthened Paul in a physical sense. Once, when Paul was in Lystra, Timothy's hometown, the people turned against Paul: "They stoned Paul and dragged him outside the city, thinking he was dead. But after the disciples had gathered around him, he got up and went back into the city. The next day he and Barnabas left for Derbe" (Acts 14:19b–20).

The account contains few details, but we can imagine what took place. The people stoned Paul until he was unconscious, then dragged him outside the city and threw him onto a trash heap. When the disciples—Paul's converts—learned what had happened, they went out and gathered around Paul's seemingly lifeless body. They prayed for him, and God answered their prayers. Paul rose up and walked back into the city. The next day, he went on as if nothing had happened because God had restored his strength.

Elsewhere, Paul writes of the fact that he draws his physical strength from Jesus Christ: "We proclaim him [Christ], admonishing and teaching everyone with all wisdom, so that we may present everyone perfect in Christ. To this end I labor, struggling with all his [Christ's] energy, which so powerfully works in me" (Colossians 1:28–29).

Our Lord supplies physical strength—not only to Paul and the other apostles and preachers but to all believers whose strength is faltering. Christians never need to say, "I can't do it." Instead, we say, "I can't, but God can. Therefore, I can. Let's go!" Paul shared this principle with Timothy to encourage him.

Mental and emotional strength

Sometimes the strength God supplies is mental strength. In Ephesians, Paul speaks of the insight God gave him into the mystery of Christ (see Ephesians 3:4). God had opened the eyes of his mind, giving him understanding of truth he would not otherwise have seen. We see this same principle in the writings of the apostle John: "We know also that the Son of God has come and has given us understanding, so that we may know him who is true" (1 John 5:20a).

At other times, the strength God supplies is emotional strength. Paul writes, "But God, who comforts the downcast, comforted us by the coming of Titus" (2 Corinthians 7:6). We hear this theme all too seldom in Christian circles. Christianity is not merely a set of doctrines. It's a way of life. It's the power to sustain us in the trench warfare of this life. It's the mental, spiritual, and emotional power to live an effective life, even when the whole world is crumbling all around us.

As Paul wrote, "But we have this treasure in jars of clay to show that this all-surpassing power is from God and not from us" (2 Corinthians 4:7). In other words, you and I don't have the power to live effectively and victoriously for Jesus. We are merely jars of clay—but God pours His power into us. When we feel powerless, He fills us with His power, which is more than adequate for any challenge we face.

A prison ministry team once came to our church and reported on their work. One young man on the team, a relatively new Christian named Michael, said that when he shared his testimony of what God had done for him while he was a prisoner, people broke down and cried. Michael couldn't believe it. He was constantly amazed that God affected people through his simple testimony.

What was true for Michael is also true for Timothy—and for you and me. We don't have to do anything alone. God's strength and encouragement are always available to us—not just for sharing our testimony or preaching the gospel but for any challenge. Whenever you feel inadequate, ask God for the strength to face the day.

Doing evil with the best of intentions

Paul also encourages Timothy with a message of God's abundant grace and mercy. He writes with amazement that the Lord Jesus "considered me faithful, appointing me to his service. Even though I was once a blasphemer and a persecutor and a violent man, I was shown mercy because I acted in ignorance and unbelief."

The apostle never got over the wonder of his astonishing encounter with the Lord Jesus on the Damascus Road (see Acts 9). Paul was on his way to Damascus to arrest the Christians there, when he suddenly fell to the ground. Jesus appeared to Paul (or, as he was then known, Saul of Tarsus). In that dramatic encounter, Paul discovered that his view of reality was upside-down. He had been persecuting Christians, thinking they were enemies of God—but then he discovered that he was behaving as God's enemy.

In spite of all of that, the Lord chose Paul. What grace! What mercy!

Nobody else has ever come to the Lord in quite the same way Paul did. Every believer's conversion story is unique, but we all have this in common: We were all once enemies of Christ. At some point in your life, a moment came when the Holy Spirit quietly called to you and said, "I have chosen you. You have been my enemy, but now it's time for you to surrender to me." The moment of your encounter was probably not as dramatic as Paul's, yet it was equally important and transforming. The entire course of your life changed—by the grace and mercy of God.

Paul goes on to tell Timothy:

> Even though I was once a blasphemer and a persecutor and a violent man, I was shown mercy because I acted in ignorance and unbelief. The grace of our Lord was poured out on me abundantly, along with the faith and love that are in Christ Jesus.
>
> Here is a trustworthy saying that deserves full acceptance: Christ Jesus came into the world to save sinners—of whom I am the worst. (1 Timothy 1:13–15)

This is an amazing statement. Paul says, first, that he received mercy because he was ignorant. As horrible as his actions were, he was not deliberately rebelling against God. The evil he did, he did out of ignorance and unbelief. Saul of Tarsus thought he was doing a good thing by persecuting the church! And the truth is, we human beings do many evil things with the best of intentions.

Islamic terrorists kill innocent people thinking they are doing the will of Allah. Japanese fighter pilots attacked Pearl Harbor in December 1941, thinking they were serving the will of their divine emperor. And there have been shameful episodes in Christian history, such as the Inquisition or the Crusades, where people have killed, tortured, and waged war in the name of Christ. And that is precisely the kind of well-intentioned evil that Saul of Tarsus engaged in.

You might say, "Saul should have known better. He had studied the Scriptures. He should have known that Jesus was the promised Messiah." Yet we, too, have the Scriptures—and how many times have we violated God's Word? How many sins have we committed when we should have known better?

In point of fact, Paul did not know any better. He was spiritually blind. He knew the Scriptures, but he didn't understand that those Scriptures pointed to Jesus of Nazareth as the promised Messiah. He thought that Jesus was a false teacher and that Christianity was a false cult. He was blinded by ignorance and unbelief.

When the Lord was dying on the cross, He prayed, "Father, forgive them, for they do not know what they are doing" (see Luke 23:34). This prayer probably covered the sins of Paul as well as the sins of those who crucified Him. This great compassionate prayer of our Lord underscores the deceptive power of sin.

For some reason, it's easier to spot deception in other people's lives than our own. We can look around us and see other people who think they are 100 percent right, yet they are tearing up their families, wrecking their marriages, ruining their lives, and destroying their health. That is the deceitful power of sin.

There is no human being who understands life and reality very well. We all think we know the truth and do what is right—yet we are all, to one degree or another, following error and fantasy. So we must continually ask God to shine His light into the darkness of our ignorance and lead us into an understanding of His truth.

The gift of faith and the gift of love

One of the questions I'm asked most often is, "What is the unpardonable sin? I'm afraid that I've committed the unpardonable sin. What do you think?"

Jesus tells us clearly that the unpardonable sin is to turn your back on Him. When the Holy Spirit has shown you unmistakably who Jesus is, yet you resist Him and turn away from Him, you run the risk of passing the point of no return with God. The Scriptures tell us:

> It is impossible for those who have once been enlightened, who have tasted the heavenly gift, who have shared in the Holy Spirit, who have tasted the goodness of the Word of God and the powers of the coming age, if they fall away, to be brought back to repentance, because to their loss they are crucifying the Son of God all over again and subjecting him to public disgrace. (Hebrews 6:4–6)

These words describe the most dire spiritual condition imaginable. Yet there are many stages you must pass through before reaching this point of no return. I always tell people that if they are concerned in their hearts about their spiritual condition, then they have not committed the unpardonable sin. Once a person reaches the point of no return, he or she no longer cares about his or her spiritual condition. That person is spiritually dead.

Saul of Tarsus had undoubtedly passed several stages of spiritual decline. He was moving toward the point of no return—but before he could descend to the depths of the unpardonable sin, he had an encounter with the risen Lord on the road to Damascus. His proud ignorance was shattered by a face-to-face encounter with Christ. He received mercy—though God's mercy nearly had to destroy him in order to save him!

Reflecting on that encounter, Paul writes, "The grace of our Lord was poured out on me abundantly, along with the faith and love that are in Christ Jesus." When you come to Jesus Christ, Paul says, you receive two important gifts.

The first gift is faith. Faith is the ability to see life realistically and to have all illusions stripped away. The world is filled with confusion, and the worldlings all around you are wasting their lives chasing fantasies. But when you see life from God's perspective, you see reality as it is.

The second gift is love. When you come to Jesus Christ, you experience a love and compassion for people that transcends all other loves. You become more aware of human need, especially spiritual need. Your eyes are opened and your heart is warmed with a love for God, a love for God's people, and a love for the lost.

Paul goes on to give us a simple formulation of a profound gospel truth: "Here is a trustworthy saying that deserves full acceptance: Christ Jesus came into the world to save sinners—of whom I am the worst" (1 Timothy 1:15).

Notice Paul's emphasis—his way of underscoring and highlighting this truth: "Here is a trustworthy saying that deserves full acceptance." When Jesus spoke, He used a similar rhetorical device to make people sit up and take notice of His words: "Truly, truly, I say unto you." Anytime you see such emphasis in the New Testament, highlight the phrase that comes next. In God's Word, such phrases mean, "Pay close attention: This is important!"

In our study, we will see Paul use such phrases five times in his letters to Timothy—"Here is a trustworthy saying that deserves full acceptance." Each time, Paul makes a statement of profound and foundational importance. These statements were the memory verses that the early Christians learned from the letters of Paul.

The first of these trustworthy, noteworthy truths was: "Christ Jesus came into the world to save sinners." This sounds like a simple formulation of the gospel—yet it is amazingly profound. We were all darkened in our understanding and alienated from God until Jesus Christ came to save us. He took away our darkness, bridged the gulf between us and God, and awakened our spirits to know Him.

The worst of sinners

Note that Paul relates this truth in a profoundly personal and humble way. He says, "Christ Jesus came into the world to save sinners—of whom I am the worst." He doesn't say, "I was the worst." He says, "I am the worst." He truly considers himself to be the chief of all sinners.

You may say, "But what about Paul's own words in 2 Corinthians 5:17—'Therefore, if anyone is in Christ, he is a new creation; the old has gone, the new has come!'? If Paul is a new creation, why does he still call himself the worst of sinners?"

Some commentators have suggested that these words are false humility on Paul's part. I disagree. I don't think God would allow even a mildly dishonest statement in His Word. I believe Paul means it sincerely when he says he is the worst of sinners. He is not thinking of his position in Christ. He is thinking about himself as a human being, living in the world—and though he was made whole in Christ, the flesh is still active in his life. He struggles against it, but the flesh is strong—an alien invader in the life of the Christian. We must constantly be on guard against it.

That's what Paul is talking about. He's looking back over his life, remembering when he thought he was pleasing God yet doing so much harm that he is now appalled. He remembers how pride once deceived him. That's what the Bible calls "the sin that so easily entangles" (see Hebrews 12:1).

Paul's biggest struggle involved the sin of pride. His struggle was even more difficult because God had revealed many wonderful truths to him, and these revelations tempted him toward the sin of pride. In 2 Corinthians 12:7, Paul writes, "To keep me from becoming conceited because of these surpassingly great revelations, there was given me a thorn in my flesh, a messenger of Satan, to torment me." So Paul acknowledges that the struggle against the flesh is a lifelong struggle—but he also says, "For that very reason I was shown mercy so that in me, the worst of sinners, Christ Jesus might display his unlimited patience as an example for those who would believe on him and receive eternal life" (1 Timothy 1:16).

Here is the second reason Paul gives for why he received mercy from the Lord. He says that God looked out over the whole human race and found the proudest man of all, a man who was so conscious of his own abilities that it blew the fuse of reality in his mind. Because of Paul's excessive pride, he says, the Lord deliberately chose him that he might be an example to others who had to struggle with any kind of sin.

How patient Jesus Christ can be! How patiently the Lord worked with this apostle! How often God forgave him!

Paul now holds himself up as an example to Timothy and says, "Don't be discouraged. You may fail from time to time, but God is patient with you. He will pick you up and use you again. He demonstrated His patience toward me in all of my pride, in all of my opposition to Christianity—and He will be patient toward you." Then, unable to contain himself, Paul breaks out in a hymn of joyful praise: "Now to the King eternal, immortal, invisible, the only God, be honor and glory for ever and ever. Amen" (1 Timothy 1:17).

Paul's heart is moved to remember how gracious the Lord Jesus has been to him; how many times he has forgiven and restored this proud, arrogant Pharisee. So he gives thanks and praise to the King of the ages, who deserves honor and glory from you and me, forever and ever—

Amen!

CHAPTER 5

Wage the Good Warfare

1 Timothy 1:18–20

Craig Brian Larson, contributing editor for *Leadership Journal,* suggests an analogy between the Christian life and the life of the Alaskan bull moose. Every fall, the bulls in the moose herd battle each other for dominance, using their antlers as weapons. If a bull moose's antlers are broken in battle, he must surrender. The moose with the strongest antlers always triumphs.

But though the battle may be fought in the fall, it is won or lost during the summertime, when the moose is nourishing himself. The moose who consumes the most complete diet for gaining muscle and growing antlers will prevail in the fall.

There's a lesson here for all of us. We all must face spiritual warfare. Our enemy, Satan, will attack at a time and season of his own choosing. Will we be victorious in the battle? Or will our antlers be broken and the battle lost? The battle is decided not in the time of warfare but in the time of preparation. Are we nourishing ourselves for battle? Are we gaining spiritual muscle and growing spiritual antlers in preparation for the clash ahead? Victory depends not on what we do in the battle but on what we do today.

Now is the time to prepare for spiritual warfare. Tomorrow will be too late.

Fight the good fight

Paul's overarching theme for all of 1 Timothy is summarized by a concise phrase that we find in these verses. Paul writes:

> Timothy, my son, I give you this instruction in keeping with the prophecies once made about you, so that by following them you may fight the good fight, holding on to faith and a good conscience. Some have rejected these and so have shipwrecked their faith. Among them are Hymenaeus and Alexander, whom I have handed over to Satan to be taught not to blaspheme. (1 Timothy 1:18–20)

The phrase that summarizes this letter is "fight the good fight, holding on to faith and a good conscience." The New King James Version puts it this way: "Wage the good warfare, having faith and a good conscience." Paul wants Timothy to know that the Christian life is warfare, and he does not want Timothy to face that battle unarmed and unprepared. We will see this battle imagery again in Paul's second letter to Timothy. There, Paul, at the end of his ministry and his life, will say of himself: "I have fought the good fight, I have finished the race, I have kept the faith. Finally, there is laid up for me the crown of righteousness, which the Lord, the righteous Judge, will give to me on that Day, and not to me only but also to all who have loved his appearing" (2 Timothy 4:7–8 NKJV)

These are sad words, but not tragic words. Indeed, it is a shout of triumph. Paul's life is not cut short. It is completed. When he writes these words in 2 Timothy, Paul is about to leave the battle of life—but he leaves as a battle-scarred victor, not a casualty.

Here in 1 Timothy, however, Paul does not contemplate the end of his ministry. Rather, he contemplates the early stages of Timothy's ministry career. Paul's word to this young Christian leader in Ephesus is that he must prepare himself to wage the good warfare and to hold fast to his faith and to a good conscience.

Notice that Paul writes in definite terms. He does not say, "Fight a good fight," or, "Wage a good warfare." This is not the word of a coach encouraging someone to get in there and do his best. Paul is talking about the Christian life. He is saying, "Fight the good fight, wage the good warfare." The Christian life is the only battle that is worth the struggle. It is not *a* fight; it is *the* fight. Because Paul understood that the Christian life is a battle, he wanted his spiritual son Timothy to know what he was up against.

What is the object of warfare? Is it to survive until the end of life? Is it to be the last soldier standing? No. Sometimes success in battle demands a sacrifice, including the ultimate sacrifice, death itself. In the motion picture version of J. R. R. Tolkien's *The Lord of the Rings: The Return of the King*, there is a scene that follows a battle in which many brave warriors were killed. In this scene, the victors gather in a great hall and drink to the memory of their fellow warriors who have fallen. The king raises his cup and says, "Hail the victorious dead!"

In battle, soldiers fall. Yet, by their very sacrifice, they are able to secure the victory for their cause. Though they die, they do not die in vain. They are the victorious dead. The Christian life is often such a war. Christians wage the good warfare, they fight the good fight, and if we are honest, we must acknowledge that Christians sometimes fall in battle. They are the martyrs, the believers who boldly profess Christ, even if it costs them everything they have, including life itself.

Those who fight the good fight are walking in the footsteps of Jesus. He went before us, fighting the battle that we now fight. He did not hide from the world and live in a monastery. He lived on the battlefields of this life. He went out into the marketplaces, the city streets, the temple courts, and He braved the dangers there. He went out into the midst of life, and subjected himself to opposition and persecution. He was our great example of what it means to wage the good warfare of the Christian life.

Who is our enemy?

Spiritual warfare is redemptive warfare, loving warfare, compassionate warfare. The most difficult challenge in spiritual warfare is to recognize that people are not the enemy. As Paul wrote to the Ephesians, "For our struggle is not against flesh and blood, but against the rulers, against the authorities, against the powers of this dark world and against the spiritual forces of evil in the heavenly realms" (Ephesians 6:12).

Who is our enemy? Rulers, authorities, powers, and spiritual forces of evil in the heavenly realms. In other words, our enemy is Satan and his demons. The moment we start to battle against other people, whether Christians or non-Christians, we have stopped fighting the good fight. We are simply fighting as the world fights.

We see Christians fighting the wrong fight all around us. Christians battle Christians over doctrinal differences and other issues in the church. Christians battle non-Christians in various forms of political and legal warfare. That's not spiritual warfare. That's not what it means to fight the good fight of faith. Our enemy is not made of flesh and blood.

People are not the problem, where spiritual warfare is concerned. People are victims of the true enemy. Some people are brainwashed by the enemy. Some are held hostage by the enemy. Some are forced to do the bidding of the enemy and fight the wars of the enemy. But people are victims. We must never treat people as the enemy. Jesus calls us to love people even when they hurt us and oppose us.

Notice the incentives Paul uses to motivate Timothy to wage the good warfare. You might expect Paul to encourage Timothy with a statement like the one the apostle John makes: "You, dear children, are from God and have overcome them, because the one who is in you is greater than the one who is in the world" (1 John 4:4). But Paul does not say that. You might expect Paul to say what the apostle Peter says, that Timothy should fight the good fight because we Christians "are shielded by God's power until the coming of the salvation that is ready to be revealed in the last time" (1 Peter 1:5). But Paul doesn't say that either.

Instead, Paul uses a much more simple and prosaic approach. He refers to Timothy's desire to please Paul, his father in the faith. Paul writes, "Timothy, my son, I give you this instruction in keeping with the prophecies once made about you."

In other words, Paul says, "Timothy, you are my son in the faith. As a son wants to please his father, I know that you want to please your spiritual father. So I am instructing you to fight the good fight of faith, knowing that you wish to fulfill the prophecies that were made about you." Paul encourages Timothy on the basis of the personal, affectionate relationship between them.

Years ago, a young man said something that struck me forcibly. His father, whom he had idolized, had just died. So this young man said to me, "What do you do when the only man you ever wanted to please is dead?" I sensed that this young man had lost his motivation to do great things. A great moral force had disappeared from his life. We all want to live our lives to please someone, and when that is taken from us, we lose a big piece of our reason for living.

Timothy was undoubtedly challenged and encouraged by Paul's fatherly words.

"I see great things ahead of you"

But notice what else Paul said about Timothy: "I give you this instruction in keeping with the prophecies once made about you." Some commentators believe these prophecies were spoken over Timothy during an ordination ceremony when Timothy was commissioned by the church at Lystra to accompany Paul in his missionary travels (see Acts 16:1–4). I used to hold this view, but I now view this passage differently.

I'm convinced that those prophecies were spoken about Timothy at the time of his conversion, not his ordination. I base this view on 2 Timothy 1:6, where Paul wrote, "For this reason I remind you to fan into flame the gift of God, which is in you through the laying on of my hands." The Scriptures teach that spiritual gifts are imparted to us at the moment of conversion, so Paul could only be referring to Timothy's conversion, not his ordination.

Paul, of course, led Timothy to the Lord. When Timothy professed his faith in Christ, the elders laid hands on Timothy and someone made a prophetic utterance, stating that Timothy would be used in a great way by God. The Scriptures do not tell us what was said. We only know that one or more elders prophetically described what Timothy's ministry would be like. So Paul encouraged Timothy, reminding him that God had indicated, through His Spirit, that this young man would have a great ministry.

I will never forget an incident in my ministry when I was a young man. I was a student at Dallas Seminary but spending my summers in Pasadena, California. I worked one summer as a youth minister in a church there, when Dr. Lewis Sperry Chafer, the president and founder of Dallas Seminary, came to town to speak. He was gracious enough to spend an afternoon with my wife, Elaine, and me.

I took Dr. Chafer to the church where I worked and showed him around the impressive buildings. The congregation at that time did not have a pastor, though they were seeking one, so Dr. Chafer said to me, "Do you think you might end up here, pastoring this church?"

"Who knows what God will do?" I said. "I don't have any particular plans."

"It would be a good place for you," he said, "because I believe God is going to give you a great ministry."

I don't know what he had in mind when he said that. I don't know if the Lord allowed him to somehow glimpse the ministry I would be privileged to have at Peninsula Bible Church in Palo Alto. But his words were a great encouragement to my heart. Many times as a young man, I remembered that Dr. Lewis Sperry Chafer had seen something in my future. I think I had a sense of how Timothy felt when he read these words of Paul.

Often, the biggest difference anyone can make in a young person's life is to see that person's potential and to say, "I see great things ahead of you. God can use your life in a great way." The elders at Lystra and Paul had seen great things ahead of young Timothy, and that prophecy of his future was an encouragement and motivator for this young leader.

Faith and a good conscience

How do you fight the good fight? Paul says that you must hold fast to two things: faith and a good conscience.

What is faith? It is believing what God has told you. Faith is accepting the radical truth that Jesus and His apostles have given to us. It is believing the truth about God's sovereign control of history and humanity, about His love for us as a lost race, and about the steps He took to redeem us and draw us back to himself.

Faith also involves learning about the nature of sin and the reason why life is often filled with trouble. By faith, we recognize and confess that much of the suffering we experience is not because of others; it is because of us. We are the problem. Something within us repeatedly sabotages our best intentions and destroys our most cherished relationships. By faith, we accept the fact that the cross of Jesus Christ is our only hope of deliverance and salvation.

Faith enables us to face the uncertainties and perils of the future with confidence in God. It has been said, "We don't know what the future holds, but we know who holds the future." So we can fight the good fight and wage the good warfare, knowing that no matter what happens to any individual soldier, the battle has already been won. Even if we fall in battle, we are victorious in death.

So we hold on to this faith. We do not deviate from it. We do not lose heart.

And with faith there must also be a good conscience. Many people, including many Christians, do not know what the conscience is or how it works.

Our conscience wasn't given to teach us the difference between right and wrong. The purpose of the conscience is to help us to act according to the truth that is found in God's Word. We need a conscience to help us to choose what is right and resist what is wrong.

Many people mistake their feelings for their conscience. They rely on their feelings to choose what is right and wrong. The problem is that our feelings are unreliable. Sometimes feelings tell us to do things we know are wrong. Many people have followed their feelings into immoral or adulterous relationships, or into unethical business deals, or into cheating on their taxes, or some other sin. Some people will rationalize sin on the basis that "it feels right."

What, then, is a good conscience? A good conscience is synonymous with an obedient heart, a heart that wants to do what God says is right. Whenever you are about to make a choice between what God says and what your feelings and flesh are telling you, obey God. If you do that, you will maintain a good conscience—and you will prepare yourself to always fight the good fight.

Your faith and good conscience work together to prepare you for battle. Faith gives you the confidence for battle. A good conscience is the armor that protects your soul. Satan cannot discourage the spiritual warrior whose faith is strong or wound the warrior whose conscience is clean. If you hold on to faith in a good conscience, you will be prepared for every battle you face.

Shipwrecked faith

What happens if we go into battle without the preparation of a strong faith and the good conscience? Paul tells us, "Some have rejected these"—that is, some have rejected faith and a good conscience—"and so have shipwrecked their faith." Paul is talking about people who know the truth but have chosen not to obey it. They not only have wandered from the faith but also have destroyed ("shipwrecked") their faith. They have started to believe that wrong is right, that dark is light. They know what is right, according to God's Word, but they are no longer willing or able to do it.

I've known a number of people over the years who have shipwrecked their faith by failing to keep a good conscience. One was a dynamic young man, the son of missionary parents. He was a pilot, and I had flown with him several times. He and his wife were members of our church, and I felt I knew him well. We studied the Bible together, and I watched him grow in the faith. He went to seminary for four years, and after he graduated, he taught in a Bible school.

At some point, he began living according to his own will and descended into sin and rebellion. He left his teaching position at the Bible school. His marriage fell apart. He told people he left the Christian faith and had become an atheist. The last I heard, he was on his third marriage. He had made a shipwreck of his faith and his family.

This story is hardly unique. We often hear of pastors, elders, or laypeople in the church who "go off the deep end." From the outside, it seems that their faith and Christian testimony collapse unexpectedly and catastrophically. But the reality is that their faith was being gradually undermined over a period of years because they failed to hold on to a good conscience.

In this passage, Paul speaks of two men who had shipwrecked their faith, Hymenaeus and Alexander. He writes, "Among them are Hymenaeus and Alexander, whom I have handed over to Satan to be taught not to blaspheme" (1 Timothy 1:20).

We do not know much about these men, though they are mentioned elsewhere in these letters to Timothy. In the second letter, Hymenaeus is said to be a person who taught that the resurrection was already past. This false teaching had overthrown the faith of some in the church (see 2 Timothy

2:18). Paul does not say that Hymenaeus had begun by deviating from doctrine. Rather, Paul suggests that Hymenaeus had gradually rejected conscience until, eventually, he began to espouse error.

In his second letter to Timothy, Paul also speaks of Alexander, a man who had done great harm to Paul and his ministry: "Alexander the metalworker did me a great deal of harm. The Lord will repay him for what he has done. You too should be on your guard against him, because he strongly opposed our message" (2 Timothy 4:14–15). Paul does not tell us what harm Alexander caused him, though it sounds like an act of betrayal, but we know that Alexander shipwrecked his faith because he rejected conscience.

Paul says of Hymenaeus and Alexander, "I have handed [them] over to Satan to be taught not to blaspheme." Paul was not being bitter or vengeful. Rather, he was pursuing the four-step course of action commanded by our Lord in Matthew 18. First, Paul went privately to these men who had harmed him. Then he went back to them with witnesses and appealed to them to repent. Then he took the matter before the entire church. Finally, he now treats these two offenders as unbelievers.

This final step is what Paul means when he says he has handed Hymenaeus and Alexander over to Satan. Paul is not saying that he has cursed them or that he has somehow subjected them to demonic attack. He is saying that these two offenders have been cut off from fellowship with the church and are now outside of the church's protection.

Delivered to Satan

Why does Paul say that Hymenaeus and Alexander are guilty of blasphemy? It's because their actions are harmful not only to Paul but also to the gospel of Jesus Christ. The word *blaspheme* comes from a Greek root word that means "evil-speaking." It is possible to speak evil of God and the gospel through our actions as well as our words. Hymenaeus and Alexander defamed and blasphemed the gospel by behaving in a way that was inconsistent with the Christian walk. Paul clearly intends this action to be remedial. He hopes that these two men will be brought to repentance.

Don't take a chance of ending up like Hymenaeus and Alexander. Prepare your soul for battle and the good fight. Hold fast to the faith. Hold on to a good conscience. Win the victory in Christ.

CHAPTER 6

The First Thing: Prayer

1 Timothy 2:1–7

A church elder once had a disagreement with his pastor. He went around to various people and complained about the pastor. Finally, word reached the pastor that this elder was spreading gossip about him.

So the pastor went to the elder and said, "Would please tell me my faults to my face? This way, I can profit by your candor, and you can help me correct my faults."

The elder was caught off guard. He hadn't expected his complaints would reach the pastor's ears. "Well, yes," he said. "Let's talk."

So they went to the pastor's office. The pastor said, "Before we begin, would you kneel with me and pray? I especially need you to pray for me that my eyes would be open to see my faults as you tell them to me. Please pray that God will enable me to correct these errors in my life."

The two men prayed together. Then the pastor said, "Now, I'm ready to hear any complaint you have for me."

The elder shook his head. "Pastor," he said, "please forgive me. After praying with you, I can see that my complaints were not worth talking about. By gossiping to others, I've been serving Satan's cause, not the Lord's. Thank you for praying with me. It was prayer I needed all along."

As we come to the second chapter of Paul's first letter to Timothy, we will see Paul set before this young leader a plan for public worship in the Ephesian church. Public worship is a revealing indication of what is taking place in the inner life of the church. And Paul says Timothy needs to make prayer the first priority of the Ephesian church.

The elements of public worship

There are three foundational elements in Christian worship, and these three elements will always be a part of the public worship experience in any healthy Christian church. Those three elements are prayer, praise, and preaching. And the first of these three elements is prayer. Paul writes, "I urge, then, first of all, that requests, prayers, intercession and thanksgiving be made for everyone—for kings and all those in authority, that we may live peaceful and quiet lives in all godliness and holiness" (1 Timothy 2:1–2).

Notice that Paul gives us a priority list of the elements of public worship that should be emphasized. First, he underscores the importance of public prayer—an entire congregation praying together as one in a public worship service. When Christians gather together in worship, they should begin with prayer. If we do not follow that pattern, we have drifted away from God's priorities.

The apostle Paul places prayer first on the list for two important reasons.

First, prayer focuses the eyes and hearts of the people on God at the beginning. A church service is a distinct kind of public gathering. Anyone entering a worship service should not be confused about the purpose for the gathering. A church service is not a Kiwanis or Rotary Club meeting. A church service recognizes God and acknowledges that He is present among us.

Second, prayer helps us put our own humanity in perspective. Prayer quiets the human heart and clears away the distracting debris of our everyday lives. We generally come to church with many things on our minds: the children who misbehaved, the upsetting phone call last night, the problems at the office, the unpaid bills.

But when we come together as a church and join our hearts in prayer, all of those other problems recede from our thoughts. We focus on the grandeur and power of God. That is one of the functions of worship—to renew our minds and bring them back into a realistic and godly perspective.

I hear people say, "I don't need to go to church to worship God. I can worship God at home, or while working in my garden, or while walking on the beach. I don't have to go to a building to worship God." Well, that's true. We can worship God anyplace and anytime.

But God has specifically told us that we are to regularly come together and worship Him as a church body. The New Testament tells us, "Let us not give up meeting together, as some are in the habit of doing, but let us encourage one another—and all the more as you see the Day approaching" (Hebrews 10:25). Yes, we can pray and worship God in the forest or on the beach or even on the living room sofa. But we should not forsake the habit of meeting together for worship as the church, the body of Christ.

The psalmist once wrote of a difficult problem in his life, a series of questions he could not answer. He wrote:

When I tried to understand all this,
    it was oppressive to me

till I entered the sanctuary of God;
  then I understood... (Psalm 73:16–17)

When we go to the sanctuary of God and worship Him along with His people, we are better able to see reality as it is. We learn to see our lives from God's perspective, which is the true perspective. That experience of worshiping God begins with prayer, with the recognition of His presence and involvement in our lives.

Three forms of prayer—and one of praise

Next, Paul goes on to list three forms of prayer and one form of praise.

Requests. The first form of prayer Paul lists are prayers for the requests of the people. In every church, there are people going through times of struggle, pain, sorrow, and pressure. A caring church prays for people who hurt. The Scriptures tell us that we have a spiritual duty to care for one another and pray for one another: "Carry each other's burdens, and in this way you will fulfill the law of Christ" (Galatians 6:2).

As a member of your local church and of the body of Christ, you have a responsibility for the burdens of your Christian brothers and sisters. So when you read about needs and hurts within your congregation, don't just shake your head and think, "That's too bad." Take those requests seriously; pray over them at home, with your family, when you're alone, and in your small group Bible study. God wants to be in partnership with us through prayer. When we bring these requests before Him and ask Him to intervene, He answers.

Prayers. The second category of prayers is simply called prayers. The English translation doesn't help us very much. In the Greek, Paul used a special word that refers to prayer requests that can be met only by God.

The previous term, "requests," referred to prayer requests that we human beings can become involved in. For example, if you are praying for someone who doesn't have enough food, you might sense the Spirit of God saying to you, "What about those cans of food in your cupboard? And perhaps you could go to the store and purchase a ham to go with them. While praying for that needy family, why not make yourself available as the answer to that prayer?"

By contrast, this term "prayers" in the Greek referred to prayer requests that are beyond human ability to fix. These are prayer requests that only God can answer. If someone has an incurable disease, a critical injury, a devastating loss, then that is a crisis that only God can resolve. That's the kind of prayer Paul writes about here. We are to bring these prayer needs before God as a congregation, and we are to pray about them together.

Intercession. The third form of prayer is intercession, a term that means "a petition on behalf of another person." The original Greek term was used when one person would petition the king on behalf of another person. This is a beautiful expression of what congregational prayer should be like. We are children of the King. We come to our heavenly Father, with whom we have an intimate relationship. He gives us the right to intercede on the behalf of other people.

Next, Paul links to these forms of prayer a form of praise, *thanksgiving.* When we gather as Christians, it's fitting to give thanks to God. One way we give thanks is through the hymns and songs we sing. So I would urge you never to sing hymns in a mechanical or thoughtless way. If you do not mean the words of a song, please don't sing them. Listen to the words and let the music minister to your heart—but sing only if you mean it.

It's amusing to look out over a congregation and see people singing words I strongly suspect they do not mean. For example, there's a hymn that says, "Take my silver and my gold / Not a mite would I withhold." And as the congregation sang that song, I thought, "Oh, how I wish they meant that! Then the church's financial problems would be over!"

I want all of my songs to God to be sincere expressions of gratitude from the depths of my heart. That's why I love the grand old hymns such as:

Amazing grace!
How sweet the sound
That saved a wretch like me!

Or:

And can it be that I should gain
An interest in the Savior's blood?
Died He for me, who caused His pain?
For me, who Him to death pursued?
Amazing love! How can it be
That Thou, my God, shouldst die for me?

When the entire congregation joins as one to sing a beautiful expression of praise to God, the people are blessed and God is glorified. That's why the apostle Paul tells us that our worship together should be filled with prayer and praise to God.

For whom should we pray?

Next, Paul deals with the question: As a congregation, whom should we pray for? Paul's answer: Everybody! He writes, "I urge, then, first of all, that requests, prayers, intercession and thanksgiving be made for everyone—for kings and all those in authority, that we may live peaceful and quiet lives in all godliness and holiness" (1 Timothy 2:1–2).

Note that word *everyone*. Understand, Paul is not saying that we should pray for all of humanity without exception. If we prayed that way, we'd never finish praying! When Paul says we should pray for everyone, he means we should pray for everyone without distinction. In other words, we should pray for all kinds of people and all kinds of needs, without distinction or discrimination.

We should not draw a line and say, "These people are beyond the power of prayer." This means that if you are a Baptist, you cannot say, "I can't pray for Episcopalians and Presbyterians and atheists." This means you can't say, "I don't agree with those people and I don't like those people, therefore I refuse to pray for them." In many cases, those are the people who most need your prayers. You need to pray for them so that you can learn to overcome your resentment and prejudice toward them.

Paul lists certain categories of people that we should be sure to pray for. He begins with "kings and all those in authority." This is a form of prayer we often neglect—to our peril! We should not ignore the needs of our governmental leaders and politicians. What if they are ungodly people? We are still to pray for them.

When Paul wrote these words to Timothy, the king of Rome was Nero, one of the cruelest of all Roman emperors. By that time, Nero had already launched a vicious program of persecution against Christians. Yet Paul urged Timothy to pray for the king, for the tyrant Nero. Here is a recognition that all government operates under God's sovereign hand (see also Romans 13:1–7).

Tertullian (c. A.D. 160–225) was a scholar and writer in the early Christian church. He lived under oppressive Roman rule, yet he prayed for the Roman leaders and urged his fellow Christians to do the same. Tertullian had a list of six requests he continually brought before the Lord whenever he prayed for the Roman emperor:

1. Long life for the emperor.
2. Secure dominions.
3. A safe home.

4. A faithful senate.
5. A righteous people to govern.
6. A world at peace.

We can all learn from this example as to how we should pray for our own leaders.

Paul also tells us that we are to pray for "all those in authority." By this, Paul refers to people at all subordinate positions in government, down to the local level, such as the mayor, city council, and school board officials. Again, Paul is not saying that we should pray for all such officials without exception but for all without distinction. We pray for these leaders whether we voted for them or not, whether we agree with them or not, whether they represent our political party and leanings or not.

In *The Hiding Place,* Corrie ten Boom tells how, during World War II, her Dutch family hid Jewish refugees from the Nazis. When the Nazi soldiers came to their house, her father was always courteous to them. He never told them he was hiding Jews in his attic, but he always treated these soldiers with respect. He believed that everyone deserves respect because everyone is made in the image of God.

God can use the wicked as well as the righteous. As the book of Proverbs reminds us, "The king's heart is in the hand of the LORD; he directs it like a watercourse wherever he pleases" (Proverbs 21:1). And in the Scriptures, we see that various pagan kings, including Nebuchadnezzar and Cyrus the Persian, are called the servants of God, even when they are being used to punish the people of God. So God calls us to pray for our leaders.

God wants all to be saved

When we pray, we should expect results.

First, Paul says we should pray in order "that we may live peaceful and quiet lives in all godliness and holiness." Did you ever consider the fact that the peace of our community is related to the prayers of God's people? In these days of global terrorism, nuclear proliferation, political extremism, racial tension, and gang violence, we need this message more than ever. I believe one of the reasons there is so much violence and fear in our society is that we Christians have not been praying as we should.

I once had a conversation with young Christians at the California State Prison, Solano, in the city of Vacaville. Some had found Christ while in prison; others had rededicated their lives to Christ there. They told me they regard themselves as the control apparatus that keeps the peace of the prison.

When riots threaten, the Christian prisoners gather and ask, "What has gone wrong with us?" Then they recommit themselves to Christian love and unity. They've learned that God keeps the prison peaceful when the Christians are in a right relationship with each other and with Him.

The California State Prison Board once asked the chief psychologist of the prison system why the Vacaville prison had less unrest at that time than any other prison in the state. The psychologist replied, "There's a group of Christians there who pray for the prison. That's what seems to make the difference."

This confirms what the apostle Paul stresses here. We can lead quiet and peaceful lives when we are faithful in prayer for those who rule over us.

The second result we should expect from prayer is that God's will is fulfilled. Paul writes:

> This is good, and pleases God our Savior, who wants all men to be saved and to come to a knowledge of the truth. For there is one God and one mediator between God and men, the man Christ Jesus, who gave himself as a ransom for all men—the testimony now given in its proper time. And for this purpose I was appointed a herald and an apostle—I am telling the truth, I am not lying—and a teacher of the true faith to the Gentiles. (1 Timothy 2:3–7)

Prayer opens the hearts of men and women to salvation. The apostle Peter tells us that God is patient toward us, "not wanting anyone to perish, but everyone to come to repentance" (see 2 Peter 3:9). Paul agrees, saying that God "wants all men to be saved and to come to a knowledge of the truth." When we pray for people, we can expect that they will hear truth they have never heard before. We can expect that they will see things in a different way than they have ever seen them before.

Prayer does not change people immediately. It's not a magic wand. But prayer can produce a gradual dawning and realization of the truth in human hearts. The darkness ebbs away, and people begin to understand their own nature and the reality of God's love.

Again, when Paul says God "wants all men to be saved and to come to a knowledge of the truth," he means all without distinction, not all without exception. Paul is not preaching universal salvation in this passage—the belief that all human beings will be saved. He is preaching that there are no human barriers to prevent any person from coming to God. He desires all kinds of people to be saved.

There is one God

People sometimes tell me, "You have your God, others have their God, and I have my God. Who is to say who is right?" It's as if they believe there are many gods, perhaps billions of gods—one for each person on the planet. But there is only one God. As Paul tells us, "For there is one God and one mediator between God and men, the man Christ Jesus, who gave himself as a ransom for all men." All of humanity must answer to this one God, in spite of differences in culture, race, or background.

While God does want all people, without distinction, to be saved and come to knowledge of the truth, He has made only one provision for their redemption. There is not a God for the Hebrews and another for the Gentiles. There is not a God for the Buddhists and another for the Hindus. There is only one God and one Mediator, Jesus Christ. His nature is unique. He is fully man and fully God. When you commit your life to that magnificent Man who solved the basic problems of life, you meet God.

That is what the disciples discovered. They did not come to Jesus because they thought He was God. They believed it was blasphemy for a man to claim to be God. They came to Him because he was such an amazing man. They saw Him to be such a wonderful, wise teacher and prophet that they were powerfully drawn to Him. Within His chest beat a human heart; but somewhere along the way, the disciples realized that the heartbeat of Jesus was the heartbeat of God.

Jesus said, "I am the way and the truth and the life. No one comes to the Father except through me" (see John 14:6). People come to Jesus in many ways. Some are led to Christ by a friend. Some find Him in an evangelistic service or a church service. Some find Christ through a tract or Christian book. Some have even been led to Christ by non-Christians! Jerry Cook tells this story in *Love, Forgiveness, and Acceptance.*

A young man, a drug pusher, was living in a free love commune in the 1970s. One day, he and a young woman were sitting in the house, smoking marijuana together. He said to her, "I wish I could stop using dope. I don't know how to get free of the stuff."

The young woman was from a Christian home but had rejected the faith of her parents. She knew the gospel, but she wanted nothing to do with Christianity. When the drug pusher told her he wished he could be free of drugs, she replied, "I know how you can do that. If you put your trust in Jesus as your Lord and Savior, He'll set you free."

The young man was baffled. "What do you mean?" he asked.

"I'm not going to tell you," she said. "If I tell you, you'll become a Christian, and you'll stop smoking dope with me, and I won't see you anymore."

But he begged her to explain the gospel to him, and finally she told him. She quoted John 3:16, which she had learned as a child, and told him that Jesus was the only way to God.

So he prayed and received Jesus Christ as his Lord and Savior, and he was delivered from his addiction to drugs. Just as the young woman had feared, he left the commune and continued on in his relationship with the Lord. He had been led to Jesus Christ by a nonbeliever![1]

People find Christ in many different ways, but there is only one way to God, and that is Jesus. That's why He said, "But small is the gate and narrow the road that leads to life, and only a few find it" (see Matthew 7:14). Paul says, that Jesus "gave himself as a ransom for all"—again, not "all" in the sense that all of humanity is saved but in the sense that there are no distinctions and all of humanity may come.

Finally, Paul says there is only one gospel, "the testimony now given in its proper time. And for this purpose I was appointed a herald and an apostle." If you are going to come to God, there is only one way to do so, and that is by the gospel, the good news that Jesus is the way, the truth, and the life. This is the nature of His work.

Down through the centuries, wherever the gospel has been preached, lives have been changed and people have come out of spiritual darkness into light. They have come out of superstition, out of violence, out of sexual immorality, out of drunkenness, out of drug abuse, out of occultism and Satanism, and they have been healed.

Broken homes have become whole. Broken hearts have become filled with joy. Broken lives have been restored. There is no greater testimony to the truth of the gospel than the record of thousands and thousands of transformed lives.

We in the church are the repository for the greatest truth ever known. We hold the solution to all the problems that have baffled the greatest minds in history. We hold the answer to the questions of human meaning and human misery. We are the body of Christ, and because He is our head, we are His hands and feet, carrying out His work in a suffering and dying world.

CHAPTER 7

Adam's Rib... or Women's Lib?

1 Timothy 2:8–15

If you are a fan of old movies, you may remember a 1949 film called *Adam's Rib,* starring Spencer Tracy and Katharine Hepburn. It's a classic romantic comedy—but it's also a serious examination of the gender roles. Spencer Tracy plays a prosecutor named Adam Bonner. Katherine Hepburn plays his wife, defense attorney Amanda Bonner.

When Adam indicts a woman for attempted murder, Amanda agrees to defend the woman. At first, the two attorneys agree not to let their courtroom battle spill over into their marriage. But the legal battle quickly escalates into a full-blown battle of the sexes.

I couldn't help thinking of *Adam's Rib* as I approached this next section of Paul's first letter to Timothy. We are about to examine one of the major battlefields of Scripture, a controversial passage that deals with the role of women in the church. Down through the centuries, people have fought (and still are fighting!) over this section of Scripture.

Over the past half-century, the church has been heavily influenced by various movements in the culture, including the feminist movement, which used to be called women's liberation or women's lib. To an extent, it's valid for the church to be responsive to the culture in which it ministers. But as we in the church seek to witness to the culture, we must be careful never to compromise or dilute God's Word. The Bible sits in judgment on human society, not the other way around.

So the dichotomy that we face as we come to 1 Timothy 2 is: Adam's rib? Or women's lib? Are women to be viewed as second-class citizens in the church? Or have women in the church been liberated, as the feminist movement would define the term?

Or does Paul, in 1 Timothy 2, offer a third and more accurate way of looking at the role of women in worship?

Holy hands

We should remember that the subject under discussion in 1 Timothy 2 is prayer and worship. This passage, then, deals with the role of women and their ministry within the praying, worshiping congregation. Paul continues his discussion of the subject of prayer. He focuses on the atmosphere in which prayer should take place within the context of a worship service:

> I want men everywhere to lift up holy hands in prayer, without anger or disputing. I also want women to dress modestly, with decency and propriety, not with braided hair or gold or pearls or expensive clothes, but with good deeds, appropriate for women who profess to worship God. (1 Timothy 2:8–10)

When Paul says, "I want men everywhere to lift up holy hands in prayer, without anger or disputing," he does not mean that only men should pray. Some denominations and churches have misinterpreted this phrase in that way, so that only men are permitted to pray in public or to lead the congregation in prayer. But that is not what Paul means. He is saying that public prayer should be conducted by people lifting up holy hands and doing so without anger or quarreling in their hearts.

Christians make a big mistake when they think that Paul is emphasizing a form of prayer. It is not the form that concerns Paul. It is the heart. It is the attitude. It is the righteousness of spirit that is at issue here.

The first characteristic Paul describes here is "holy hands." Raised hands were a common posture of prayer in those days, derived from the posture of prayer in use in Jewish synagogues. The Jews led congregational prayer by standing with their arms raised.

What, then, are "holy hands"? Paul is not saying that the person who prays needs to have some religious ritual done, like sprinkling his hands with holy water. Rather, Paul is using a figure of speech that addresses the heart of the one who prays. In order to have holy hands, we must have lives, thoughts, and hearts that are clean and holy before God. Our lives must be honest, sincere, and righteous.

Second, Paul says that these prayers must be offered "without anger or disputing." This means that the one who prays must have right relationships with other believers. The one who prays must not harbor bitterness or resentment against others in the church. And if other people have any grievance against the one who prays, that grievance needs to be brought out and settled. A person's relationships must be whole and healthy in order for that person's prayers to be honoring to God.

When I was a boy in Montana, we had Methodist services once a month because there was no Methodist church in town. Each month, one man would always stand and lead in prayer. His prayer was anywhere from ten to fifteen minutes in length, and it invariably put many parishioners to sleep. Worst of all, everyone in town knew that this man was putting on a show of being religious. He was the biggest rascal in town. His dishonest business practices were legendary. So the longer he prayed, the more people despised him as a hypocrite.

A person who stands before the congregation and leads prayer must have holy hands and healthy relationships with his Christian brothers and sisters. If not, his prayers are not only meaningless—they are an offense. Our private lives must match our public prayers—or our prayers condemn us as hypocrites.

The prayers of women

Paul goes on to say that women also should be involved in congregational prayer. The wording of this section does not specifically say that women should pray, but the context makes it clear that this entire passage deals with prayer. Paul is designating, first, how men should pray in the worship service. Then he moves to talking about how women should pray. This is clear from Paul's transition, "I also want women to..."

The use of this word *also* in English is a weak translation. In the Greek, the sense of this term is strong. The clear implication is "in like manner, women are to pray." Like the men who pray, women who pray are to be characterized by godly lives, not merely outward display. So Paul is saying that when women pray before the congregation, they should do so with modest dress and a life record of good deeds.

Viewed in this way, Paul's teaching in 1 Timothy 2 agrees perfectly with his teaching in 1 Corinthians 11. In both places, Paul speaks of the role of women in the congregation. In Corinthians, he acknowledges that women are permitted to pray and prophesy in the church. (To "prophesy" in the New Testament does not necessarily mean to foretell future events; rather, it means "to comment on the Scriptures or to expound God's Word.")

Paul goes on to say, however, that women who pray or prophesy in the congregation must have their heads covered as a demonstration of their agreement with the biblical principle of headship. Paul deals extensively with this principle of headship in 1 Corinthians 11. To state the principle succinctly,

Paul says that the head of the body is the direction-setter for the body. He states that the head of the woman is the man, that the head of every man is Christ, and that the head of Christ is God the Father. So, everyone at every level is under submission to a head, and ultimately to God the Father, who is the head of all.

Now, many people look at Paul's statement to Timothy as an attempt on the apostle's part to regulate the way women dress. Paul does write, "I also want women to dress modestly, with decency and propriety, not with braided hair or gold or pearls or expensive clothes, but with good deeds, appropriate for women who profess to worship God." If you read those words as meaning simply that Paul is imposing a dress code on women in the church, then you have missed the point.

When Paul talks about matters of braided hair or jewelry or clothing, he is not attacking the way women dress. He is using the external adornment that women wear as a lens through which to see a woman's attitude. As the Lord said to the prophet Samuel, "Man looks at the outward appearance, but the Lord looks at the heart" (1 Samuel 16:7).

Often, the way we dress and the way we behave reveal the reality of our hearts. If a woman comes to church adorned in such a way as to stir up envy in the women of the church and lust in the men, then we have an insight into the condition of her heart. She is not trying to get God's attention; she is seeking attention from people.

I recall a woman who came to our congregation many years ago as a new Christian. She had come out of a worldly lifestyle, and she brought vestiges of the old worldliness with her. I'm sure you've heard of strapless evening gowns. Well, this woman was dressed in gownless evening straps! It's a compliment to refer to a woman as a vision—but this woman was a sight!

Over the next few weeks, however, I saw a gradual transformation in this woman. No one criticized her or gossiped about her. I think that as the Lord spoke to her week by week, she began to experience an inner change. She stopped dressing to impress, and she began dressing to reflect the new priorities in her heart.

Paul is not saying in this passage that Christian women should dress in a way that is frumpy and unattractive. It's no sin to have a pleasing appearance. And it's no sin to be stylish. Christian women should be concerned first to have hearts that are sincere and responsive to the Spirit of God. If a woman's inner reality is right with God, then her outer adornment will be right with God as well.

The role of women in teaching

Next, Paul turns from prayer to the subject of teaching in the congregation. What is the role of women in teaching? Paul writes:

> A woman should learn in quietness and full submission. I do not permit a woman to teach or to have authority over a man; she must be silent. For Adam was formed first, then Eve. And Adam was not the one deceived; it was the woman who was deceived and became a sinner. (1 Timothy 2:11–14)

Here we come to an area of great controversy: What part can a woman play in a church service? Is it valid for women to lead, to speak, and to teach in church? Paul says that a woman should "learn in quietness" and "be silent." I have visited churches where this teaching of Paul's was taken so literally that women were prohibited from speaking a single word in church. They were not even allowed to say "hello" once they entered the church sanctuary.

This is religious extremism based on a misinterpretation of Paul's counsel to Timothy. It's important to note that the same Greek word that is translated "quietness" and "silent" here is also used in 1 Timothy 2:2, where Paul says that we should pray "for kings and all those in authority, that we may live peaceful and quiet lives in all godliness and holiness." Obviously, Paul is not saying that it is desirable for us to live in absolute silence. He is saying that it's desirable to live an undisturbed life, a life that is tranquil and not marred by trouble with the authorities.

Now if you carry this understanding of the word *quietness* over to the verses regarding women in the church, it changes Paul's meaning completely. Clearly, Paul is not saying that women are forbidden to speak in church. He is saying that the church service should be conducted in an orderly and peaceful way. We find a parallel concept in another letter by Paul, where he writes, "We hear that some among you are idle. They are not busy; they are busybodies. Such people we command and urge in the Lord Jesus Christ to settle down and earn the bread they eat" (2 Thessalonians 3:11–12).

In this passage, the same word that is elsewhere translated "quietness" or "silent" is used to say that busybodies in the church should "settle down." Another translation says that the busybodies in the church should be told to "do their work in quietness." Paul is not telling people to shut their mouths. He is telling people to go about their business, including the business of worship, in a peaceful, respectful, orderly way.

Paul is talking about the attitude we should have in a worship service. It is disruptive in a worship service to have people interrupt a sermon or prayer or other act of worship with arguments or persistent questioning. When a few individuals stubbornly insist on having their own way or asserting their own viewpoint or demanding answers to their questions, the result is a disruption of the entire worship experience. So Paul is counseling Timothy to require a standard of orderly behavior in the worship service.

Some people misinterpret Paul's words and suggest that he is saying that men should always be the teachers in the church and women should be the learners. But the roles of teacher and learner are not determined by gender. Paul is saying that when women are learners in the church, they should learn in a peaceable and orderly way. They should not interrupt or disrupt the teaching process with challenges to the teachers.

It may be that Paul's teaching in this passage does not so much reflect gender discrimination in Paul's thinking so much as it reflects a problem that had arisen due to the Greek culture. In Ephesus, as in other Greek-influenced cities, women often participated in city government. The women in that culture were often aggressive and vociferous and didn't hesitate to disrupt any proceedings to voice their opinions. So Paul needed to instruct Timothy on how to handle disruptions that arose from the unique character of the culture.

The meaning of "authority"

Next, the apostle Paul sets forth the key principle for this passage of Scripture:

> I do not permit a woman to teach or to have authority over a man; she must be silent. For Adam was formed first, then Eve. And Adam was not the one deceived; it was the woman who was deceived and became a sinner. (1 Timothy 2:12–14)

As we have already seen, Paul is not issuing an absolute prohibition against teaching by women in the church. He does not say, "I permit no woman to teach, anywhere, anytime, to anyone, period!" This passage has been misinterpreted in this way, but that is not what Paul is saying. Other New Testament passages make it clear that women did teach in the early church with the blessing of Paul. As we will see when we look at Paul's letter to Titus, Paul instructs Titus to tell the older women to teach younger women how to love their husbands and rule their children.

Women were expected to teach in the church. One notable case was when Aquila and his wife, Priscilla, took Apollos, the eloquent orator of the early church, and instructed him in a more complete understanding of the doctrines of Jesus. Priscilla is linked with her husband as one of those instructors. So women clearly did teach.

The key to this passage is the phrase "have authority over a man." In the Greek, the word used in this phrase is *authentein,* which means "to domineer, to usurp authority, to take what is not rightfully yours." In this context, clearly, the term refers to domineering by teaching. In other words, women are not to take over in a church and become the final, authoritative teachers.

Does this mean that women are not permitted to be elders or pastors in the church? If by pastor you mean (as the Scriptures mean) a shepherd of a flock, then we have to acknowledge that women have been pastors for centuries. In every church there are women who teach Sunday school classes. Her class is her flock, and as their pastor and teacher, she is the guide and guardian of that flock. In that sense she is a biblical pastor.

But what if you are using the word *pastor* in the conventional sense, meaning the person who is to be a voice of authority as to what the Scriptures mean? For that is what Paul is talking about here. In this sense, we must faithfully acknowledge that a woman is not to be a pastor or elder. That is Paul's teaching in this passage.

This teaching is confirmed by incontrovertible historical fact. In the New Testament church, there were no women apostles and no women elders. Jesus could have settled this controversy at the beginning of the church by appointing Mary Magdalene or another woman as an apostle—but He did not do so. Neither Paul nor any of the apostles ever chose a woman to be an elder of any church they founded. If it was biblically permissible to do so, though, they easily could have done so. There were many godly women available, but no woman was ever made an elder in the early church.

Many churches today operate on an unbiblical model, because they have a single pastor or a single elder as their final authority. No church in the New Testament era operated that way. Churches in the first century always had pastors and elders (plural). No one person was ever given a final voice of authority. Elders reached unanimous decisions after prayer and deliberation as to what the final teaching of the Scriptures meant. It is that role that is denied to women by the apostle Paul in this passage.

Adam versus Eve

There are two reasons why Paul disallows women from such roles. It is important to note that Paul does not take these reasons from culture but from creation. It would be a mistake to think that Paul bases his counsel on the cultural patterns of the day. Paul clearly states that this edict regarding the roles of men and women in worship stems from the differences between men and women in the story of creation and fall in Genesis.

Paul begins by appealing to the order of creation. He writes, "For Adam was formed first, then Eve." This order of creation was evidently important in the mind of God. The Lord deliberately formed the male first and gave him a job to do in Eden before the woman was created. Adam may have been living for a considerable period of time (years, decades, or more) before Eve was taken from his side and brought to him.

Adam was given the task of naming all the animals, which means that he was involved in a research project. He had to study all the animals, because in the Bible names are given to things in order to reflect their true nature. Adam had a time-consuming task to perform, because there were many animals. As Adam worked at this task, he was looking for something. He noted that all of the animals came in pairs, a male and a female of each kind. Yet there was no corresponding human female to complement his own humanity (see Genesis 2:20).

At this point, God performed the first surgical operation, complete with anesthesia. God put Adam to sleep and took a rib from his side, made of it a woman, and brought her to Adam. The first response of Adam was, in effect, "At last!" He said:

> "This is now bone of my bones
> > and flesh of my flesh;
> she shall be called 'woman,'
> > for she was taken out of man." (Genesis 2:23b)

The word *now* is significant. Adam is saying, "Finally! At last! I have found that which completes me, corresponds to me, is equal with me, is sent to help me fulfill the task that God has given me to do!"

Maleness and femaleness complement each other. The specific quality given to male leadership is that of initiation. That is why the man was sent first into the world; he had something to do first.

In nature and in the church, each gender has a role to fulfill. There are differences between men and women that we in the church should recognize and respect. Neither gender is superior or inferior to the other. As Paul wrote in another letter, in the church there is "neither Jew nor Greek, slave nor free, male nor female, for you are all one in Christ Jesus" (see Galatians 3:28). As men and women live in mutual respect for each other's contributions to life and worship, peace and joy will reign—and the church will influence the world greatly for God.

CHAPTER 8

The Lord's Leaders

1 Timothy 3:1–7

Different churches and denominations use different titles to describe their leaders. The Baptists have deacons. The Presbyterians have elders. Methodists have stewards and bishops. Episcopalians have rectors and vicars. Catholics have bishops and priests. Most denominations refer to the preaching leader as the minister or pastor.

When you turn to the Scriptures, you discover that the whole subject is simple. There are only two classes of leaders designated in the early church. They were called elders (or overseers) and deacons. In 1 Timothy 3, Paul deals with the subject of leadership and talks about the qualifications and responsibilities of leaders in the church. He writes, "Here is a trustworthy saying: If anyone sets his heart on being an overseer, he desires a noble task" (1 Timothy 3:1).

Paul begins by emphasizing that anyone who wishes to be a leader or overseer in the church has desired a "noble task." In other words, the role of an overseer or elder entails a sober responsibility. The apostle underscores the importance of this leadership role for several reasons.

First, Jesus, in founding the church, made provision for elders or overseers to serve as leaders in the church. The role of overseer was not invented by human beings. It was ordained by Jesus, and He is the head of the church. He designated the kind of leaders who would govern the operations of the church, and He determined the way that those leaders would function within the church.

Unfortunately, too many churches today are operated like corporations. Decisions are made by a board of directors according to the business practices of the world. That is not the New Testament model for the church.

The church was born from the death and resurrection of Jesus Christ. The first distinctive mark of a true church is that it shares the life of Christ. Every true member of His church is born by the Spirit and filled with the

Spirit. This means that the church is not an organization like any other human organization. The methods of the corporate world are not adequate to the task of governing the church of Jesus Christ.

The elders and deacons

When our Lord, after His resurrection, sent the disciples out as apostles, He instructed them to lay the foundation of the church. Paul said, "By the grace God has given me, I laid a foundation as an expert builder" (see 1 Corinthians 3:10). That foundation was the apostolic teaching concerning the work and the person of Jesus. He goes on to say, "For no one can lay any foundation other than the one already laid, which is Jesus Christ" (1 Corinthians 3:11). It was the apostle's task to proclaim these distinctive doctrines about Jesus that define the church and guide its development.

When you read about the early church in Jerusalem in the book of Acts, you discover that the elders of the Jerusalem church were the apostles. They were the first human leaders of the church.

In Acts 6, when a problem arose in the early church concerning the care of widows, the matter was brought to the apostles. They, as overseers of the church, knew they had two priorities that should occupy their time and their thoughts: First, they were to give themselves continually to prayer. Second, they were to devote themselves to the ministry of God's Word (see Acts 6:4). So when this problem was brought before the apostles, they urged the church to appoint seven men to serve as deacons. The deacons were to be in charge of distributing food to the widows, so that the elders would be relieved of that responsibility.

As the church spread beyond the city limits of Jerusalem, the apostles tried to keep up with the growth. Local church bodies sprang up throughout the regions of Judea and Samaria, and a great spiritual awakening even broke out in the pagan city of Antioch in Syria. The apostles traveled around to the different churches, helping these local bodies to become organized and established. The apostles soon discovered, however, that the church was expanding faster than they could travel.

So they began to appoint elders in every church. These elders or overseers were appointed from among the congregations. Many elders were recent converts who had come to Christ out of a pagan background. So the apostles would visit these churches and make sure that these recently converted elders were operating the churches in accordance with God's will, as revealed through the apostolic witness. Often, the apostles sent representatives, such as Timothy and Titus, to go to these churches, appoint elders, and instruct the leaders and the people in the Christian faith.

The elders had two primary tasks: Like the apostles in the church at Jerusalem, they were to devote themselves to prayer and the ministry of the Word. They were to study, teach, and preach the Word of God. And through prayer, they were to discover the will of the Lord Jesus, who is head of the church.

Equipping member-ministers

Question: Who is the minister at your church?

Answer: You are.

Many people think that a church consists of one minister and many members—that is, one preacher and many spectators. But that is a mistaken notion. If a church is operating according to the biblical model, then it has as many ministers as there are members. So a church of a hundred people consists of a hundred ministers, and a church of a thousand people consists of a thousand ministers. In any truly biblical church, there are no spectators. Everyone is a minister.

The moment you became a member of the body of Christ, my friend, you entered the ministry. Don't expect the elders to do all the work of the ministry, and don't expect the deacons to do it all. The Spirit of God has given you gifts for ministry, so go do the work of the ministry!

The Lord Jesus says to you, "I have placed you in your community, in your neighborhood, on your street, for a reason. Look around. There are needy, lost people all around you. I have placed you where you are so that you will reach them. You are my representative. You are my hands and feet. Go, do the work I have given you. Be the hands and feet and voice of Jesus to the people all around you."

What is the elders' role? In his letter to the Ephesians, Paul wrote about spiritual gifts, and in one section he focused on the leadership gifts and how those gifts should be used in the church. "It was [the Lord Jesus] who gave some to be apostles, some to be prophets, some to be evangelists, and some to be pastors and teachers, to prepare God's people for works of service, so that the body of Christ may be built up" (Ephesians 4:11–12).

Paul here describes various functions of overseers, and these functions are apportioned as spiritual gifts—gifts of apostolic leadership, prophesying (in the New Testament sense of expounding God's Word), evangelism, pastoral ministry (shepherding God's flock), and teaching. The purpose of these leadership gifts is to prepare and equip God's people for works of service. In other words, the overseers of the church have the noble task of encouraging, instructing, training, and motivating all of us as ministers to move out into our neighborhoods and our world.

That's why the Greek word for "elder" or "overseer" is *episkopos,* a word that means "overseer, one who watches over something.' Elders are to be watching and guiding the member-ministers of the church, instructing them in the truth of God's Word, guiding them, teaching them how to do the work of the ministry—and correcting them, if need be.

To be an elder is to sit at the control board of the most exciting work that is going on in the world. Why? Because the church, in God's estimation, is the most important body in the world. God has set the church at the center of life. He has given us the opportunity of sharing His truth with the people around us—and the privilege of watching people respond to his Word. No wonder Paul calls the work of an elder a "noble task."

Individually, elders have no special authority. No elder is to be a boss in the church. Churches that allow pastors or elders to become tyrants and dictators fail to fulfill the New Testament pattern. Elders are brothers, not commanders.

Corporately, as a body of elders, they are to meet together to seek the mind of the Lord. They know they have succeeded when, in the most re-markable way that only God could bring about, they agree together about the Lord's will. When the Spirit of the Lord is at work in a body of elders, He leads them together through all the problems, difficulties, resistance, and personality differences—and He brings them all to a sense of harmony and unity. It is a beautiful thing when a body of elders has found the mind of the Lord for their church.

What a noble task that is!

The qualifications of an elder

The apostle Paul gives us the guidelines for the kind of people who should serve as elders. First, he gives us a list of character qualities that should char-acterize elders. Why are these qualities important? Because they mark the people whom the Holy Spirit has selected for the task of overseeing God's church. Please note: The congregation does not select elders; the Holy Spirit selects them. The Spirit chooses men in every congregation and develops within them the character qualities needed, leading them through various experiences in order to prepare them for that task.

Let's examine the character qualities that Paul lists for us. He writes, "Now the overseer must be above reproach, the husband of but one wife, temperate, self-controlled, respectable, hospitable, able to teach, not given to drunkenness, not violent but gentle, not quarrelsome, not a lover of money" (1 Timothy 3:2–3).

First, an elder must be above reproach. That doesn't mean he has never made a mistake or stumbled in life. Paul is not saying that an elder must be perfect. If that were so, no one would qualify. Rather, a person who is above reproach is one who has demonstrated a desire to live a godly, righteous life. If he errs or stumbles, he admits it and corrects it.

Second, an elder is to be "the husband of but one wife"—that is, a one-woman man. Many people have struggled with this qualification, because sometimes elders' wives die and the elders remarry, or the elder is divorced and remarried. This provision has given rise to a lot of controversy. But the word means that an elder is not to be a philanderer, an adulterer, a man who is often eyeing and lusting after other women. An elder must be lovingly committed to his wife. He must demonstrate fidelity.

Third, an elder must be known for his good habits. He must be "temperate"—that is, calm and serious-minded, not given to outbursts of extreme emotion. He must be "self-controlled"—that is, governed by an inner peace and the ability to manage his behavior at all times; he must be level and steady. He must be "respectable"—that is, dignified and orderly, a man who by his demeanor commands respect.

Fourth, an elder must be "hospitable." This means his home should be open to friends and strangers alike. Moreover, he should be the kind of man who, like the Good Samaritan, will stop and help strangers in a time of need.

Fifth, an elder must be able to teach. This is a crucial requirement. There are many godly men in a congregation who have excellent character but lack the gift of teaching. An elder *must* teach. He must be able to expound the Scriptures, recognize error, and correct those who misuse God's Word.

Sixth, an elder must not be "given to drunkenness." Wine was commonly consumed in the culture of the first century, and it was consumed by Christians as well as by pagans. But Paul makes it clear that elders should not drink wine to the point of intoxication. People who have a drinking problem are disqualified.

Seventh, an elder must be "not violent but gentle." In other words, an elder must not be an angry, contentious man who is constantly attacking others, intimidating others, and demanding his way. Elders are to be characterized by a gentle spirit.

Eighth, an elder must not be "quarrelsome." In the Greek, the word used here conveys a sense of being stubborn and insisting on his own point of view at all costs. Such people are disqualified from serving as elders.

Ninth and finally, he must not be in it for what he can get. He must not be greedy or obsessed with gaining influence or affluence.

These are the character qualities that qualify a person to be an elder. But character qualities are only half the picture. Paul goes on to say that elders must demonstrate a record of accomplishments.

The accomplishments of an elder

In the next section, Paul lists the accomplishments that should be part of the resumé of an elder: "He must manage his own family well and see that his children obey him with proper respect. (If anyone does not know how to manage his own family, how can he take care of God's church?)" (1 Timothy 3:4–5).

The first accomplishment to look for is a well-managed family. Look at the man's children. Are they obedient? Are they respectable? Or are they the scandal of the church? Let's face it. The children of a pastor and elders are under closer scrutiny than any other children in the church.

In the original text, the word *children* in this passage suggests small children. Paul seems to recognize that there are many influences in a child's life that determine his or her outcome. Often, in adolescence or the teen years, a well-instructed child from a good Christian home may go astray due to influences of peers, bad schooling, or the corrupting influence of the culture. So an elder who has a rebellious teenager in the home should not be automatically disqualified.

In general, however, the way an elder manages his home and his children is a good indicator of how he would manage the Lord's church. There are problems in every family, and it is helpful to look at an elder's approach to those problems and see whether he evades them or meets them head-on. It is instructive to see whether he uses worldly approaches or biblical solutions.

Next, the apostle Paul lists the accomplishment of maturity. He writes, "He must not be a recent convert, or he may become conceited and fall under the same judgment as the devil" (1 Timothy 3:6).

If you have ever known a new convert, especially someone who has gone from a life of sin to a radically new life in Christ, then you have probably seen how joyful and enthusiastic a new convert can be. Young Christians (that is,

Christians who are young in the faith, regardless of their chronological age) are exciting to be around. They are eager to tell others about their faith. They are filled with a newfound love for the Lord. They stir up and inspire the people around them.

So why does Paul say that recent converts should not be made elders in the church? The problem with a recent convert is that, regardless of how earnest and sincere the convert may be, regardless of how eager he is to follow the Lord with all his heart, he is still immature. He doesn't know the Scriptures. He lacks the wisdom that comes from experience in the faith.

Also, there is always the danger that when a new convert is given a position of public leadership and public trust, he may become proud and conceited "and fall under the same judgment as the devil." Satan's undoing, of course, was pride. If a new convert becomes an elder, he may become like the twelve recently converted disciples of Jesus who argued among themselves about which of them was the greatest. Whenever you give responsibility to someone who is spiritually immature, you can expect that young leader's ego to expand exponentially!

When the ego gets in the way, ministry crumbles. God will not use human flesh to bring about success in His kingdom. Anything that is not built by the power of God, through the wisdom of God, according to the will of God, will not succeed.

Avoiding the devil's trap

Finally, Paul adds this requirement of an elder: "He must also have a good reputation with outsiders, so that he will not fall into disgrace and into the devil's trap" (1 Timothy 3:7).

Some years ago, I was visiting with a pharmacist whose store was not far from our church. I mentioned to him a man who attended our church, and this pharmacist surprised me by speaking disparagingly of the man.

"Why do you say that about him?" I asked.

"I know him," the pharmacist said. "He may attend your church, but I know more about him than you do. He has owed me money for six months, and he has never paid a dime. I have no respect for him."

I was a young pastor at the time, and I didn't know how to respond. The church member was respected by everyone in the church. The only negative word I had ever heard about him came from this disgruntled pharmacist.

I decided to watch the life of this man and avoid placing too much responsibility on him, at least for a time. Within a few weeks, this man experienced a sudden disgrace. The entire church learned that he had been hiding a serious moral defect. He had fallen into "the devil's trap." He went from being one of the most respected men in our congregation to being disgraced and fallen. Afterwards, I was thankful that the Lord had led me into a conversation with the pharmacist who was outside our congregation.

Leaders in the church must be people of good reputation, not only within the church but also within the larger community beyond the church. It is easy to fool fellow Christians by putting on a Sunday face week after week. But there are people in the community who know what we are like Monday through Saturday. If we do not have a good reputation among those people, then our character is defective and we are not qualified to serve as elders and overseers of the Lord's church.

These, then, are the qualifications for leaders in the body of Christ. When we see these qualifications, then we are probably looking at someone whom the Spirit has chosen as an overseer. It's an exciting and noble task to be a church leader, a human channel through whom the mind of the living Lord is revealed in our midst.

And as a congregation, our responsibility does not end when our overseers have been recognized, chosen, and ordained for service. Their noble task is just beginning—and so is ours! We need to pray for our elders and lift them up before the Lord. They will be under satanic attack (note that the devil is mentioned twice in this passage). If Satan can destroy their work, damage their faith, undermine their family life, then he will strike a blow against the Lord's church.

So support your elders. Pray for them. Learn from them. Become partners in ministry with them. In this way, you will become a kind of church member and church minister God intends you to be.

CHAPTER 9

The Lord's Servants

1 Timothy 3:8–13

Ron Ritchie is the founder of Free at Last. He is also the husband of Anne Marie and the father of two sons, Ron, Jr., and Rodd. Years ago, when Ron was on the pastoral staff of Peninsula Bible Church and Roddie was eight years old, Roddie's teacher asked the class to write a few sentences about what their fathers did for a living.

Roddie wrote, "My father is a rabbi, or a priest, or a minister, or something like that." Young Roddie knew his dad was a clergyman—but he wasn't sure what kind!

Many believers are in the same boat. They are a bit confused as to what the New Testament prescription for church leadership is. If we study Paul's counsel to Timothy, all of our confusion will be swept away, for Paul's direction is clear and specific.

We have previously examined Paul's instructions to Timothy about the leaders called elders. These are people who serve by leading. Next, we shall look at those in the church who lead by serving, the people called deacons.

Leading by serving

There is an old story about a disgruntled church member. When asked why he was upset, he said, "The preacher won't preach, the teachers won't teach, and the deacons won't deek!" Here, in this section, Paul talks about the role of the deacons and tells us how deacons are to "deek." He writes:

> Deacons, likewise, are to be men worthy of respect, sincere, not indulging in much wine, and not pursuing dishonest gain. They must keep hold of the deep truths of the faith with a clear conscience. They must first be tested; and then if there is nothing against them, let them serve as deacons. (1 Timothy 3:8–10)

The function of deacons in the early church arose from a dispute over the distribution of food to needy widows, as described in Acts 6. There were two cultural divisions in the church at Jerusalem, the Hebraic Jews who spoke Aramaic and the Hellenized Jews who spoke Greek. The Greek-speaking Jews in the church felt that their widows were not being as well cared-for as the widows of the Aramaic-speaking Jews. The problem was brought to the apostles, who told the people to designate seven men from among themselves to be in charge of the distribution of food. These seven men were the first deacons.

The apostles set three qualifications for the role of deacons: The deacons were to be men of good reputation; they were to be filled with the Spirit (that is, they were to understand the revelation of life that the Spirit of God had taught); and they were to possess the spiritual gift of wisdom (the spiritual ability to apply the truth of God's Word to specific situations).

The deacons were to serve by handling the practical problems of administration and compassionate caring for human needs in the church. The deacons in Acts 6 were chosen by the congregation and confirmed by the elders.

The qualifications for deacons

Now, let's examine the qualifications Paul lists for deacons.

First, deacons are to be "men worthy of respect, sincere, not indulging in much wine, and not pursuing dishonest gain." These are personal qualifications. Deacons are to be worthy of respect—men who have earned a reputation for being reliable, admirable, and wise. And they are to be sincere—men who say what they mean and mean what they say. They are to be sober and self-controlled, not given to intoxication. And they are not to be greedy or always looking for opportunities to make money.

Second, deacons are to be men with tested records of Christian behavior and strong Christian faith. Paul writes, "They must keep hold of the deep truths of the faith with a clear conscience. They must first be tested; and then if there is nothing against them, let them serve as deacons." A deacon should be one who understands God's Word, applies it to his life, and relies upon it to solve problems and make decisions. When Paul says that they must hold to the deep truths of the faith "with a clear conscience," he is saying that a deacon not only must know God's Word but also must behave accordingly. He must practice what he preaches. And deacons must be people of proven character—and the way to prove someone's character is to put them into service and see how they conduct themselves.

The qualifications for women as deacons

Next, Paul writes, "In the same way, their wives are to be women worthy of respect, not malicious talkers but temperate and trustworthy in everything" (1 Timothy 3:11).

I believe the *New International Version* has mistranslated this verse. While it's true that the original Greek language could refer to the wives of male deacons, I don't think that is Paul's meaning. I believe the context makes it clear that Paul is not speaking of the wives of deacons but of deacons who are women. There is no corresponding counsel regarding the wives of elders in the preceding passage. If Paul were truly concerned about the behavior of the wives of the deacons, he would be just as concerned about the behavior of elders' wives.

In Romans 16, there is a woman named Phoebe whom Paul refers to as a deacon. Phoebe, Paul says, was a deacon of the church at Cenchreae, which was the port city for the city of Corinth. She had been a great help to Paul in his ministry. So there clearly were women deacons in the early church. It's clear that Paul is writing about women deacons in verse 11.

Paul says that four traits should characterize women deacons.

First, like men, women deacons are to be worthy of respect. They are to be temperate and self-controlled, not given to gossip or slander. They must never speak maliciously of anyone but must be worthy of the trust they hold.

Deacons go into people's homes and deal with people's hurts, so it's important that they be trustworthy. Clearly, Paul did not want the deacons, whether men or women, to spread tales or divulge the confidences of the people they served.

Many people, including Christians, do not take the sin of gossip seriously. What's the harm, they think, of a little sweet tea and spicy talk? Yet the Scriptures treat the issue of gossip as a one of the most destructive of all sins. The book of Proverbs says that perverse people stir up dissension "and a gossip separates close friends" (see Proverbs 16:28). And Paul, in Romans, lists gossip and slander alongside such horrible sins as murder, lying, and hating God (see Romans 1:29–30).

I know of a congregation that was plagued for years with unrest. The pastors and the board of elders were continually at odds, and the church's ministry was undermined. No one could explain the source of the disunity in the church. One day, the reason came to light: A woman in the church, the wife of one of the elders, had been deliberately planting rumors and suspicions throughout the church. She was sly and subtle and never accused anyone directly, but her hints and insinuations were devastating. She destroyed many reputations and relationships. That's the kind of behavior Paul warns of here.

Note also that word *temperate*. This word means that a deacon should practice moderation in all things. A temperate person is not addicted to strong drink, or to any other substance. Temperate people live balanced lives and are not given to overeating or gambling or any other vice. I would even say that temperate people are not inclined to be workaholics; they keep all things in balance, including work, family time, worship time, and time for rest.

Finally, Paul says that a woman deacon is to be "trustworthy in all things." Trustworthy people are responsible. If given an assignment, they carry it out. If they see a need, they meet it without being told to. They work faithfully and humbly behind the scenes, not for glory or applause but simply because they want to serve God and others.

A final word of instruction

Paul closes with a general word of instruction that applies to all deacons, both men and women: "A deacon must be the husband of but one wife and must manage his children and his household well" (1 Timothy 3:12).

Some people have mistakenly interpreted this verse to mean that a deacon must be married. Yet, as far as we know, neither Paul nor Timothy was married at this point. So it seems clear that the point of this verse is not that a deacon must be a married individual but that a deacon must, if married, be faithful to his or her spouse.

Paul also says that deacons are to manage their children and their households well. You can tell a lot about a deacon and his or her ability to function in the congregation by the way he or she handles family responsibilities and family relationships. Relationship skills and management skills that are exercised within a family tend to serve a person well in the church.

Finally, Paul sums up his instruction regarding deacons with this statement: "Those who have served well gain an excellent standing and great assurance in their faith in Christ Jesus" (1 Timothy 3:13).

Notice that two things result when a deacon serves God and the church in the right way.

First, that deacon gains an "excellent standing." This means that a deacon who serves well gains the gratitude and appreciation of the congregation.

Paul also says that deacons earned for themselves "great assurance in their faith in Christ Jesus." That word *assurance* means "boldness." When you serve the Lord with all your heart in whatever ministry He gives you, God gives you a sense of partnership in His work and a bold confidence in your Christian faith.

This is a profound truth: God always rewards His servants, and He promises that those who serve as deacons in the congregation will be rewarded with great boldness in their faith. That is a great promise to be claimed by all who serve by leading and all who lead by serving.

CHAPTER 10

God's Chosen Instrument: The Church

1 Timothy 3:14–15

Years ago, during an airline flight, I picked up the in-flight magazine from the seat pocket and flipped through the articles. I came upon a full-page advertisement with a headline that read, "When you understand that you can change the world, your life will never be the same again."

Those were startling words. I thought, "How true!"

Then I looked at the bottom of the page and saw that it was an advertisement for *Playboy* magazine. Well, I was irritated. The last publication in the world I would want to agree with is *Playboy*.

And yet, on reflection, I have to agree that there really is truth to that headline: *Playboy* magazine has definitely changed the world—and not for the better. Since Hugh Hefner published the first issue of the magazine in 1953, we have steadily seen an increasing approval of immoral behavior in our society.

Our films, television shows, and popular music have become openly pornographic and degrading. We have seen an explosion in teenage pregnancies, abortion, child molestation, video and Internet pornography, and even pornography involving the sexual abuse of children. Because the *Playboy* philosophy has become accepted in our society, we are sacrificing our homes, our children, and our souls upon the altar of our lusts.

Even so, I can't help thinking the headline I read in that magazine would make a great slogan for Christians: "When you understand that you can change the world, your life will never be the same again." We are the church of Jesus Christ, and we can change our world for the better. We can introduce the world to the Savior. We can point the world toward hope and healing.

And that is the theme we encounter in the next section of 1 Timothy.

An exalted view of the church

At this point, it would be helpful to look at the cultural background of Ephesus. Paul had left Timothy in charge of the church in Ephesus—a city that I would liken to Los Angeles. In *Letters to a Troubled Church: 1 and 2*

Corinthians (Discovery House Publishers, 2008), I compared the Greek city of Corinth with modern-day San Francisco. And if that is so, then Ephesus would certainly qualify as the L.A. of its day.

Ephesus was the second largest city in the Roman Empire, and it was the center of commerce, culture, and sexual immorality in the empire. Its most prominent feature was the Temple of Diana, which was dedicated to the worship of sex. In that decadent and immoral city, the Ephesian church had been established for a number of years, and Paul had sent Timothy there to correct certain problems in that church.

Thus far in this letter, Paul has already reminded Timothy of the need for strong, clear, biblical teaching to counteract the growing problem of error in the church. He has also instructed Timothy regarding public worship, prayer, and preaching, and the selection of leaders and servants—elders and deacons—in the church. Now Paul writes about the nature and mission of the church: "Although I hope to come to you soon, I am writing you these instructions so that, if I am delayed, you will know how people ought to conduct themselves in God's household, which is the church of the living God, the pillar and foundation of the truth" (1 Timothy 3:14–15).

What an exalted view of the church! And how far removed is this view from the often contemptuous view of the church we hear so often today. Many people, including many Christians, regard the church as an anachronism, a relic from the past, with nothing to say to the present hour. According to these critics, the church has nothing to say about the real problems of today's world.

Well, that is not my view, and it certainly wasn't Paul's. He makes it clear that the church is a tremendously significant body—and the mission of this body is nothing less than the transformation of the world.

God's household

Don't mistake the meaning of this phrase in verse 15: "you will know how people ought to conduct themselves in God's household." The apostle Paul is not talking about how Christians should behave in a church service. He is not saying that Timothy should instruct the Ephesian Christians in how to sit quietly and stay awake during the sermon, or how to pass the offering plate, or how not to criticize the preacher.

God's household, the church, is not a building, nor is it a meeting in a building. God's household is the body of Christ, the fellowship of believers. We, as Christians, need to understand how to conduct ourselves with one another, how to treat one another, love one another, forgive one another, encourage one another, and so forth. That is what Paul means.

A friend of mine once chatted with the owner of a coffee shop he frequented during the week. He asked the owner of the shop, "What do you think of the church?" The man made a face and replied, "To me the church is nothing but a great big dark building."

Many would agree with this man. To them, the word *church* evokes mental images of stone walls, spires or steeples, stained glass, people sitting in rows listening to boring sermons or singing dreary hymns. But Paul would never have had such an idea in his mind. The church in his day did not meet in church buildings with stained glass. In the book of Acts, we see that Christians met in the synagogues, temple courts, public forums, and rented facilities, but for the most parts they met in private homes.

I'm not saying it's wrong for a church to have a nice building with beautiful architecture; I want to make sure we understand what Paul truly means when he speaks of God's household. The church is not a building. Rather, the church consists of people who have been born by the Spirit of God and have entered into a new lifestyle because of the presence of Jesus Christ in their midst. That is the biblical definition of the church.

Now, if that is our definition of the church, then why do we divide Christian ministries into church and parachurch ministries? Why do we say that Peninsula Bible Church or the First Presbyterian Church on the corner or the First Baptist Church on the next block is the church but Christian organizations like Child Evangelism Fellowship, Young Life, Campus Crusade, The Navigators, Wycliffe Bible Translators, and so forth are parachurch ministries? To be candid, I dislike the word *parachurch*. I think the division between church and parachurch is an invalid dichotomy.

If an organization is made up of Christians who are born by the Spirit of God and are to live according to the presence of Jesus Christ in their midst, then that group of people is the church. They are not parachurch. They are the church. Jesus did not die on the cross for parachurches; He gave himself for the church. The Holy Spirit did not come to build parachurches; He builds churches, and everyone who is involved in Christian ministry is part of the church at work.

The local church, the so-called parachurch ministry, the home Bible study, and the individual Christian who seeks to represent Christ in the neighborhood and the workplace—these are all part of God's household.

These are all the church. This is a vision for the church and a definition of the church that we need to recapture.

The symbol and the reality

When Christians gathered together in the first century, they always valued that experience. You cannot read the book of Acts without seeing how the early believers dearly loved to join together in worship and in fellowship, in large groups or in small groups.

The apostle Paul chose his words wisely when he referred to the church as God's household. This term suggests the intimacy and warmth of a genuine loving family. And that is what the early church truly was.

Paul also writes of "the church of the living God, the pillar and foundation of the truth." This phrase suggests the exciting power and profound importance of the church. It would transform our view of ourselves and our relationship to the world if we could recapture Paul's wonderful vision of the church as God intended it to be.

We Christians are the house of God. The Creator of the universe chooses to make His dwelling place among human beings through the church. Does that send a tingle down your spine? Almighty God lives in us! Wherever you find a follower of Jesus Christ, you find the house of God.

That is why, whenever we Christians gather together, whether in large groups or small, our hearts should be moved by the marvel of this truth: The God of the universe is our intimate friend. He dwells with us and in us. We are the household of God.

The church of the living God

Paul goes on to say that we are "the church of the living God." That phrase was probably intended as a direct contrast to that world-famous Ephesian landmark, the Temple of Diana. It was, after all, a temple dedicated to a lifeless idol. It was said that a strangely-shaped meteorite had fallen from the sky. The superstitious pagans of Ephesus thought that it resembled the goddess Diana, so they built a temple around it and worshiped it as Diana of the Ephesians. A lifeless piece of rock was the central glory of Ephesus.

But Paul says we are not like the temple of a dead goddess. We do not have a powerless, impersonal God. We are connected to the living God. As Paul told the citizens of Athens, "For in him we live and move and have our being" (see Acts 17:28).

As imperfect as the church may be, it is God's chosen instrument for change. He will not use anything else. He has committed himself to this body of imperfect people, so do not ignore it. As Jesus announced at the beginning, "On this rock I will build my church, and the gates of Hades will not overcome it" (see Matthew 16:18).

We Christians sometimes forget who we are. We forget the source of our power and what we can do through Him who strengthens us. Collectively and individually, we have with us a silent, invisible power unlike any other power known to humanity. This power is not available to unregenerate people. It's called resurrection power. We can do immeasurably more than we ask or even imagine through "his power that is at work within us" (Ephesians 3:20). This power is available to every local gathering of authentic believers, and it's available to every individual believer.

The greatest creativity

Christians are also empowered and equipped through spiritual gifts. Every Christian, without exception, has spiritual gifts. They are given to us by the Spirit of God to prepare us for works of ministry in the church and in the world. Because of spiritual gifts, we can live each day with a sense of expectancy about what God is going to do in our lives. We may be under pressure, under satanic bombardment, but we will never be bored because God is at work through us.

Each local congregation and individual Christian has an arsenal of weapons we can use to change lives and change the world. These are powerful, nonviolent weapons of faith, hope, love, prayer, and righteousness. With such weapons as these, we can go out into the world and attack the social problems and crises of our day. And our weapons do not merely attack the surface symptoms. They attack the root problems and solve them.

Nothing is more frustrating to me than to see God's people living powerless and ineffectual lives. Nothing is more frustrating than the knowledge that we have God's power at our fingertips, yet we fail to use it. Instead, we use the world's methods and resources, and then we wonder why nothing changes. When will we learn what it truly means to be "the church of the living God"?

Paul uses two powerful words to describe the church. He calls it "the pillar and foundation of the truth." The great reason for the existence of the church is to invade the world with God's truth. This world is saturated with error and satanic deception. Sin is paraded through the streets of our world. Foolishness and rebellion are exalted as the epitome of wisdom.

The church is called upon to speak the truth in the midst of falsehood and confusion. The church is called upon to point out that the emperor has no clothes—that, in fact, the emperor of this world is Satan. That's why Paul calls the church the pillar and foundation of truth.

What is a pillar? Ancient temples were constructed with massive pillars, several feet thick, to support the roof. Paul's imagery suggests that the church is the strong and durable structure that supports the weight of God's truth. In a world riddled with problems and chaotic with confusion, the pillar of the church elevates the structure of God's truth for everyone to see.

Is there any hope that our society will ever recover from its current downhill slide? Yes, there is hope—but that hope does not lie with the White House or the Congress or the Supreme Court. That hope cannot be found in the Democratic Party or the Republican Party, the Libertarian Party or the Green Party. That hope cannot be found in the National Rifle Association or the Sierra Club. It cannot be found in the Army, Navy, Air Force, or Marines, as admirable as they are. There is only one hope our nation has for turning aside from corruption and despair.

That hope is the church.

But herein lies the tragedy of the untaught church—the congregation that has not been adequately instructed in the truth. As I have traveled around this country, I have been shocked and saddened to see that the church in the United States is a biblically illiterate church. People do not know the Bible. The depths of God's truth are not being revealed to the people in compelling and life-changing ways.

Instead, people are being served pablum—simple and superficial truths that do not challenge anyone to go deeper into their faith. People are not being inspired to trust God and dare great things for him. The true depths of God's Word remain unplumbed.

How can the church become the pillar and foundation of the truth if it is not being taught the truth? The apostle Paul understood that the church had been sent into the world to make a difference. So he instructed Timothy to help the Ephesian Christians to understand their great purpose of the world. In effect, Paul urged Timothy to tell the Christians in Ephesus, "When you understand that you can change the world, your life will never be the same again."

Some years ago, I went to San Antonio, Texas, for the dedication of the new buildings for Bible Study Fellowship (now called BSF International). The dedication speaker was Dr. Francis A. Schaeffer, a man who has been a true twentieth-century prophet for God. It was about three years before his death from cancer, and his body and voice were weak due to the treatments he was receiving. But his mind and spirit were strong, and he delivered a powerful message from the Word of God.

In that message, he made a statement that has stuck with me ever since: "The greatest creativity ever given is the ability of men, by their choices, to change the course of history." God has given that creativity to human beings, to you and me and to everyone in His church. That's the source of human dignity—the ability to affect the course of events through the obedience and perseverance of our will. The church has the power to change the world, and that's why the church is here.

CHAPTER 11

The Great Mystery

1 Timothy 3:16

O ur faith is a mystery.

We believe in a man who was born of a virgin, who was fully man and fully God, who was crucified and buried, who rose again and ascended into heaven and now lives within us and among us. If that's not the greatest mystery in the world, what is?

C. S. Lewis described the mystery of the Christian faith in a 1943 BBC radio broadcast, later incorporated into *Mere Christianity*:

> I am trying here to prevent anyone saying the really foolish thing that people often say about Him: I'm ready to accept Jesus as a great moral teacher, but I don't accept his claim to be God. That is the one thing we must not say. A man who was merely a man and said the sort of things Jesus said would not be a great moral teacher. He would either be a lunatic—on the level with the man who says he is a poached egg—or else he would be the Devil of Hell. You must make your choice. Either this man was, and is, the Son of God, or else a madman or something worse. You can shut him up for a fool, you can spit at him and kill him as a demon or you can fall at his feet and call him Lord and God, but let us not come with any patronising nonsense about his being a great human teacher. He has not left that open to us. He did not intend to.[1]

Now we come to 1 Timothy 3:16, a verse I view as the centerpiece of Paul's first letter to Timothy. Everything the apostle has said so far points ahead to this verse, and everything he will say afterward is built upon it. This verse constitutes a powerful confession of faith—faith in the mystery of the incarnation, death, and resurrection of Jesus our Lord.

The mystery of godliness

Many Bible scholars believe that the rhythm and phrasing of 1 Timothy 3:16 shows that it was originally a hymn that was sung in first-century churches. This verse contains the most profound and astonishing truth to be found in Scripture:

Beyond all question, the mystery of godliness is great:
> He appeared in a body,
>> was vindicated by the Spirit,
> was seen by angels,
>> was preached among the nations,
> was believed on in the world,
>> was taken up in glory.

Paul underscores the importance of this great truth, saying, "The mystery of godliness is great." When Paul says that this truth is a mystery, he is not saying that it is obscure or hidden, like the clues in a murder mystery. Whenever the New Testament speaks of truth as a mystery, it means that it is an insight into a deeper reality, hidden from secular wisdom. The spiritual mind can understand it, but the worldly mind cannot.

Why can't worldly wisdom understand this truth? Because this truth can be understood only in light of the revelation of God's Word—and human wisdom does not accept the validity of God's revealed Word. If secular minds cannot locate this truth in an encyclopedia of human discovery or in a university or in a scientific laboratory, then they say, "It must not be true!"

The fact is that the truth expressed in this verse is ultimate Truth, the most important truth of all—yet it is a mystery, a secret insight into the true nature of life. As such, it is hidden from secular minds and made known only to believing hearts.

Human beings are continually trying to understand themselves: Why do we continually do the things we don't want to do? Why do we become slaves to our worst impulses and habits? Why can't we maintain healthy, happy relationships? Why can't we solve the great problems of our race—crime, poverty, ignorance, racial strife, religious strife, and war? Where can we find the missing elements of truth about ourselves?

The reason the answers to these questions are so elusive is that the missing elements can be found only in the pages of Scripture. That is what makes the Bible the most important book in the world. There is no other book like it. Nothing reveals the truth about our true nature except the mind and will of God.

The secret is a person

Next, the apostle Paul uses the phrase "the mystery of godliness." Some translations render this phrase "the mystery of our religion." But "religion" is a mistranslation. The Greek phrase in this verse, *eusebeia musterion*, literally means the "godliness mystery" or the "holiness secret."

The same Greek word, *eusebeia,* appears again in the next chapter, where it is translated "godly" and "godliness":

Have nothing to do with godless myths and old wives' tales; rather, train yourself to be *godly.* For physical training is of some value, but *godliness* has value for all things, holding promise for both the present life and the life to come. (1 Timothy 4:7–8, emphasis added)

So the proper translation in 1 Timothy 3:16 is "godliness," not 'religion." The English word *godliness* comes from an Old English word meaning "God-likeness." But that does not convey an accurate sense of the Greek word, because the name of God is not part of the original word. In reality, an even better translation might be "goodliness." That is truly what Paul is talking about.

Another synonym for "goodliness" might be "wholeness." The Greek word conveys a sense of wholeness, balance, and completeness. Every human being in this world wants to be a whole and complete person, well-balanced in every way. So Paul tells us that the secret of wholeness, of goodliness, of godliness, has been revealed. This secret, of course, is Jesus.

People everywhere are looking for the secret of wholeness. They are chasing after philosophies and pop psychology and Eastern religion and every other mystery imaginable. But the secret is not a philosophy or an esoteric belief system. The secret is a person, Jesus.

As Paul tells us, "He appeared in a body." Or as some translations put it, "He was manifested in the flesh." Some ancient manuscripts of the original Greek text use the word *God* there: "God appeared in a body" or "God was manifested in the flesh." Most Bible scholars believe that in his original letter, Paul probably used the word *he.* It makes no difference, since even the pronoun "he" still refers to verse 15, where Paul refers to "the church of the living God." Whether the proper noun "God" or the pronoun "he" is used, it refers to God, and it is a statement that God came to earth in human form through Jesus Christ.

Unfolding the mystery

In this hymn, we see six unfoldings of the mystery of Jesus. These six unfoldings are divided into three sets of couplets. Each couplet expresses two contrasting and complementary truths about Jesus. One line of each couplet expresses His visible nature; the other expresses an aspect of His invisible nature. The combination of these two contrasting, complementary truths contains the secret of His perfect life.

Let's take a closer look at each of these couplets. The first couplet is:

He appeared in a body,
>   was vindicated by the Spirit

Again, I believe that there is a subtle mistranslation here. I would like to suggest a slightly different version of these two lines that I think would better express the mind of the apostle Paul.

First, I would eliminate the English-language articles "a" and "the." Those words do not occur in the original Greek; they are supplied by the translators, and there is no justification for placing them there. Second, I would change "Spirit" to "spirit." The translators thought that Paul was referring to the Holy Spirit, but I don't think so. Third, I would change the word *vindicated* to *justified,* because that is how the Greek word is normally translated throughout the rest of the New Testament.

So in my translation, those lines would read:

He appeared in body,
>   was justified by spirit

In other words, this hymn is telling us that Jesus was visibly and outwardly manifested in his bodily flesh; and he was inwardly justified in spirit—that is, his human spirit. The first line tells us that Jesus appeared as a normal human being, no different from the rest of us. He entered life as we do, through human birth. He enjoyed life. He loved His family, worked hard to earn a living, ate and slept, suffered losses and sorrows, and understood poverty, pain, and rejection. He was like us in every way. He even bled and died and was buried like any other human being.

Within Jesus, however, there was a hidden glory that would break out in remarkable, astonishing ways. There was something about Him that was more than human, and people were attracted to the hidden glory they sensed in Him. The apostle John spoke of it this way: "We have seen his glory, the glory of the One and Only, who came from the Father, full of grace and truth" (see John 1:14).

Though outwardly He came as a human being like every other human being, we have seen His inner glory. What was that inner glory? Grace and truth, as revealed by the spirit He demonstrated. We saw His grace exemplified through His compassion, love, mercy, and forgiveness. We saw His truth exemplified through the amazing words He spoke, from His breathtaking Sermon on the Mount to the profoundly moving high-priestly prayer He prayed before going to the cross. Even His enemies were forced to confess, "No one ever spoke the way this man does" (see John 7:46).

That's what Paul meant by the phrase "justified by spirit." The way He lived, taught, and dealt with people revealed His spirit, the secret of His inner life. And when this secret was revealed, He was justified as righteous. The word *justified* that Paul uses in 1 Timothy 3:16 is the same Greek word he uses in Romans 5:1: "Therefore, since we have been justified through faith, we have peace with God through our Lord Jesus Christ."

To be justified means to be made righteous in God's sight. The words and actions of Jesus revealed His spirit, and His spirit justified Him, bearing continual witness that He was righteous before God. He was fully accepted by God and acceptable to God. The Holy Spirit bore witness that this was so: "You are my Son, whom I love; with you I am well pleased" (see Mark 1:11; see also Matthew 3:17; 17:5; Luke 3:22). That was the secret of His serene and untroubled character. That is what kept Him panic-proof in the midst of all the pressure and opposition He faced.

This profound truth about Jesus was so remarkable that the early Christians incorporated it into this hymn, which Paul now quotes. Jesus was justified by His spirit. We are justified and made acceptable to God through faith in Jesus Christ. Just as He was made acceptable to God, so are we. And God the Father now says of you and me, "These, too, are my beloved children, in whom I am well pleased." And because our heavenly Father loves and accepts us, we too can remain panic-proof in the midst of all the pressure and opposition we face.

Eyeballed by angels

The second couplet Paul quotes from this hymn states that Jesus

was seen by angels,
>was preached among the nations

Here again, we see the blending of the invisible and visible realities of Jesus. He was "seen by angels," an event that could only take place in the invisible realm. Yet He was also "preached among the nations," an event that was visible throughout the known world.

In the phrase "seen by angels," the word *seen* is the Greek word *optanomai,* from which we get such English words as *optometrist,* meaning a doctor who deals with issues of vision and the eye. *Seen* is a weak English word to convey what this Greek word means. There are other Greek words that mean to merely see or observe—words such as *blepo, eido,* or *skopeo.* But this word *optanomai* means to gaze wide-eyed, to stare in wonder and amazement with protruding eyeballs. It is a descriptive and vivid term. It literally means that Jesus was eyeballed by the angels.

The Gospels tell us that angels announced His coming and were present at His birth. They sang when the tiny newborn baby was laid in a manger in that cold and flea-ridden cave. They gazed in wide-eyed wonder that God, the Lord of Glory, should be born as a baby in a manger. They were with Him to strengthen Him when He was tempted by the devil after forty days of fasting in the wilderness. Angels strengthened Him during His time of struggle and agony in the Garden of Gethsemane. They guarded His tomb. They announced His resurrection. They comforted the disciples when He ascended into glory.

The angels had known of His majesty, power, and greatness since the beginning of time, but only when God became a man did they begin to understand the depths of His love. Imagine their wide-eyed amazement as they watched Him endure the beating and mocking and scourging, and as He poured out His life blood upon the cross. They eyeballed Him with awe and amazement.

Seen by angels? Perhaps now you begin to see why "seen" is far too weak and passive a word to capture the depth of meaning that is expressed in this brief phrase! There is a wonderful old hymn, with lyrics by Johnson Oatman Jr., that captures a sense of what Paul is saying in this verse:

> "Holy, holy!" is what the angels sing,
> And I expect to help them make the courts of heaven ring;
> But when I sing redemption's story, they all fold their wings,
> For angels never felt the joy that our salvation brings.

Angels can never experience the joy that is ours because we have been redeemed. They can only stare in wide-eyed wonder at all that Jesus has done for us.

Remember the second line of the couplet: Jesus "was preached among the nations." Only human beings can preach the gospel of Jesus Christ throughout the nations. Angels do not have that privilege. We, the saved, have been commissioned by Jesus to preach His word of salvation throughout the world.

Taken up in glory

Finally, we come to the last couplet, which again links the visible with the invisible:

was believed on in the world,

was taken up in glory

"Believed on in the world" was an evident, visible fact in the first-century world. By the time this letter was written, the good news of Jesus Christ had been preached in Jerusalem, and Judea, and Samaria, and unto the uttermost parts of the known world.

Wherever the gospel was preached, new communities of transformed people sprang up and affected the moral climate around them. These new communities, called churches, were populated by every category of people: Jews and Gentiles, rich and poor, patricians and slaves, men and women. Wherever the church of Jesus Christ took root, thousands of lives were changed. Jesus was believed on in the world.

Like Humpty Dumpty, the entire human race has had a great fall, and no power on earth, not all the king's horses or all the king's men, can put the human race together again. But what was impossible for the king's horses and men is easy for the King himself. King Jesus puts human beings back together again. That is the good news of the gospel.

I recall a couple I met in the late 1950s named John and Helen. John was a successful dental surgeon in the Bay Area, and he and Helen were on the verge of divorce. Their relationship had deteriorated to the point where they could not stand to speak to each other. They were separated and deeply embittered toward each other.

But John's nurse was a Christian, and she invited him to attend a Billy Graham Crusade in San Francisco. "I'm sorry," he said. "I am an atheist, and I'm simply not interested in anything Dr. Graham has to say."

The nurse wouldn't take no for an answer. She continued to invite him, gently but persistently, until finally he decided to go. He attended the first night, and he returned the next night and the next. On the final night, John went forward and yielded his life to Jesus Christ.

It was instantly apparent that his life was under new management. There was a radical change in his attitudes, especially toward his wife, Helen. He went to his wife, told her about his decision to follow Christ, and asked her to forgive his sins against her. She decided to try working on their marriage again. As John talked to her about his newfound faith, she too became a believer.

John and Helen began attending Peninsula Bible Church, and people who met them were so impressed by their love for each other that they became known as "the honeymooners." John often taught Bible classes and counseled people in need, and he became one of our elders. When he passed away in the early 1980s, his funeral was a celebration of the life joyfully completed.

John's story is a testimony to the power of Jesus to change lives. That's what the phrase "believed on in the world" means. For two thousand years, Jesus has been believed on in the world, and He has been changing lives, relationships, homes, and entire communities. From the first century to the twenty-first, this good news has gone out into the world, and people have believed—and they have found hope, deliverance, forgiveness, and restored relationships.

The last phrase of the couplet states that Jesus "was taken up in glory." That statement is often misunderstood. People take it to mean that Jesus was taken up into glory, meaning he ascended into heaven. But Paul says "in glory," not "into glory." In other words, Jesus was already glorified when he was taken up. His glorified state explains the miracles of transformed lives that have taken place throughout two thousand years of ministry.

We tend to think of the ascension of Jesus as the moment when He was taken up into the sky, where heaven is. But that's a false assumption, based on cultural stereotypes about heaven. Many people think of heaven as a place that floats among the clouds. But heaven is not in the sky, and neither is Jesus. The heavenly realm is not up there; it's everywhere—and it's right here. When Jesus was taken up in glory, He entered the realm of heaven so that He was no longer confined by his earthly body. As William Temple observed in *Readings in St. John's Gospel:* "His ascension means that he is perfectly united with God; we are with him wherever we are present to God; and that is everywhere and always. Because he is 'in heaven' he is everywhere on earth; because he is ascended, he is here now."[2]

That's why, throughout two thousand years of church history, Jesus Christ has been the answer to the puzzles of life. When He ascended, He was not taken away from us into the sky. He was made available to us in an even more powerful and meaningful way than when He walked the earth in His flesh. Because He was taken up in glory, He is with you right now.

A friend of mine once said, "Jesus did the most ordinary kind of jobs. It takes all God's power in me to do the simplest things—His way. Christianity is not a way of doing special things. It is a special way of doing everything."

Because Jesus was taken up in glory, everything we do is transformed. Our daily drive with our carpool partners, our interactions with co-workers and clients at the office, our wait in the supermarket checkout line, a chat with a neighbor over the backyard fence, a restaurant meal with friends—all of these should be acts of holy devotion to our Lord. Everything we do is transformed by the fact that He was taken up in glory.

Ruth Graham, the wife of evangelist Billy Graham, kept a framed motto over her kitchen sink: "Divine service performed here three times daily." That is the attitude of a person whose life is lived through the lens of the Lord's glory. As Paul wrote to the Corinthians, "So whether you eat or drink or whatever you do, do it all for the glory of God" (1 Corinthians 10:31).

Because Jesus was taken up in glory, He is everywhere. The church is everywhere. Everything we do, even eating or drinking, can be a spiritual act of devotion to our Lord. It's all in how we choose to look at life.

Authentic Christianity has nothing to do with religion. After all, what is religion? It is humanity's faltering, fumbling search for something bigger than itself, something it can believe in. But genuine Christianity is not a philosophy or a belief system or a religion. It's a person. Christianity is, above all, a person who appeared in body, but was justified by spirit; was beheld in wonder by angels, yet was preached on earth among the nations; was believed on in the world, yet was taken up in glory and lives among us now.

That is great truth in which we live. That is the great mystery of godliness and wholeness for our lives.

CHAPTER 12

Fraudulent Faith

1 Timothy 4:1–5

When I was in my early twenties, the mainstream denominations in America were undergoing a major conflict, the Fundamentalist-Modernist Controversy. On the fundamentalist side were those who held to the Bible as God's inspired and inerrant Word. On the modernist side were liberal churchmen, heavily influenced by the higher-criticism scholars who questioned the reliability of the Scriptures.

During that time, I came across 1 Timothy 4:1 in the King James Version, which reads, "Now the Spirit speaketh expressly, that in the latter times some shall depart from the faith, giving heed to seducing spirits, and doctrines of devils." I had been taught that the phrase "the latter times" referred to the days shortly before the second coming of Christ. Therefore, this verse seemed to say that the Lord's return would be preceded by a great apostasy or falling away from the truth within the church.

Looking around at the church in the United States and seeing the raging controversy between the fundamentalists and the modernists, it was easy for me to believe that I was in the latter days and that the Lord's return was imminent. In fact, many church leaders at that time were quite explicitly saying that this was so. There are other New Testament passages that warn of an increasing departure from the faith as the return of the Lord draws near, but those passages connect the falling away from faith with the appearance of a man known as "the Antichrist" (see 2 Thessalonians 2:3; 1 John 2:18). This satanically controlled world leader will draw many people away from the faith.

I no longer believe that 1 Timothy 4:1 speaks of the period just prior to the Lord's return. I believe Paul, in this verse, is speaking of the times in which we now live. Let's take a closer look at what Paul is saying to Timothy, and to us, about the problem of fraudulent faith within the church.

Waves of deception

We'll begin by examining this passage as translated in the *New International Version*: "The Spirit clearly says that in later times some will abandon the faith and follow deceiving spirits and things taught by demons" (1 Timothy 4:1).

The King James Version used the phrase "in the latter times." The NIV uses the phrase "in later times." I believe that a proper translation of this phrase would be "in succeeding seasons" or "in times to come." In other words, I believe this phrase suggests that people will abandon the faith and follow false doctrines throughout succeeding seasons of time.

Just as there are four seasons in a calendar year, the world goes through successive seasons of human events. There are seasons of war, seasons of peace, seasons of unrest and upheaval, seasons of calm and social unity, seasons of economic depression, seasons of surging prosperity, and so forth. The apostle Paul tells us that there will also be seasons of deceit, when error gushes forth like a fountain, when people forsake God's truth and chase after satanic lies. Over my lifetime, I have seen several such seasons come and go.

These seasons of deceit were predicted by the Holy Spirit, though we do not know how the Spirit made this revelation known to Paul. Perhaps the apostle gained these insights through direct visions and visits from Jesus. Perhaps the Spirit spoke through one or more New Testament prophets. At any rate, the Spirit predicted that seasons of deceit would come.

The late nineteenth century was a season of deceit, when many new cults arose. Those cults have occupied center stage in religious history ever since: Mormonism, Jehovah's Witnesses, Christian Science, and many other fraudulent faiths. These cults all claim to be Christian, but they distort the truth of the Scriptures. The end of the nineteenth century was followed by decades of relative quiet.

Then, in the mid-1960s, it all broke loose again. A torrent of error flooded our culture, our media, and even our churches. The Unification Church (the Moonies) came into existence under the Korean leader, Sun Myung Moon. The Hare Krishna—cadres of young people in saffron robes with shaved heads—appeared at airports, passing out literature and selling flowers. Scientology, with its strange and pseudo-scientific doctrines, was born. Transcendental Meditation soared in popularity. And many other false faiths exploded in popularity.

These seasons of deceit should not catch us off guard. The apostle Paul told us that waves of deception would occur down through successive seasons of time. He told us that many would depart from the truth of the apostolic Scriptures.

These deceptive cults use various means to recruit new members. Some appeal to the intellect, some to the emotions, some to the will, some to human pride. But they all have one common characteristic: They deceive people by presenting a different Jesus from the Jesus of the Gospels.

If you want to know whether a certain group is truly Christian or if it is a deceptive cult, all you have to do is answer the question, "What do they say about Jesus? Do they say that Jesus is God in human flesh? Do they say He is the Savior of the world who died on the cross, was buried, and rose again?" If not, then, as Paul said, they "follow deceiving spirits and things taught by demons." The unseen forces of evil in this universe know that Jesus is the centerpiece of God's plan of redemption, so they continually try to distort and corrupt His image.

Lying spirits

All around us we see indiscriminate acceptance of every non-Christian belief system: Buddhism, Hinduism, Islam, Wicca, Druidism, and more. But if a Christian individual or organization wants to present the biblical truth of Jesus Christ, there is often protest, censorship, and sharp opposition. Why is Christianity, among all faiths, so often singled out for attack? It's because we are engaged in spiritual warfare. The satanic forces that oppose us are allied with those false faiths. They war against us and our Lord.

Where do these deceiving spirits come from? The Scriptures tell us they are fallen angels. Even before the world was created, these angels followed their leader, Lucifer, the highest of the angels of God, into a rebellion against God. They became identified with Lucifer's nature, which Jesus says is that of a murderer and a liar (see John 8:44).

Yet this strange, malevolent being, Satan, is also called "the god of this age" (2 Corinthians 4:4). What a frightening thought! This world ignorantly follows a murdering, lying spirit—a demon-god who gleefully leads them to slaughter. This is the enemy Paul warned the Ephesians about: "For our struggle is not against flesh and blood, but against the rulers, against the authorities, against the powers of this dark world and against the spiritual forces of evil in the heavenly realms" (Ephesians 6:12).

These rulers, authorities, powers, and spiritual forces of evil in the heavenly realms are the very spirits who originate the false and twisted ideas about Jesus. These spirits have access to the inner thoughts and feelings of human beings, including Christians. We are all affected by strange urges and ideas that arise within us—but these impulses do not always originate with us. Sometimes they come as "flaming arrows of the evil one" (see Ephesians 6:16). These unseen beings mislead us and assault us with intricate arguments and clever rationalizations, seeking to deceive us with "doctrines of demons."

Take, for instance, the philosophy called humanism. This is probably the most widespread philosophy of our day. All the great universities of the world are dedicated to the propagation of humanist ideals. Humanism is appealing to many people because it affirms the dignity and worth of all people. Unfortunately, humanists reject the authority of God's Word while elevating human intellect to a supreme position. Humanists deny that there is a creator to whom we are ultimately accountable. This is a fraudulent faith, propagated by lying spirits.

Another fraudulent faith comes from the realm of science. While scientific knowledge has greatly improved our lives, the belief that life arose spontaneously and evolved by random processes has done great harm to our culture. Many young people are taught in school that all of life, including their own existence, can be explained without reference to God. They are told that God the Creator is a myth and that they themselves are nothing but highly evolved animals. When people believe they are animals, they behave as animals. Many of the ills of our society can be traced to the fact that young people are taught that they are the product of random processes, living meaningless lives in an uncaring universe. This, too, is a doctrine of demons.

Christians generally fail to recognize the seriousness of our battle. We easily fall into the trap of thinking of church as a series of Sunday services, youth meetings, and family picnics. But God views the church as serious business. We are in a death struggle against a murderous, lying foe. Our enemy seeks to destroy us, body and soul. Satan is dead serious about this conflict. We need to take it seriously as well.

A seared conscience

Paul says that doctrines of demons were being spread in Ephesus by human teachers. "Such teachings come through hypocritical liars, whose consciences have been seared as with a hot iron" (1 Timothy 4:2).

Demons are the source of these fraudulent faiths, but deceived human beings act as propaganda agents for our invisible enemy. The apostle suggests two identifying marks of the human propagators of spiritual error.

First, false human teachers deal in pretentions. They are "hypocritical liars." They come to us with lofty-sounding claims. They claim to have access to secret sources of truth that other people do not have. They claim to have a privileged relationship with God, and He grants them access to the secrets and mysteries of life. These teachers are often able to elevate themselves in subtle ways, so that other people think of them as amazingly humble and self-effacing. But their humility is an act; everything they do is calculated to draw attention to themselves.

Second, they have seared consciences. Our conscience is that ethical and moral compass within us that motivates us to do right and inhibits us from doing wrong. These false teachers have had their consciences burned out of them with a hot iron. They have sinned so often and told so many lies that nothing restrains them. They feel the rules don't apply to them. They never feel guilty or sorry. They may have learned how to sound sincere, but they are utterly self-centered.

One such person was Jim Jones, founder of the People's Temple. Jones was originally ordained a minister in the Disciples of Christ denomination. But over time, he became fascinated with his ability to manipulate audiences with his preaching skills. He left the Disciples of Christ and founded his own church. In his preaching, he claimed that the Bible was a mixture of truth and error. Of course, there was only one person qualified to determine what was truth and what was error: Jim Jones.

In time, Jones claimed to be the incarnation of Jesus, the Buddha, and the Communist leader V. I. Lenin. Members of his San Francisco-based church were encouraged to call him father and view him as a savior. When the government began investigating the church for tax evasion, Jones moved the People's Temple to Guyana in South America. There, he said, they would build a utopian society in the jungle.

On November 18, 1978, when a California congressman arrived to investigate the cult, Jones ordered his men to murder the congressman and his entourage. Then Jim Jones and all nine hundred members of his cult died of either suicide (cyanide poisoning) or gunshot wounds.

The world was shocked at the news photos of hundreds of bodies scattered on the ground. But the apostle Paul would not have been surprised. This is what happens when hypocritical liars with seared consciences preach doctrines of demons.

The trap of asceticism

Paul goes on to describe the twisted religious practices that result when false teachers preach a fraudulent faith: "They forbid people to marry and order them to abstain from certain foods, which God created to be received with thanksgiving by those who believe and who know the truth" (1 Timothy 4:3).

Religious error is often accompanied by ascetic practices—that is, by the denial of the natural, pleasurable experiences of our humanity. One of these experiences is marriage. Down through the centuries, there have been cults that controlled every aspect of their members' lives, including forbidding people to marry. These cults often teach that all sex, including sex in marriage, is sin.

Some cults also control their members' diet. This is not to say that there is anything wrong with dieting for the sake of one's health. But there have been numerous cults that have taken the issue of dietary restriction to absurd extremes. We often see an affinity between dietary restrictions and religious extremism and error.

Why are cultists attracted to asceticism? It's because of the conviction—which is common wherever there is religious error—that self-denial pleases God. People who engage in ascetic practices are often sincere, but sincerely wrong. Genuine Christians, especially in the early stages of their faith, sometimes deny themselves in some way so that God will be pleased with them. It's not wrong to discipline ourselves, to fast, to spend a night in prayer, or to memorize hundreds of Scripture verses—but if we do these things thinking that God will be pleased by our self-denial, then we have fallen into the trap of religious asceticism.

You may ask, "But didn't Jesus say that we should deny ourselves, take up our cross, and follow him?" Yes, in Luke 9:23, Jesus did say that. But we should be careful not to confuse self-denial (asceticism) with denying self, as Jesus called us to do. Self-denial is giving up something perfectly good, such as marriage or food, in order to win favor with God.

But true denial of the self, which the Lord commands, is not an attempt to earn God's favor. Because Jesus purchased our redemption on the cross, we willingly put His agenda ahead of our own out of gratitude for what He has done for us. We do not have to punish ourselves to earn God's favor. Jesus already took our punishment upon himself at Calvary. We now follow Him out of thankful, joyful hearts.

One way that we deny the self is by honoring God with our bodies. That means we do not yield to sexual immorality. The apostle Paul put it this way:

> Flee from sexual immorality. All other sins a man commits are outside his body, but he who sins sexually sins against his own body. Do you not know that your body is a temple of the Holy Spirit, who is in you, whom

you have received from God? You are not your own; you were bought at a price. Therefore honor God with your body. (1 Corinthians 6:18–20)

What is our motivation for sexual purity? It's not to earn favor with God. Our motivation is gratitude. We are grateful to God because we have been bought with a price—the price of our Lord's own blood, shed upon the cross.

Received with thanksgiving

Paul answers the false teachers by going back to the doctrine of creation. He writes:

They forbid people to marry and order them to abstain from certain foods, which God created to be received with thanksgiving by those who believe and who know the truth. For everything God created is good, and nothing is to be rejected if it is received with thanksgiving, because it is consecrated by the word of God and prayer. (1 Timothy 4:3–5)

The false teachers are wrong to teach self-denial, because everything God created is good. Instead of denying ourselves good things like marriage and food, we should receive these things with thanksgiving and consecrate them by God's Word and by prayer.

What does it mean to be thankful? It means that we recognize that we are incapable in ourselves of producing the wonderful things we enjoy. Marriage is a gift of God. Good food grows from the earth that God created. All good things that we enjoy are gifts of God's grace. So, with thankful hearts, we praise Him for His goodness to us.

Since God gave these gifts to us to for our enjoyment, why should we refuse them? If we deny ourselves the good things God has given us, we insult God. How would you feel if you gave a wonderful gift to your child, and your child refused to receive it? God did not give us good things just so we could practice asceticism. He gave us good gifts because He loves us.

God's gifts should be "received with thanksgiving" and "consecrated by the word of God and prayer." Consecration means to put something to its proper use. A good example of consecrating our gifts by the Word of God and prayer is when we sit down to a meal and give thanks to God. Food is the most basic element of life. We are to give thanks for our daily bread because, as an anonymous poet reminds us,

Back of the bread is the snowy flour,
and back of the flour the mill.

Back of the mill is the field of wheat,
the rain and the Father's will.

A young man demonstrated what it means to truly be thankful for the gifts God has given us. After his wife of four years fell gravely ill, he awoke in the middle of the night, thinking about what she meant to him and how much he loved her. Then he wrote these words:

My wife may die before morning, but I have been with her for four years. Four years! There is no way I can feel cheated if I didn't have her another day. I didn't deserve her for one minute.

And I may die before morning! What I must do is die now. I must accept the justice of death and the injustice of life.

I have lived a good life, longer than many, better than most. I have had thirty-two years. I couldn't ask for another day.

What did I do to deserve birth? It was a gift. I am me. That is a miracle. I have no right to a single minute. But some are given a single hour, and yet I have had thirty-two years.

Few can choose when they will die, but I choose to accept death now. As of this moment I give up my right to live and I give up my right to her life.

Those are the words of a thankful heart. I am challenged and convicted by those words—just as I am challenged by these words on a little plaque that hangs in our home:

There is no thought worth thinking
Unless it is the thought of God.
There is no sight worth seeing
Unless it is seen through his eyes.
There is no breath worth breathing
Without giving thanks to him
Whose very breath it is.

What paupers we are in ourselves! Yet how rich we are when we gratefully receive the gifts of God's grace.

CHAPTER 13

A Good Servant

1 Timothy 4:6–10

While in seminary, I spent two summers as an intern with radio Bible teacher J. Vernon McGee. After seminary, I spent three months traveling with Dr. Harry Ironside, recently retired pastor of Moody Memorial Church in Chicago. So I was privileged to be mentored by two legendary Bible teachers.

In 1950, I was called as the first pastor of a two-year-old fellowship in Palo Alto, California, which would later become Peninsula Bible Church. So, at age thirty-two, I became the pastor of people who were older and wiser than I, some of whom were nationally known Christian leaders. I was expected to be not only their Bible teacher but also their partner in ministry. I might even be called upon to correct their viewpoints or challenge their actions from time to time.

I often felt inadequate to the challenges I faced. Many times, I wished I could talk to Dr. McGee or Dr. Ironside and draw upon their depths of Bible wisdom and ministry experience.

I eventually spent four decades as pastor of Peninsula Bible Church, retiring in 1990. During that time, I saw many young pastors come out of seminary. As my hair turned white and my face grew lined with age, many of these newly minted ministers apparently mistook my superannuated condition for wisdom, and they came to me with the same kinds of questions I used to inflict on my mentors.

These young pastors reminded me of my younger self—and of Timothy, a young pastor left alone in Ephesus, having to face the problems of a fast-growing church in a pagan city. I'm sure that Timothy often longed to have Paul there to give him answers and guidance for the various problems he faced.

I think Timothy must have been overjoyed to receive this letter from Paul, his spiritual father and mentor in the ministry. It must have encouraged him greatly in the midst of his dangerous and demanding life. This letter undoubtedly helped to make up for all the times Timothy must have said, "What do I do now? How do I solve this mess? Where is Paul when I need him?"

In the twenty centuries since this letter was written, hundreds of thousands of pastors and churches have richly benefitted from Paul's counsel in this letter.

What do you feed on?

Paul never minced words when he wrote to Timothy. He helped Timothy face every problem and issue in the church with unflinching realism. Paul knew this young man was up against a dangerous situation that called for a cool head, a loving heart, and unwavering faith and courage. Several times in this letter, Paul reminds Timothy of the importance of maintaining his steadfastness in the face of challenges. This passage is one of these reminders:

> If you point these things out to the brothers, you will be a good minister of Christ Jesus, brought up in the truths of the faith and of the good teaching that you have followed. Have nothing to do with godless myths and old wives' tales; rather, train yourself to be godly. For physical training is of some value, but godliness has value for all things, holding promise for both the present life and the life to come.
>
> This is a trustworthy saying that deserves full acceptance (and for this we labor and strive), that we have put our hope in the living God, who is the Savior of all men, and especially of those who believe. (1 Timothy 4:6–10)

When Paul urges Timothy to be "a good minister of Christ Jesus," he is not referring to our current concept of a minister, that is, a clergyman who is hired by a congregation to stand behind a pulpit and preach. The Greek word Paul uses here is *diakonos,* which means "deacon" or "servant." So Paul is urging Timothy to be a good deacon of Jesus Christ. A deacon is one who serves.

So Paul is using the word in the widest sense possible: "a good servant of Jesus Christ." In that sense, the word includes everyone, not just pastors. All Christians are called to be servants of the Lord Jesus. In order to be a good servant of Jesus Christ, Paul says, you need to follow certain guidelines.

Paul's first admonition to Timothy is: Watch what you feed on! Be sure to consume only "the truths of the faith" and "the good teaching that you have followed." In other words, you are what you eat, so be sure to nourish yourself on the words of the faith and the good doctrine that you have received.

What do you feed on? What do you put in your mind? The sports pages? Soap operas? The Dow Jones averages? Movies on cable television? Fiction best sellers? A steady diet of these substances can leave you spiritually undernourished at best—and consuming certain things (demonic horror movies or Internet pornography, for example) could even leave you with a fatal dose of food poisoning. What you feed on determines what you become as a servant of Jesus Christ.

There's nothing wrong with a certain amount of sports, news, or entertainment in your daily diet. I'm not saying you should abstain from such foods, but you do need to practice moderation. If these things monopolize our time or control our thoughts, then our lives are out of balance and need to be brought into line with God's priorities.

Paul urges Timothy to feed on the things that are essential to a strong spiritual life—things such as "the truths of the faith and of the good teaching that you have followed." He is talking about sound doctrine, the teaching of biblical truth. All Christians need to feed on sound teaching that flows from God's Word.

The Bible is the greatest book ever written, the only place where we can find eternal, undiluted truth about life. The Scriptures contain God's view of reality, and His view is the objective view—the view of the One who created reality out of nothing. No book is more important to feed upon than the Word of God. It's a big book, and it requires careful study and meditation in order to understand what it says to us.

It's a book of many layers and incredible depth, and you can read a passage dozens of times and still find new facets of meaning embedded there. No other book has ever influenced and transformed so many lives. So if you wish to be well nourished and strengthened to face the challenges of life, feed upon God's Word.

Living under the authority of Scripture

How well do you know the Bible? You probably feel you have a pretty good working knowledge of the Scriptures. If someone asked you to identify Sodom, you'd probably know better than to answer, "The husband of Gomorrah." If someone asked you to identify the epistles, you'd certainly know better than to answer, "The wives of the apostles." But how are you at applying the truth of God's Word to your everyday life? Do you truly live under the authority of Scripture? Does the truth of God's Word permeate your words and actions?

Have you learned to bless those who persecute you? Before you answer, consider these situations. The last time your boss yelled at you for some minor mistake, how did you respond? What were your thoughts and emotions? Did you pray for your boss? Or did you inwardly curse him? And how did you respond to that person in the next car who tailgated you or cut you off on the freeway? How did you respond to that obnoxious landlord, or the officer who gave you that ticket, or that university professor who belittled your faith? How are you responding in times of conflict with your spouse or your rebellious teenager?

Is your home open to strangers? Scripture tells us to practice hospitality. Are you planning this week to have someone over for dinner? Are you thinking of ways to share your faith with that person?

Can you honestly say you are applying God's Word to your everyday life and your most important relationships? Are you truly living under the authority of Scripture?

Knowing the truth does not help ourselves or anyone else. Only doing the truth makes an impact on the world. If we are only *hearers* of the Word and not doers of the Word, then we are deceiving ourselves.

So Paul's message to Timothy is this: Nourish yourself on the good words of the faith; understand sound teaching, and apply it to your life. Learn God's truth; then do it. That is how to change the world.

Godless myths and old wives' tales

Paul has begun with positive instruction. He has told Timothy how to spiritually nourish himself. But there is also a negative instruction—that is, a warning about what Timothy needs to avoid. Paul writes, "Have nothing to do with godless myths and old wives' tales; rather, train yourself to be godly" (1 Timothy 4:7).

Some things never change. We are as plagued today by "godless myths and old wives' tales," as were the people of Paul's day. I don't know what particular myths and tales Paul had in mind, but the details hardly matter. The term "old wives' tales" referred to the kinds of stories, laced with superstition and falsehood, that might be spread by foolish people with too much time on their hands. Paul tells Timothy not to waste any time on such matters.

There are many examples of contemporary "old wives' tales" we could point to. People are often fascinated by bizarre tales of supernatural occurrences. Some "researchers" claim to be able to regress people into past lives. They use guided hypnosis to put a person into a trance and get him or her to recall a past life as an Egyptian pharaoh or an Indian princess. People who believe the godless myths of reincarnation neglect to do the math: There were only a few million people in the world in the days of the pharaohs and Indian princesses—and there are well over six billion people in the world today. If reincarnation were true, then we'd have far too many bodies and not nearly enough souls to go around!

It doesn't take a lot of thought to realize that reincarnation is sheer superstitious nonsense. Moreover, it directly contradicts God's Word, which tells us that human beings are "destined to die once, and after that to face judgment" (Hebrews 9:27). Yet millions of people, including some unwise Christians, have fallen for the godless myth of reincarnation. To believe in reincarnation is to reject belief in the resurrection. You cannot believe in both reincarnation and the resurrection because they are contradictory views of reality.

As Paul urged Timothy, so I urge you: Don't waste time listening to godless myths and old wives' tales. Study the Scriptures and gain God's view of reality. Avoid myths that would lead you into error and spiritual self-destruction. Nourish your mind and your spirit on sound words of faith in Jesus Christ.

Wholly lean on Jesus

Next, Paul turns to the question of physical training versus spiritual training. He writes, "For physical training is of some value, but godliness has value for all things, holding promise for both the present life and the life to come" (1 Timothy 4:8).

This is a great verse for all the physical exercise enthusiasts. If you have ever wondered if Paul was a jogger, then this first tells you that he was at least knowledgeable about the importance of exercise. Throughout his letters, he uses athletics-related metaphors, speaking of the Christian life in terms of foot races, boxing matches, and gladiator battles. It may well be that Paul was a sports fan and that he was an athlete in his younger days.

Here in this verse, he states clearly that physical exercise has value. But he also makes it clear where our priorities should lie. Godliness, he says, has far more value than physical training. Though exercise has value for this life, training in godliness is valuable both for this life and for the life to come.

There's evidence in Acts that Paul was physically fit. Luke writes, "We went on ahead to the ship and sailed for Assos, where we were going to take

Paul aboard. He had made this arrangement because he was going there on foot. When he met us at Assos, we took him aboard and went on to Mitylene" (Acts 20:13–14).

He sent his companions by ship around a point that jutted into the sea, a voyage of about forty miles, while he cut across the peninsula on foot, a hike of about twenty-five miles. He walked alone, perhaps because he wanted to think and pray (Christians today might do well to combine meditation and prayer with an hour on the treadmill). Paul believed in exercise, but he kept it in balance. He maintained his spiritual fitness first, then his physical fitness.

Many Christians say, "I wish I had more time for prayer and Bible study." But Paul didn't wish for more time. He *made* time. He made spiritual fitness his first priority. Spiritual training through prayer and meditation in the Scriptures will strengthen your spiritual muscles and trim away your spiritual flab. By steeping your spirit in God's Word, you will gain confidence to witness to others, plus the power to resist temptation and face your fears. That's the value of spiritual training and spiritual fitness.

Paul goes on to write, "This is a trustworthy saying that deserves full acceptance (and for this we labor and strive), that we have put our hope in the living God, who is the Savior of all men, and especially of those who believe" (1 Timothy 4:9–10).

Five times in this letter Paul underscores his words with this statement: "This is a trustworthy saying that deserves full acceptance." In other words, "Listen! This is important!" Here Paul tells Timothy—in fact, he practically shouts to Timothy—about the motivation that drives him in ministry. "We labor and strive," Paul says—words that suggest an intense degree of effort, commitment, and action.

Godliness doesn't happen by accident. You don't get zapped by godliness, nor do you drift into godliness. A godly spirit is the result of effort, labor, and commitment to God's Word and prayer. We must make time for these spiritual disciplines, and that usually means that we have to forego something else. We must pursue godliness by a deliberate act of the will. There's a song that expresses what it means to pursue a life of godliness:

My hope is built on nothing less
Than Jesus' blood and righteousness.
I dare not trust the sweetest frame
But wholly lean on Jesus' name.

Do you wholly lean on Jesus' name all day long? Do you nourish your mind and your spirit on the great truths of His Word? As Paul says at the conclusion of this passage, "We have put our hope in the living God, who is the Savior of all men, and especially of those who believe." Salvation is available to all who will come to Jesus and receive it. He alone has made it possible. There is no other Savior.

In the book of Acts, the apostle Peter stood before the Sanhedrin, the same council of religious rulers who had demanded the crucifixion of Jesus. At the risk of his own life, he boldly declared, "Salvation is found in no one else, for there is no other name under heaven given to men by which we must be saved" (Acts 4:12).

Jesus is the Savior of all people, without distinction, yet that salvation becomes effective only to those who believe.

Do you believe in Jesus? It's one thing to say, "I believe in Jesus" and give assent to a doctrinal statement about Jesus. But it is quite another thing to boldly risk everything—your career, your reputation, even life itself—for the sake of following Him. But when you look at your life objectively, from God's point of view, you can come to only one conclusion: Knowing Jesus is the only thing that matters.

CHAPTER 14

Advice to a Young Pastor

1 Timothy 4:11–16

In the early twentieth century, the seaport town of Monterey, California, was home to dozens of fish canning factories. Fourteen canneries lined the waterfront street called Ocean View Avenue. By the 1930s, the street and its fish factories had become unofficially known as Cannery Row, a name that novelist John Steinbeck adopted as the title of his 1945 novel.

Cannery Row was home to many interesting and oddball characters, many of whom were immortalized in Steinbeck's novel. It was also home to thousands of pelicans. The birds had migrated to Monterey and settled around the fish canneries because of the plentiful supply of food. The fishermen would bring in their catch, clean it on the waterfront, and discard hundreds of pounds of scrap fish parts for the pelicans to feast on.

This arrangement worked well for decades. The fishermen could dispose of the waste fish, and within hours it would all be cleaned up by the pelicans. That all changed in the mid-1950s when the fishing industry collapsed and the Monterey canneries closed their doors.

Hundreds of pelicans waited for the fishermen to arrive with food, but the fishermen didn't come. The pelicans began to starve. In the wild, pelicans would dive into the water to get their meals. But over the decades of being fed by the fishermen, the Monterey pelicans had forgotten how to fish for themselves.

The pelican population in Monterey would have starved to death if wildlife experts hadn't come up with a solution. They captured wild pelicans in other coastal sections of California and brought them to Monterey. The wild pelicans immediately started hunting their own food. The Monterey pelicans watched, learned, and joined in. The Monterey pelicans were saved by the good example of the imported pelicans.

In the church as in nature, we all need good examples to follow. That is Paul's message to Timothy in the fourth chapter of this letter.

The danger of youthful arrogance

The apostle Paul opens this section of his letter with these words of counsel to his spiritual son Timothy: "Command and teach these things. Don't let anyone look down on you because you are young, but set an example for the believers in speech, in life, in love, in faith and in purity" (1 Timothy 4:11–12).

Timothy faced a difficult challenge in Ephesus. He was a young man, probably in his mid-thirties, having spent about fifteen years traveling around the Roman Empire with the apostle Paul. Timothy undoubtedly felt intimidated by some of the elders of the Ephesian church. As Paul made clear earlier in this letter, he expected Timothy to correct some of the problems that were taking place in that church:

> As I urged you when I went into Macedonia, stay there in Ephesus so that you may command certain men not to teach false doctrines any longer nor to devote themselves to myths and endless genealogies. These promote controversies rather than God's work—which is by faith. (1 Timothy 1:3–4)

That was a tough assignment! Timothy would have to approach these situations with great care. He needed to be bold, yet he also needed to handle the situations with diplomacy and sensitivity. Paul had not placed Timothy in Ephesus to make enemies. Timothy was there to solve problems. Paul knew what Timothy was up against, so he instructed his spiritual son in how to minister among people who were older than he was.

Paul begins by telling Timothy, "Don't let anyone look down on you because you are young." Please understand, Paul isn't telling Timothy to pick a fight with anyone who looks down on him. He's telling Timothy to be aware of how he comes across to people, especially older people. He should be sensitive toward their feelings and be careful not to cause any offense.

Young people often don't realize how they sound to older people. One of the most common causes of the rejection of a young man's ministry is an attitude that might be called youthful arrogance. The young person often doesn't mean to come across as arrogant. He's simply not aware that his words and actions are interpreted that way.

Youthful arrogance can take various forms, such as a dogmatic, know-it-all attitude. The Old Testament reminds us: "One who puts on his armor should not boast like one who takes it off" (1 Kings 20:11). In other words, a young and untested warrior who is just strapping on his armor has nothing to brag about, compared with a battle-tested veteran who is removing his armor after returning from the fields of war.

You might say, "But doesn't Paul urge Timothy to take charge and issue orders? After all, he says, 'Command and teach these things.'"

But in the Greek, the word Paul uses is *paraggello,* which means proclaim or announce. Paul is not telling Timothy to order the Ephesian Christians around. He is telling Timothy to announce and teach the good news of Jesus Christ to the people in Ephesus. The phrase "these things" refers to verse 10, where Paul told Timothy that Jesus is "the Savior of all men, and especially of those who believe." Timothy should proclaim this message to everyone in Ephesus—not in a domineering way, but respectfully and humbly.

Francis Asbury was an outstanding young Methodist missionary in America. John Wesley sent him from England to the eastern American colonies. Asbury arrived when he was just twenty-six years of age. He rode on horseback through the Colonies, preaching everywhere he went. He is estimated to have ridden 250,000 miles during the course of his ministry. Here is a brief entry from one of Francis Asbury's journals:

> I packed up my clothes and books to be ready for my departure, and had an agreeable conversation with Mr. O. The next day some of my friends were so unguarded and imprudent as to commend me to my face. Satan, ready for every advantage, seized the opportunity and assaulted me with self-pleasing, self-exalting ideas, but the Lord enabled me to discover the danger, and the snare was broken. May He ever keep me humble and little and mean in my own eyes.

Francis Asbury was the prototype for the Methodist circuit riders who later rode west, spreading the gospel as they went. It's hardly surprising that a young man with such a humble attitude accomplished great things for God.

A good example in speech and conduct

In verse 12, Paul goes on to say that a young servant of Jesus Christ should "set an example for the believers in speech, in life, in love, in faith and in purity." As Christians, we are to be role models in our speech and conduct, and three qualities ought to come through: love, faithfulness, and purity. In other words, our speech should be loving, faithful, pure speech. And our conduct should be loving, faithful, pure conduct.

To be loving is to exemplify all the qualities Paul describes 1 Corinthians 13, the famous love chapter: patient, kind, not envious, not boastful, not proud, not rude, not self-seeking, not easily angered, quick to let go of grudges, rejoicing with the truth, not delighting in evil, always protective and trusting and hopeful and persevering, and unfailing. That is what love is like. That is what our speech and conduct should be like.

To be faithful is to be reliable in all of our commitments. We do not flatter or use insincere words. We say what we mean and mean what we say. We keep promises. We set an example of absolute dependability.

To be pure is to be moral, clean, righteous, good, honorable, and holy. I can think of no single failing that has destroyed more young ministers than impurity. Paul had probably seen a number of Christian leaders fall into this trap.

Moreover, Paul knew the danger Timothy faced in a city like Ephesus, which was given over to sexual immorality. So Paul's counsel to Timothy was to maintain a standard of purity in his speech and conduct. Implicit in this counsel was the fact that there should be no vulgar, obscene, or profane words in his speech, no dirty stories, no sexual misconduct, no indulging in making out or fornication or pornography or sexually suggestive entertainment. Purity is the platform from which an effective ministry proceeds. Without a pure life, Timothy's gospel would mean nothing.

Next, Paul turns to the public preaching of God's Word. Here, Paul gives us a glimpse behind the scenes of the pulpit ministry of the first-century church. He writes:

> Until I come, devote yourself to the public reading of Scripture, to preaching and to teaching. Do not neglect your gift, which was given you through a prophetic message when the body of elders laid their hands on you.
>
> Be diligent in these matters; give yourself wholly to them, so that everyone may see your progress. Watch your life and doctrine closely. Persevere in them, because if you do, you will save both yourself and your hearers. (1 Timothy 4:13–16)

Paul tells Timothy that an effective preaching ministry consists of reading the Scriptures in public, exhorting, and teaching. Notice the centrality of the Scriptures. Timothy is to first read the Scriptures; then he is to exhort, urge, proclaim, open up, and make clear what the Scriptures say; and he is to teach and explain the Scriptures.

The Word of God is the focus for everything that takes place in the preaching ministry. Why does the congregation come together? They come to praise God, worship God, sing hymns to God, and fellowship together.

But there is one aspect of the worship service that is at the hub of everything else that is done: The congregation meets in order to hear the Word of God, taught by a man of God, led by the Spirit of God, who implants that Word into every individual life and heart.

Use your gift!

Next, Paul gives us three steps to an effective preaching ministry. Here is the first of those three steps: "Do not neglect your gift, which was given you through a prophetic message when the body of elders laid their hands on you" (1 Timothy 4:14).

Paul begins with Timothy's spiritual gift. Paul referred to the prophetic message regarding Timothy's gift earlier in this letter when he said, "Timothy, my son, I give you this instruction in keeping with the prophecies once made about you" (see 1 Timothy 1:18–20). Paul will also refer to Timothy's gift in his second letter to Timothy: "For this reason I remind you to fan into flame the gift of God, which is in you through the laying on of my hands" (2 Timothy 1:6).

We don't all receive a prophetic affirmation through the laying on of hands, but all Christians have spiritual gifts. There is no believer who does not have spiritual gifts. Don't make the mistake of thinking that spiritual gifts are merely for pastors or elders. All of us, without exception, receive at least one spiritual gift when we come to Christ.

The Scriptures list at least twenty-one different spiritual gifts: apostle, prophet, evangelist, pastor, teacher, service, exhortation, giving, leadership, mercy, helps, administration, wisdom, knowledge, discernment, prophecy, tongues, interpretation, faith, healing, and miracles. You'll find these gifts listed in Romans 12:3–8; 1 Corinthians 12:1–12, 27–30; and Ephesians 4:11.

Paul's point is this: You, Timothy, have been given a spiritual gift; make sure that you put it to good use. Bible scholars have debated what Timothy's gift might have been. Some think it was the gift of evangelism because, in his second letter to Timothy, Paul says, "Do the work of an evangelist, discharge all the duties of your ministry" (see 2 Timothy 4:5). I doubt that, because the gift of an evangelist usually accompanies a strong, outgoing personality; Timothy was shy and introverted, so I doubt that this was his gift.

Timothy undoubtedly had the gift of a pastor-teacher, and probably other gifts besides (God generally gives clusters of gifts to his people, not just one). Every human being is a kaleidoscope of gifts, and God uses all of these facets and hues to convey his truth in the richest and deepest way possible.

Timothy was certainly aware of his gifts, and he knew what Paul meant when he urged Timothy to put his gifts to good use.

Often, Christians in the congregation find themselves attracted to this minister or that, and they even pit one person's ministry against another, behaving jealously and quarreling because a certain cluster of spiritual gifts appeals to them. In 1 Corinthians 3, Paul makes it clear that this is a worldly and immature response. We should not choose sides and say, "I follow Paul," or, "I follow Apollos." It's childish to speak that way, Paul says, because all of God's preachers, teachers, and evangelists are mere servants of Christ. And we should remain united in following our Lord and Savior, Jesus Christ.

Be prepared and keep it personal!

Next, Paul reveals the second step to effective preaching and teaching of God's Word: Be thoroughly prepared. He writes, "Be diligent in these matters; give yourself wholly to them, so that everyone may see your progress" (1 Timothy 4:15).

We owe it to God to give Him our best, including our most thoughtful preparation whenever we approach His holy Word. Most people have no idea how much work goes into preparing a sermon. A diligent preacher of the Word does not get up on Sunday morning and share whatever rolls off the top of his head.

A preacher must examine Scripture carefully. He must meditate on it, research it, ask and answer questions in his own mind about it, look up the meanings of words in lexicons and commentaries, think through an introduction and a conclusion to his message, and do it all without seeming mechanical or artificial. That takes a lot of work. Preaching demands thorough preparation of the heart as well as the mind.

The third step to effective preaching and teaching that Paul suggests to Timothy is: Keep it personal. "Watch your life and doctrine closely. Persevere in them, because if you do, you will save both yourself and your hearers" (1 Timothy 4:16).

Here Paul states a profound psychological principle: You can only give to others what you yourself have first experienced, nothing more. A pastor can never bring anyone to a maturity that he himself does not possess. Pastors, preachers, and teachers must continually experience growth in their relationship with God's Word.

When Paul says, "you will save both yourself and your hearers," he is not talking about redemption. Timothy was already saved by the grace of God, and so were most of his hearers. Paul uses the word *save* in the same sense as the word *salvation* is used when he writes, "Continue to work out your salvation with fear and trembling, for it is God who works in you to will and to act according to his good purpose" (see Philippians 2:12–13). Paul is talking about salvation in the sense of fulfillment, maturity, and being delivered from temptation and evil. He is talking about being saved from spiritual harm and destructive choices.

Sharing the good news is for everyone

I have to confess that I will sometimes read back over my past sermons. Am I doing this to bolster my ego? Hardly! I find it humbling and embarrassing to do so. As I read, I become painfully aware of the awkward phrasings, the unclear sentences, the grammatical errors, and more. I become intensely aware of what a feeble instrument the Lord has to work with in me.

But embedded amid all of my mistakes and flaws are nuggets of God's truth—insights that God unveiled to me as I studied His Word and prepared the message. Reading God's truth woven through my poor message always blesses me anew. I recall how, as I labored over the message, God opened my eyes in new ways. Reading through those messages affects me as though I were reading someone else's words.

This is a great affirmation to me that God is able to do His work through me despite my limitations. There's always something in my sermons that is God's work, not mine. And the same is true for you, whether you minister in a pulpit, an office, a factory, a retail shop, a classroom, or a military base. Whatever you do, wherever you minister, God wants to speak His Word through you.

When you use your spiritual gifts, prepare your heart and mind through God's Word. When you speak, keep it personal; simply tell your story. Don't worry about your flaws or feelings of awkwardness. Make yourself available to God, and He will use you to touch hearts and minds. His strength will be perfected in your weakness, and He will influence many lives through you.

There is no more exciting way to live than that. I can't imagine any greater adventure than the adventure of sharing God's Word with other people. It's the adventure of seeing eyes opened and light streaming into human hearts for the first time. It's the adventure of seeing lives transformed and relationships healed. It's the adventure of seeing people brought out of the darkness and into God's kingdom of light.

And your life will be transformed as well. You don't have to be a pastor, a preacher, or an evangelist to proclaim God's Word to others. In fact, Jesus has commissioned all of us to go into the world and share the good news with everyone we meet. We can do that in the lunchroom at work. We can do that in the supermarket line. We can do that in the hallway after class. We can do that over a cup of coffee with a neighbor.

All it takes is a willingness to speak and live a lifestyle of Christian love, Christian faithfulness, and Christian purity.

CHAPTER 15

Caring for Widows

1 Timothy 5:1–16

An issue of *Our Daily Bread* featured the story of Margaret, a widow in her nineties. She faced increasing pain and infirmity as her life neared its completion. She had become too weak to walk and was nearly deaf. She rarely left the confines of her nursing home.

Yet Margaret had a ministry that circled the globe. Every day, she sat in her chair for hours at a time, going through a stack of prayer cards. She would read one card after another and diligently pray for each missionary. Author Dave Branon concluded:

> Margaret doesn't have much more than prayer to offer her Lord. She is the essence of the answer to the question in Psalm 116:12, "What shall I render to the Lord for all his benefits toward me?" Verse 13 answers, "I will… call upon the name of the Lord."
>
> A lifetime of being sustained by God's love, grace, and mercy is just about over for Margaret. In the face of mounting physical weakness, she is staying spiritually strong to the end. O, to have her courage and dedication—at any age![1]

We sometimes forget about the widows in our midst. After all, they don't come to worship services anymore, they don't sing in the choir anymore, and they don't take part in the prayer meetings or missionary conferences anymore.

But God doesn't view widows that way. Perhaps all a widow like Margaret can do is pray—but prayer is a more powerful ministry than most churchgoers are involved in. Widows who pray are on the front lines of the church as it advances against the gates of hell. The church needs its widows, and widows need the care of the church.

So as we come to the fifth chapter of Paul's first letter to Timothy, we find the apostle addressing certain problems in the church at Ephesus.

Timothy must deal with problems between various classes within the congregation. He must teach people of different generations, different economic classes, and different cultural backgrounds to love one another and unite together as a single body of believers.

Christian relationships are family relationships

Paul opens this section with some insights into how we should view and treat one another in the church. He writes, "Do not rebuke an older man harshly, but exhort him as if he were your father. Treat younger men as brothers, older women as mothers, and younger women as sisters, with absolute purity" (1 Timothy 5:1–2).

Here we find another psychological insight from God's Word. Paul tells us that the way we treat people depends on how we view them. Paul wants Timothy to know that if he will view the older men in the congregation as fathers, he will treat them with a natural deference and respect.

The mindset of the world is to divide people into two categories: allies and competitors. If you are a worldly person with worldly goals, you will tend to take advantage of your allies while trying to gain advantage over your competitors. Either way, you are using other people to advance yourself. This is why the mindset of the world is a self-centered mindset.

We Christians, however, are to have a different approach to people. As followers of Christ, we are not to take advantage nor gain advantage. We are called to love and serve others. This is especially true of older people, those who have survived trials and crises and have gained a degree of wisdom through years of experience.

Paul says that in addition to treating older man as fathers, Timothy should view younger men as his brothers. Again, Paul instructs Timothy to view church relationships as family relationships. Young men are not Timothy's rivals or competitors; they are his brothers, and he is to treat them with brotherly caring and respect.

Next, Paul tells Timothy to treat the older women as mothers. If we view older women in the congregation as mothers, then we will treat them with genuine Christian compassion and respect.

The apostle Paul goes on to tell Timothy that he should view younger women as sisters. In other words, he should demonstrate a brotherly love and protectiveness toward them. Note that Paul adds, "with absolute purity." A young pastor, Paul says, should be pure in his intentions and dealings with young women in the church. There should be no hint of sexual advances.

Paul is not saying that a chaste romantic relationship is out of the question. Certainly, it's conceivable that Timothy might develop a romantic relationship that could lead to marriage. But Paul wants Timothy to set a goal of viewing all young women in the church as sisters, so that he will treat them with a love and respect that is appropriate for brothers and sisters.

Young Christians would have fewer relationship problems if they would view each other and treat each other as brothers and sisters. In this way, they would have the opportunity to truly get to know each other as people before sexual attraction clouds their perceptions. If romantic love is right, it will come in its own time.

Sexual attraction has a blinding and obscuring effect; it prevents people from seeing each other accurately and objectively. A young man and a young woman get to know each other better as friends than they do as lovers. So, if you want to truly know someone, maintain purity in your relationship with that person.

Caring for widows

Paul now turns to the problem of widows. In this first-century culture, widows were a real concern to the churches. When a wife lost her husband, there were few ways she could support herself. Independent businesswomen were a rarity in New Testament times. We see a few examples, such as Lydia, the seller of purple, whom Paul met at Philippi, and Phoebe, the deaconess from Cenchrea (see Romans 16:1). But independent women of means were the exception rather than the rule.

In those days, women got married and depended on their husbands for their livelihood. When a woman found herself without a husband, she often needed assistance in order to survive. A widow who had no family to take her in could end up in desperate circumstances.

There were no government programs to help people in poverty. So Paul gave Timothy instruction in how to deal with widows in the church. He wrote:

> Give proper recognition to those widows who are really in need. But if a widow has children or grandchildren, these should learn first of all to put their religion into practice by caring for their own family and so repaying their parents and grandparents, for this is pleasing to God. The widow who is really in need and left all alone puts her hope in God and continues night and day to pray and to ask God for help. But the widow who lives for pleasure is dead even while she lives. Give the people these

instructions, too, so that no one may be open to blame. If anyone does not provide for his relatives, and especially for his immediate family, he has denied the faith and is worse than an unbeliever. (1 Timothy 5:3–8)

Strong words! Clearly, this was a crucial matter in the early church. Though times have changed, the principle remains the same. We should take these matters seriously in the church today.

In the early church, a special pension fund was set up to provide support for widows. Those widows who were placed on the pension roll pledged themselves to a ministry of helping and praying. They also pledged not to remarry. They were to put their hope in God alone.

Certain limitations and qualifications had to be fulfilled by the widows on this pension roll. Some widows were qualified for inclusion; some were not. To be included, women must fulfill at least five qualifications that the apostle gives here.

First, they had to be widows with no family to provide for them. If a widow had children or grandchildren, then her family had a responsibility to care for her. Paul sets forth a clear principle: It's up to the family to care for those members who cannot care for themselves.

This principle still applies in our day. However, the social safety nets in our society have made it less likely that widows need to be dependent on their families. Those safety nets include government assistance, such as Social Security, and private insurance programs. If a woman today has the means to provide for herself, then the church has no responsibility to provide for her. That is a principle Paul clearly sets forth here.

But whether a widow requires financial assistance from the church or not, she is worthy to be honored, respected, and loved with the compassion of Christ. The church needs to be conscious of the emotional needs of widows. Christians should not allow a woman to be lonely. Every church should make sure that widows feel that they are a vital, functioning part of the body of Christ.

Second, the widows had to give themselves to spiritual ministry. Paul writes:

The widow who is really in need and left all alone puts her hope in God and continues night and day to pray and to ask God for help. But the widow who lives for pleasure is dead even while she lives. Give the people these instructions, too, so that no one may be open to blame. (1 Timothy 5:5–7)

There are many ways to include widows in the life of the church. Widows should receive regular visits or phone calls, for example, from the deacons. But it's not enough to tell widows on a regular basis, "We are thinking about you. We are praying for you." Widows need to keep busy, and there is plenty of work for them to do. The church should actively include widows in the ongoing ministry of the church, including the ministry of prayer. After all, prayer is power, and a platoon of praying widows can be an unstoppable force in the life of the church.

In his letter to Titus, the apostle Paul urges that the older women teach the younger women. This kind of cross-generational ministry provides an important service to both generations. Older widows need to know they are still useful in the life of the church. Young women need to learn wisdom from the older women. It's a beautiful thing to see women in the congregation helping each other, praying for each other, serving each other, and learning from each other.

From time to time, I see a widow who has received a large sum of money after her husband's death, and she has spent her days and her money entertaining herself. She takes cruises around the world. She attends bridge parties and goes shopping in Carmel. She has fun, but she has no ministry.

The apostle Paul bluntly states, "But the widow who lives for pleasure is dead even while she lives." In other words, she might as well be dead. She is not using her life as God intends. She is focused only on herself, not others, and is missing out on the rich life of ministry that could be hers.

The ministry of widows

Third, to be placed on the pension rolls, widows had to be at least sixty years old. Paul writes:

> No widow may be put on the list of widows unless she is over sixty, has been faithful to her husband, and is well known for her good deeds, such as bringing up children, showing hospitality, washing the feet of the saints, helping those in trouble and devoting herself to all kinds of good deeds. (1 Timothy 5:9–10)

In those days, sixty years old was generally beyond the normal human life expectancy, so a widow in her sixties was usually near the end of her life. So Paul said that such women, with only a few years left on earth, were asked to devote those remaining years to the service of the Lord.

Fourth, widows had to have been faithful in marriage. This does not mean she cannot have been remarried after the death of her first husband. It means that while she was married, she did not betray her marriage vows.

Fifth, to be placed on the church pension rolls, widows had to have a reputation for good deeds. Paul goes on to list the kinds of good deeds he means: "bringing up children, showing hospitality, washing the feet of the saints, helping those in trouble and devoting herself to all kinds of good deeds." In short, such women needed to be genuine servants.

"Washing the feet of the saints" is a reference to the fact that people in those days wore sandals, and their feet would get dusty from the road. When a traveler arrived at a house, therefore, it was the custom for someone to bring out a basin to wash the traveler's feet. In middle-class or poor households, where there were no servants, this task was usually performed by the woman of the household. Foot washing was also a symbol for any kind of menial ministry or act of servanthood. The reference to foot washing implied that the widows who were placed on the rolls should have humble spirits.

Paul also refers to "helping those in trouble." To be placed on the rolls, a widow must be the kind of woman who has given aid to the afflicted. She must have had a habit of caring for the sick, cleaning house for the infirm, providing food for people in need, and so forth. She must be the kind of woman who has devoted herself to doing good in every way. A woman who met these qualifications would reflect well upon the gospel, and her life would be a powerful witness to the community of nonbelievers.

My wife, Elaine, was born in El Cerrito, north of Berkeley, California. Her father died just a few months after she was born, and her mother was widowed and alone, with no family around. But Elaine's mother had a Christian neighbor living across the street, a godly woman named Mrs. Rasmussen.

At that time, Elaine's mother was Roman Catholic and Mrs. Rasmussen was a Protestant, but that made no difference to Mrs. Rasmussen. She took this widow and her baby daughter into her heart, surrounded them with love, and ministered to their needs. Later, when Elaine's mother left California and moved to Montana, Mrs. Rasmussen kept in touch with them by letter for the rest of her life.

When Elaine and I were married and came back from Hawaii after World War II, we stopped in California to visit Mrs. Rasmussen. What a godly woman! Her face was alight with the Spirit of God. She was cheerful, even though she was wheelchair-bound due to crippling arthritis. She was still an angel of mercy and beloved by the entire neighborhood. She brought hundreds of people to Christ by the power of her life of love and quiet service to others.

That's the lifestyle the apostle Paul encourages Christian widows to live. Without being burdened by having to raise children and care for a husband, these godly women have time for ministry tasks that can make an enormous difference for God's kingdom.

What about young widows?

Paul goes on to state that some widows were not to be supported. He writes, "As for younger widows, do not put them on such a list. For when their sensual desires overcome their dedication to Christ, they want to marry" (1 Timothy 5:11).

This practice of enrolling widows and dedicating them to ministry in the church may have been the basis for the Roman Catholic Church's institution of orders of sisters. In *The Sound of Music,* we have the story of Maria, a novitiate who wishes to join an order of sisters and devote herself to a life of celibacy and service to others. But as we see in this passage, Paul would have refused to accept Maria because she was too young. He understood the pressures on a young woman to marry and have a family.

Paul said, "Do not put them on such a list." In other words, younger widows will be strongly tempted to seek again the companionship they once had in marriage. So they should not be treated in the same way as an older widow and placed on the pension list. Instead, Paul says, Timothy should encourage young widows to marry again, because that is their natural inclination and desire.

Even though, in the moment of grief over the loss of her husband, a young woman might express a strong desire to remain celibate for the rest of her life, that feeling might pass. In time, her natural desires might overcome her initial commitment to remaining celibate. Paul does not want to put these women in a position where they would be caught between a commitment made in the emotion of the moment and a woman's understandable and natural desires.

Paul goes on:

Besides, they get into the habit of being idle and going about from house to house. And not only do they become idlers, but also gossips and busybodies, saying things they ought not to. So I counsel younger widows to marry, to have children, to manage their homes and to give the enemy no opportunity for slander. Some have in fact already turned away to follow Satan. (1 Timothy 5:13–15)

If you are a woman, please do not take Paul's words as an insult. At first glance, it may seem that he is dealing in gender stereotypes. If young men were placed on a pension roll and allowed to live idle lives, they too would likely become "gossips and busybodies, saying things they ought not to." The issue in this verse is not men versus women but busy versus idle. People who have too much time on their hands easily fall into harmful behavior, such as gossiping and talking too much.

So Paul, in addressing the question of widows in the church, says that young widows who are capable of being productive should stay busy. They should not be encouraged to become idle. This is good sound counsel from Paul to Timothy.

Paul also urges younger widows to marry and raise families. By doing so, they will take away one of the weapons that Satan uses against the church. If the young widows in the church live virtuous lives, caring for their families, then the enemies of Christianity cannot attack the church for encouraging loose morals.

This is not to say that women cannot work outside the home. But we must acknowledge the simple fact that a strong society is built upon a foundation of strong families. Once the family begins to crumble, society cannot long endure. So Paul, writing to Timothy, urges the younger widows to establish homes, to serve as wives and mothers, and thus contribute to the stability of the society around them.

Caring for older people

Paul summarizes his discussion of widows in this verse: "If any woman who is a believer has widows in her family, she should help them and not let the church be burdened with them, so that the church can help those widows who are really in need" (1 Timothy 5:16).

In his commentary on this passage, William Barclay has observed that there is an explicit responsibility of families to care for older parents and an implicit responsibility of older people to behave in a godly way. Older parents should try to be easy to live with. Sometimes older parents can be so difficult and unpleasant that no one in their right mind would ever want to take them in.

Three times in this passage the apostle underscores our Christian responsibility to take care of older people. It's not always necessary or possible to have them live in the home, though that would be the usual and best situation.

It's a privilege to spend time with older people, to learn from them and care for them. After all, our parents sacrificed to care for us at the beginning of our lives; it's only right to care for them as the end of their lives approaches.

Earlier, Paul wrote, "But if a widow has children or grandchildren, these should learn first of all to put their religion into practice by caring for their own family and so repaying their parents and grandparents, for this is pleasing to God" (1 Timothy 5:4).

God is always interested in the lonely and the hurting. As Christians, we truly put our religion into practice when we care for the weak and helpless, especially those in our own family. If we do not show Christian love and acceptance to our own parents and grandparents, how can we claim to love God?

Paul also wrote, "If anyone does not provide for his relatives, and especially for his immediate family, he has denied the faith and is worse than an unbeliever" (1 Timothy 5:8).

Tough words! And so true. How can anyone claim to be a Christian while refusing to care for family members, especially parents and grandparents? In the secular writings of the first century, it's clear that in the Roman, Greek, and Jewish world, people were naturally expected to care for older family members. In Athenian society, a statesman was not allowed to give a public speech if his record of caring for family members was blemished. Everywhere in the Roman world people considered it shocking and disgraceful to ignore the needs of older parents.

If unbelievers have such a view toward the elderly in their families, then certainly we should take this responsibility seriously in the church of Jesus Christ. We should visit older family members, call them, remember their important days (such as birthdays and anniversaries), see to their needs, make sure they are comfortable, and if necessary, take them into our homes.

Speaking personally, I am grateful that my wife's mother lived with us for twenty-seven years in our home. We loved her and enjoyed having her as part of our family throughout that time. Eventually, it became necessary for her to be in a nursing home when she required a level of care that we could not give her. But even when she could no longer live in our home, we would visit her often, and we never let her feel unwanted.

Caring for our parents and grandparents is more than our Christian responsibility. It is a ministry opportunity. Our parents and grandparents loved us when we were too small and helpless to do anything in return. Now we have the privilege of putting our faith into practice and caring for them with the love of Jesus Christ.

CHAPTER 16

Keeping Elders Healthy

1 Timothy 5:17–25

Years ago I visited with missionaries in Costa Rica, and they told me about stomach problems they experienced. They said that a few months earlier, Dr. Donald Grey Barnhouse had spent time with them, and they mentioned this problem to him. (Dr. Barnhouse was then pastor of the historic Tenth Presbyterian Church of Philadelphia.)

Dr. Barnhouse said, "If you would obey what your Bible says, you wouldn't have this problem." He quoted 1 Timothy 5:23 to them: "Stop drinking only water, and use a little wine because of your stomach and your frequent illnesses." So they followed Dr. Barnhouse's advice, and their digestive problems cleared up.

The focus of this next section of Paul's letter is on maintaining the health of the elders of the church—not just their physical health, but also their spiritual health. Here, Paul instructs Timothy in how to determine which men have the traits God wants in the elders of His church; how to treat them fairly; and how to deal with them when they sin.

The church is God's instrument for accomplishing His eternal plan in human history, and the elders are the overseers of God's church. So it's important to understand how to keep the elders spiritually strong and healthy. Paul writes:

> The elders who direct the affairs of the church well are worthy of double honor, especially those whose work is preaching and teaching. For the Scripture says, "Do not muzzle the ox while it is treading out the grain," and "The worker deserves his wages." (1 Timothy 5:17–18)

Paul refers to the church leaders he previously spoke of in 1 Timothy 3, the overseers or elders. As we have seen, an elder's responsibility is to exercise wise and prayerful oversight, to be aware of what is happening in a congregation, and to take action to solve problems. When Paul says the elders "direct the affairs of the church," he is not saying that the elders are bosses. An elder does not demand respect; he earns it through humble service to the Lord and to the congregation.

Some people have interpreted this passage to suggest that Paul divides the elders into two classes, the ruling elders and the teaching elders. But there is really only one class. In 1 Timothy 3:2, Paul says that elders should be capable of teaching as well as leading. In fact, Paul's instruction to Timothy suggests that if an elder is not teaching or preaching, he is not leading.

Double honor

Paul notes that some elders devote long hours to extensive preparation and teach on a frequent basis. As a result, they hardly have any time left to earn a living in other ways. Those elders who labor intensively in ministry are worthy of what Paul calls "double honor." What does this mean?

To receive single honor would be to receive respect. To receive double honor would be to receive money. The needs and expenses of these especially hard-working elders are to be paid so that they will be free to do the work of preaching and teaching.

People often ask why we pay preachers. Some think that since Paul earned his living making tents, preachers should not be paid. But Paul set the basis for paying a pastor's salary. If an elder is occupied fully in the work of preaching and teaching in that church, he should receive double honor.

As support for this instruction, Paul cites scriptural evidence. He quotes Moses in the book of Deuteronomy: "Do not muzzle the ox while it is treading out the grain" (see Deuteronomy 25:4). In Bible times, when oxen were used to thresh the grain, the animals were not permitted to be muzzled. They were working, so they deserved to eat. Elsewhere, Paul wrote:

> For it is written in the Law of Moses: "Do not muzzle an ox while it is treading out the grain." Is it about oxen that God is concerned? Surely he says this for us, doesn't he? Yes, this was written for us, because when the plowman plows and the thresher threshes, they ought to do so in the hope of sharing in the harvest. (1 Corinthians 9:9–10)

Whenever we read the Old Testament, we should remember that all of the regulations given to Israel are given to us as well. When God instructed Israel concerning matters of worship, diet, work, clothing, and so forth, He was using symbolic pictures to teach as spiritual truths. If you read the Old Testament with this principle in mind, you will understand its teachings in an entirely new way.

Paul also quotes the words of Jesus from the Gospel of Luke: "The worker deserves his wages" (see Luke 10:7). This quotation is interesting for several reasons. First, it shows us that the Gospel of Luke was already in circulation at the time that Paul wrote this letter. Second, Paul says that he is quoting from Scripture, so it is clear that he regards the Gospel of Luke as the inspired Word of God. Third, Paul makes it clear that he views this statement as the Lord's confirmation of this principle.

Another principle we can glean from this passage is that if an elder is not engaged in intensive teaching and feeding the flock, then it would be wrong to support him. He is worthy of honor, but the elder who is engaged in full-time teaching and preaching is worthy of double honor.

The discipline of elders

The apostle now takes up the delicate matter of the discipline of elders who engage in misconduct. Paul writes, "Do not entertain an accusation against an elder unless it is brought by two or three witnesses. Those who sin are to be rebuked publicly, so that the others may take warning" (1 Timothy 5:19–20).

Elders sometimes must say unpleasant things to people, though they should not go out of their way to cause an offense. When people take offense, they sometimes strike back by spreading slanderous rumors. So Paul sets forth an important principle: An accusation against an elder must be supported by more than one person. An elder's reputation must not hinge on the word of a single witness.

I once received a call from a young pastor who had been summarily dismissed by his board of elders. Charges were leveled at him by his secretary. She was angry over some matter, so she created a forged letter and presented it to the elders as evidence of the pastor's wrongdoing. The elders accepted this false evidence as proof. They called the young pastor in and confronted him. The pastor denied knowing anything about the letter, but the elders relieved him of his responsibilities.

This man was devastated. He was presumed guilty and unable to prove his innocence. Weeks later, the secretary confessed that she had written the letter herself. The young pastor's reputation was restored and God used this experience in his life. The board of elders learned a painful lesson. A great deal of hurt would have been avoided, however, if they had followed the counsel of the apostle Paul: "Do not entertain an accusation against an elder unless it is brought by two or three witnesses."

Now, if an accusation is lodged against an elder and the accusation is confirmed, the best resolution is for the elder to repent. If an elder repents of his wrongdoing, no public action is necessary. But if he persists in his sin, then a public rebuke is required: "Those who sin are to be rebuked publicly, so that the others may take warning."

Here, Paul appears to refer to our Lord's words in Matthew 18, that well-known passage on church discipline. Jesus said, "If your brother sins against you, go and show him his fault, just between the two of you. If he listens to you, you have won your brother over" (Matthew 18:15). Nothing more needs to be said. The matter is settled. This sort of reconciliation ought to be taking place in churches all the time.

Without partiality

But what if the matter is not resolved that simply? Jesus goes on to say, "But if he will not listen, take one or two others along, so that 'every matter may be established by the testimony of two or three witnesses.' If he refuses to listen to them, tell it to the church" (Matthew 18:16–17a). That is a public rebuke—a difficult but often important step. If the church does not follow this step, the church's witness may be impaired.

Paul is instructing Timothy in a delicate area. Timothy is not an elder in the Ephesian church. He is an apostolic representative. He represents the apostle Paul in the Ephesian church. Because of Timothy's delicate position, Paul urges Timothy to observe certain principles. These principles are still valid for us.

First, Paul says that Timothy must be careful to show no partiality. Paul writes, "I charge you, in the sight of God and Christ Jesus and the elect angels, to keep these instructions without partiality, and to do nothing out of favoritism" (1 Timothy 5:21).

Notice the solemnity with which Paul charges Timothy. He gives this command to Timothy "in the sight of God and Christ Jesus and the elect angels." Clearly, Paul wants Timothy to view this matter with all seriousness. So he reminds Timothy that nothing is hidden in the eyes of God the Father, of the Lord Jesus, and of the "elect angels," the ministering spirits who watch over human beings.

Timothy probably had close friends among the leaders of the church in Ephesus. He might have felt drawn to some personalities and repelled by others. Timothy needed to be careful not to let his personal feelings interfere with impartial judgment in matters of the church.

Don't be hasty

Next, Paul instructs Timothy to exercise great care in choosing leaders in the church. Paul writes, "Do not be hasty in the laying on of hands, and do not share in the sins of others. Keep yourself pure" (1 Timothy 5:22).

The laying on of hands was the recognition by the other elders that a man had been chosen of the Lord. Some people mistakenly think that the laying on of hands confers some supernatural virtue on someone. That is not so. This symbol indicates that a person has been chosen by God for a certain purpose. Because the symbol makes an important statement to the church, Paul tells Timothy not to administer this symbol hastily. Church leaders should be chosen because they display the qualifications for leadership that we saw in 1 Timothy 3:1–7.

Many churches have abandoned the biblical standards for leaders. Many churches seemed to elect wealthy men to their boards merely because they are wealthy. If they know how to make money, if they are successful in the business world, then (according to human wisdom) they must be eligible to be elders. But this is not so. Those who are successful by the world's standards may be the worst possible men to be in leadership. That's why Paul tells Timothy to be careful and to make sure that people who are placed in leadership have the right qualifications according to Scripture.

Paul also tells Timothy not to ignore sins and character weaknesses when selecting leaders. That is what Paul means when he writes, "Do not share in the sins of others. Keep yourself pure." If you place a man in a church leadership position while knowing about ongoing sin in his life, then you are sharing in his sins.

Water or wine?

Next, Paul gives this odd admonition: "Stop drinking only water, and use a little wine because of your stomach and your frequent illnesses" (1 Timothy 5:23).

This advice doesn't seem to fit the context. Paul suddenly shifts gears from principles of church leadership to matters of Timothy's personal health. Or so it seems. In reality, I believe Paul's counsel to Timothy here proceeds naturally from the context of the previous verse.

Paul has just told Timothy, "Keep yourself pure." Timothy clearly wanted to do that. He was a dedicated young man who had willingly set aside his personal comfort and convenience in order to focus on a life of ministry in the church. As he wrote, Paul was probably reminded of a trait in Timothy that needed correction.

Timothy, in his zeal to keep himself pure and maintain a spotless reputation, was probably abstaining from wine. Ephesus was a city given over to every kind of immorality, including drunkenness. Many Christians, including Timothy, may have reacted by adopting a lifestyle of abstinence.

While the Scriptures warn against drunkenness, they do not teach abstinence. We know that the Lord Jesus drank wine, and so did the apostles. People have often consumed wine as much for its healthfulness as its taste. In the primitive conditions of the first century, the water supply was often tainted. The small alcohol content in wine (usually less than 10 percent) was sufficient to kill any bacteria or parasites.

Timothy probably suffered from stomach problems due to contaminated drinking water. So Paul told Timothy that he should practice a healthy balance, not abstinence. He should be pure, but for his health's sake he should drink wine in moderation in place of the tainted water of Ephesus.

I have heard some tortured exegeses of this passage, especially by people who preach abstinence. Once, when I was in Texas, I heard a young preacher read this verse from the King James Version, which says, "Drink no longer water, but use a little wine for thy stomach's sake." This preacher claimed that Paul referred to two different kinds of liquid in this passage. The first liquid this preacher called "longer water." He defined "longer water" as any alcoholic beverage. Then he said that the second liquid mentioned, which the King James Version called wine, was sweet, unfermented grape juice. He had taken Paul's text and turned its meaning upside down! That's what happens when you interpret Scripture according to your biases instead of its true meaning, especially in the original Greek.

Bringing hidden things to light

Finally, Paul tells Timothy that he should observe men over a period of time to see if they are qualified for leadership. He writes, "The sins of some men are obvious, reaching the place of judgment ahead of them; the sins of others trail behind them. In the same way, good deeds are obvious, and even those that are not cannot be hidden" (1 Timothy 5:24–25).

This is wise counsel. God was at work in the church at Ephesus, and He was bringing to light things that were hidden. As the Lord once said, "There is nothing concealed that will not be disclosed, or hidden that will not be made known. What you have said in the dark will be heard in the daylight, and what you have whispered in the ear in the inner rooms will be proclaimed from the roofs" (Luke 12:2–3).

God takes hidden sins and brings them to light. Many a man thinks he is hiding his sins, but he is not. God is steadily working to bring those sins to public exposure. There are some men whose sins are conspicuous, but others are skilled at hiding sin. They appear to be dedicated, committed people, but evil festers in their hearts. Before placing people in positions of leadership, take time to observe them. Don't make hasty, superficial judgments. The closer you get, the more obvious their evil will become.

And the reverse is also true. Some men have good qualities and good works in their lives that are not immediately visible. It takes time to discover the virtue of these individuals. It may well be that the reason their good traits remain hidden is that they are genuinely godly, humble men. Take time to get to know these people, and God will bring their hidden traits to light.

These verses contain penetrating insights into how God intends His church to function. Many churches have wandered away from these principles, often with tragic results. So I rejoice that Paul's counsel to Timothy is being rediscovered in the church in our day. May we take these truths seriously, apply them diligently, and replace decades of flawed tradition with a fresh infusion of God's timeless truth. Then, and only then, will we become the church God intended us to be.

CHAPTER 17

Slaves for God

1 Timothy 6:1–5

At the time the apostle Paul wrote his first letter to Timothy, half the population of the Roman Empire—about sixty million people—were slaves. Many had been taken as prisoners of war by the conquering Roman legions. Some were taken out of their own countries, while others were forced to live as slaves within their own lands. Some were highly educated and performed tasks that involved reading and writing. Most slaves, however, were used for menial labor, such as working in the fields or in the mines.

Slavery became a serious problem in the early church, when both slaves and slave owners were converted to Christianity. People in the church wanted to know: What does the Lord say to slaves—and to the people who own them?

You may think that this passage of Scripture has nothing to say to our culture. After all, there are neither slaves nor slave masters in the church today. Yet the principles that govern the master-slave relationship are still relevant to workplace relationships.

You may, in fact, see yourself as a wage slave. You sell a portion of your time and labor to an employer, and you receive a sum of money in return. You are functioning as a servant or a slave for that period of time. True, you get a paycheck and you can resign anytime you wish. But as we study this passage together, I think you'll find that Paul has a great deal to say to us about how employers and employees should relate to each other.

The Bible's view of slavery

The apostle writes:

All who are under the yoke of slavery should consider their masters worthy of full respect, so that God's name and our teaching may not be slandered. Those who have believing masters are not to show less respect for them because they are brothers. Instead, they are to serve them even better, because those who benefit from their service are believers, and dear to them. These are the things you are to teach and urge on them. (1 Timothy 6:1–2)

Many people are troubled because the New Testament doesn't denounce slavery; in fact, the Bible seems to accommodate slavery. If Christianity is a religion of liberty, why doesn't it speak out against slavery? It's true that this passage does not explicitly denounce slavery, but neither does it approve of slavery. It accepts slavery as a cultural reality.

There is an implied sense in which slavery is condemned. Deliverance from slavery and oppression is a recurring theme throughout the Old and New Testaments. The Old Testament book of Exodus is the story of the deliverance of the people of Israel from slavery in Egypt, and slavery is clearly viewed as a condition of oppression and injustice in that book.

In the New Testament, one of the key moments in the ministry of Jesus occurs in Luke 4. There, Jesus stands before the synagogue in His hometown of Nazareth and reads from Isaiah 61, a passage that prophetically refers to Jesus in His role as the Messiah-Deliverer:

"The Spirit of the Lord is on me,
  because he has anointed me
  to preach good news to the poor.
He has sent me to proclaim freedom for the prisoners
  and recovery of sight for the blind,
to release the oppressed,
  to proclaim the year of the Lord's favor." (Luke 4:18–19)

The early church had a profound impact on the practice of trading and owning slaves. Although there were sixty million slaves in the Roman Empire during the first century, the practice of slavery had largely disappeared by the end of the second century. This was primarily due to the impact of Christian teaching throughout the empire. Wherever the Christian gospel has penetrated, slaves have ultimately been set free.

While slavery was being practiced in the United States prior to the Civil War, some slave owners used the Bible to rationalize slave holding. Ultimately, however, the Scriptures tipped the scales against the slave owners. Christian reformers such as William Wilberforce, Granville Sharp, and Thomas Clarkson in England and Benjamin Rush and John Woolman in the United States fought the slave trade because of their conviction that slavery was an offense against God. They believed that the teachings of Christ and Paul made it clear that slave holding was a sin and an injustice. As Paul wrote to the Galatians, "There is neither Jew nor Greek, slave nor free, male nor female, for you are all one in Christ Jesus" (Galatians 3:28).

With those words, Paul laid the foundation for the deliverance of the world from the curse of slavery. Once you establish the principle that the slave and the slave master are "one in Christ Jesus," you have dismantled the foundation of human slavery.

Worthy of respect

There is a great lesson in the principle embedded in the Old Testament story of Joseph, the favorite son of Jacob. Joseph's brothers sold him into slavery in Egypt. So this well-educated young Hebrew became a slave in an Egyptian household. There he served faithfully until he was falsely accused by the Egyptian slave master's wife of attempting to rape her. So Joseph was unjustly sent to prison.

Joseph must have wondered why God allowed him to undergo such injustice. Yet he found the grace to wait on God's timing, believing throughout the years of his ordeal of enslavement and false imprisonment that God was working out a plan for his life. In time, Joseph was released from prison and given a high position in the Egyptian government.

Do you have a tyrant for a boss? Do you work for someone who continually frustrates you, humiliates you, and makes you feel like a slave? Paul says, "All who are under the yoke of slavery should consider their masters worthy of full respect, so that God's name and our teaching may not be slandered." Paul does not say, "Pretend to respect your boss," or, "Act as if you respect your boss." We are to consider the boss worthy of respect, no matter how he treats us.

Why are we to respect someone who hasn't earned our respect? One reason, which is implicit in Paul's words: Bosses are made in the image of God. Even though that image is marred by sin, your boss reflects the image of God and should be treated with respect.

The Scriptures view all human beings as God's creation, made in God's image. Though human beings are fallen, they are not worthless. Human beings are deceived victims of Satan and his demons. As a result, bosses sometimes act in deceived ways, treating their fellow human beings as property or inferiors. But bosses, for all their faults, are still made in God's image, and they should be treated with respect.

If the boss is an unbeliever, we are to treat him with respect so that we will bring credit upon God and the gospel and possibly lead him to Christ. When we treat an unfair boss with respect, we show that God's love enables us to transcend our normal human impulses of resentment and anger. Our Christlike behavior toward an un-Christlike boss is a powerful witness to the world.

If the boss is a fellow believer, then we are to respect the boss all the more because of the special relationship we have as brothers in Christ—yet we should not presume upon that relationship. The fact that my boss and I are brothers in Christ does not mean we are equals in the workplace. It does not entitle me to special favors.

Apparently, some of the Christian slaves in Ephesus had begun to behave toward their bosses with a sense of entitlement. They were not showing respect to their bosses. So Paul wrote:

> Those who have believing masters are not to show less respect for them because they are brothers. Instead, they are to serve them even better, because those who benefit from their service are believers, and dear to them. These are the things you are to teach and urge on them. (1 Timothy 6:2)

I have often seen (and I'm sure you have too) Christians who feel entitled to presume upon their relationship with fellow Christians. They do business with a Christian businessman, and they feel entitled to a discount or some other favor: "After all, we're brothers in the Lord." Some Christian businesspeople have told me they hate to see fellow church members come into their stores because they often ask for special favors. This is one Christian using another Christian for his own advantage.

Paul says, in effect, "You don't deserve special favors from your Christian brothers. Instead, you owe them a special measure of courtesy and respect. You don't have to pay them more than you would anyone else, but you are not entitled to pay them less. Instead, treat them with respect because they are your brothers in Christ."

An impact on society

During the Civil War, the Confederate army was led by General Robert E. Lee. He was a paradoxical leader. Though he commanded the military forces of a slave-owning society, he was personally opposed to slavery. He inherited slaves after the death of his father and immediately set them free. He was a man of deep Christian conviction, and he opposed slavery and racism.

General Lee was originally appointed by Abraham Lincoln to command the First Cavalry of the United States Army. But when Lee's home state of Virginia seceded from the Union, Lee resigned his commission. He felt that his loyalties lay with the people of Virginia, even though he was morally opposed to slavery. His plan was to invade Pennsylvania in the summer of 1863 and end the war with a decisive victory over the North. But Lee's forces were defeated at the battle of Gettysburg. The war dragged on for another two years until Lee was forced to surrender at Appomattox in April 1865.

One Sunday morning, just a few weeks after his humiliating surrender, General Lee sat in his favorite pew at the Episcopal church in Richmond. Near the end of the service, Communion was served. A black man, a former slave, stood and walked forward. He knelt at the rail to receive the bread and wine of Holy Communion.

A murmur of anger and resentment rippled through the white congregation. The gall of this former slave!

General Lee rose, walked to the altar, and knelt beside the black man. Sharing the cup, these two Christian brothers of different races received Holy Communion together. Then Lee stood, faced the congregation, and put his arm around his black brother.

"All men are brothers in Christ," he said. "Have we not all one Father?"

That is the message Paul wants all slave masters and slaves to understand. The great American tragedy is that slave masters failed to learn this lesson until after they were defeated on the battlefield. If the Christians in the South had understood the Scriptures, I believe the institution of slavery would have disappeared without violence, without the Civil War, and without the tragic legacy of segregation and racial strife that has characterized our history ever since.

Over the years, Christians have shown far too much race consciousness and far too little Christ consciousness. It is only as Christians learn to reflect the grace and truth of Jesus Christ that we begin to influence our society for Christ.

Those who oppose

Paul knew that it would be hard for slaves to accept the idea of respecting their slave masters. And he knew it would be hard for slave masters to respect their slaves as equals in Christ. So Paul went on to write:

> If anyone teaches false doctrines and does not agree to the sound instruction of our Lord Jesus Christ and to godly teaching, he is conceited and

understands nothing. He has an unhealthy interest in controversies and quarrels about words that result in envy, strife, malicious talk, evil suspicions and constant friction between men of corrupt mind, who have been robbed of the truth and who think that godliness is a means to financial gain. (1 Timothy 6:3–5)

Paul says there will be some who will not accept his teaching. In fact, some will stridently oppose his teaching. But when they do, he says, remember two things about such people.

First, their actions are sinful, because they oppose "the sound instruction of our Lord Jesus Christ." Paul invokes the authority of the Lord. Paul has taught that slaves should be respectful toward slave owners, which is nothing more than the same sort of humble submission that Jesus taught and exemplified. Jesus told us to love our enemies and bless those who persecute us. He told us to live as servants. Through His teaching, Jesus laid the foundation for nonviolent social change.

Second, anyone who opposes Paul's teaching is sinful for opposing "godly teaching." As we have previously seen, godliness is wholeness. Godly teaching produces unity. Those who oppose godly teaching create division and conflict. As Jesus once said, "He who is not with me is against me, and he who does not gather with me, scatters" (Luke 11:23).

If you want to know whether a certain teacher represents Christ, don't listen to what he says. Look at the effect of his teaching. If that person creates division, then he is against Christ, regardless of what he claims. Satan's teaching divides human beings; the teachings of the Lord Jesus produce harmony and unity.

What prompts some people to oppose the teachings of Paul and of the Lord Jesus Christ? Paul suggests several motivations. Such a person, he says, "is conceited and understands nothing." Such people are convinced that they alone have the right view, and they become angry if anyone opposes them.

When I was a young Christian, I was involved in a church where there was a heated controversy between Christians. At one point during a meeting, a wise older Christians stood and quoted the proverb, "Pride only breeds quarrels" (see Proverbs 13:10). I never forgot that principle. Whenever there is quarreling and contention, someone is acting out of pride. Only when Christians choose to be humble and Christlike will the contention and quarreling cease.

Such people, Paul says, also love controversy. They enjoy a good fight. Paul says, "He has an unhealthy interest in controversies and quarrels."

Controversy stirs the blood. It gets the adrenaline flowing. Many people enjoy that sense of excitement when two opponents bare their claws. People who love controversy are destructive to the unity and peace of the church.

Another motivation Paul suggests is greed. There are some people, Paul says, who have a "corrupt mind, who have been robbed of the truth and who think that godliness is a means to financial gain." Some people attend church as a means of advancing themselves in the community and the business world. They feel that membership in the right church gives them a respectable position. They see the church as a place to network and gain clients for their business. Some feel that people will show them honor and deference if they display a concern for religious values. Such people do not have God's goals in mind.

What is your attitude?

The church exists to set people free. The gospel is a message of freedom and equality. Anyone who is enslaved in any way—whether economically or politically, or by habits such as drinking, smoking, drugs, sexual addictions, gambling addictions, and so forth—may come to Christ and His church for deliverance. The power of the gospel is the power to set people free.

Even if we are slaves to an unfair boss, we are free in Christ. We are free to respect that person who does not respect us. We are free to love those who mistreat us. We are free to live humbly and surrender our demands for equality. Ultimately, this means that we are free to pattern in our lives after Jesus. As Paul wrote:

> Your attitude should be the same as that of Christ Jesus:
> Who, being in very nature God,
> did not consider equality with God something to be grasped,
> but made himself nothing,
> taking the very nature of a servant. (Philippians 2:5–7a)

Jesus, the Creator of the universe, was willing to become a slave for your sake. Are you willing to be a slave for His?

CHAPTER 18

The Cost of Riches

1 Timothy 6:6–19

One night in June 1997, Billie Bob Harrell, Jr., sat in his easy chair and checked his Quick Pick lottery ticket against a sequence of numbers in the newspaper. His heart skipped a beat when he saw that the numbers matched. The lottery ticket in his hand was worth $31 million. Billie Bob and his wife, Barbara Jean, were instant millionaires.

After being laid off from several jobs, Billie Bob's financial struggles were over. With his windfall, he bought a ranch for himself and vacation home. He, his wife, and each of his kids got new cars. He made a huge donation to his church.

But his blessing soon turned into a curse. Relatives, church members, and strangers begged him for financial assistance. He quickly lost track of how much he spent and lent. He and his wife began arguing about money.

One day in 1999, less than two years after winning the lottery, he sat down with his financial adviser and grimly confessed, "Winning the lottery was the worst thing that ever happened to me." A few days later, he took his shotgun into the bedroom of his expensive home, pressed the barrel to his chest, and pulled the trigger. In a very real sense, he was killed by his good fortune.

Such stories are amazingly common. A man who won $16.2 million in the Pennsylvania lottery in 1988 discovered that his brother was plotting to murder him in order to inherit the winnings. The brother went to prison, and within a few years the lottery winner was broke, having spent or lost all his money. He was living on Social Security when he died.

A New Jersey woman won her state's lottery in 1985 and again in 1986. Her winnings totaled $5.4 million, which she frittered away. Within a few years, she had to give up her mansion and ended up in a trailer park. She still bought lottery tickets every week but never won again.

A Minnesota woman who won an $11 million Powerball jackpot used her winnings to finance a drug and alcohol habit. While intoxicated, she caused a car crash that killed one person and left another paralyzed. She ended up in prison.

Financial advisors Michael Begin and Darl LePage have researched the lives of lottery winners and observe, "The reality is that 70 percent of all lottery winners will squander away their winnings in a few years. In the process, they will see family and friendships destroyed and the financial security they hoped for disappear."[1]

Wealth is a trap for the unwary. I'm sure you would like a chance to get caught in that trap! But in this closing section of Paul's first letter to Timothy, the apostle warns us against the dangers of money, and he gives us a practical, biblical perspective on the godly use of wealth.

Godliness with contentment

Paul plunges into the heart of the matter, showing us what true wealth is. He writes, "But godliness with contentment is great gain. For we brought nothing into the world, and we can take nothing out of it. But if we have food and clothing, we will be content with that" (1 Timothy 6:6–8).

What does it take to be wealthy?

Twice in this passage, Paul says that true wealth doesn't consist of possessions—a fat bank account, new cars, a mansion, a vacation house, a yacht in the harbor. True wealth is an attitude of contentment.

Paul links contentment with godliness. If you feel blessed by what God has given you, then you have all you need. You have a contented heart. Those who are godly tend to view all of life as a gift from God. That godly attitude engenders contentment in the hearts of those who trust in the Lord.

One of the great sicknesses of our hedonistic, materialistic age is the epidemic of restlessness. Those who don't know God are constantly looking for experiences and anesthetics to take away the pain of their empty lives. They either try to numb the pain with drugs and alcohol or distract themselves with thrills, sexual pleasure, gambling, or entertainment.

Restless people continually seek escape from life. Contented people are busy enjoying life. The apostle Paul defined contentment in another of his letters: "I have learned to be content whatever the circumstances. I know what it is to be in need, and I know what it is to have plenty. I have learned the secret of being content in any and every situation, whether well fed or hungry, whether living in plenty or in want" (Philippians 4:11b–12).

Paul's godliness produces his sense of contentment. True godliness means that we understand that God is the source of our food, our clothing, our housing, and everything else we need in life. When we have learned to place our trust in Him, then we have nothing to be anxious or restless about. We are content.

The Lord Jesus made this point while speaking to a crowd. As He spoke, a man in the crowd shouted to Him, "Teacher, tell my brother to divide the inheritance with me."

Jesus replied, "Man, who appointed me a judge or an arbiter between you?" Then He turned to the crowd and said, "Watch out! Be on your guard against all kinds of greed; a man's life does not consist in the abundance of his possessions" (see Luke 12:13–15).

Not by bread alone

Paul goes on to support his contention with the examples of birth and death. He writes, "For we brought nothing into the world, and we can take nothing out of it." What do you have when you are born? Nothing. You come into the world a red-faced, squalling baby. You don't own a thing. Even your diaper was furnished to you. And what will you take with you when you leave this world? Nothing.

I once picked up a young hitchhiker. We chatted for a while, and he said, "My uncle died a millionaire." I said, "No, he didn't. Your uncle died with nothing." Looking surprised, he said, "What do you mean? You don't know my uncle." I said, "Who has the million now?"

"Oh, I see what you mean."

Nobody dies a millionaire. We all die paupers.

The apostle goes on to say, "But if we have food and clothing, we will be content with that." All we need is provision for the maintenance of life and shelter from the elements. Since God provides that for us, we should be content.

Jesus linked godliness and physical contentment when He said, "It is written: 'Man does not live on bread alone, but on every word that comes from the mouth of God.'" Yes, we need food in order to maintain our physical existence, but knowledge of God and His truth enables us to live authentically. Fellowship with the Lord of glory makes the heart rejoice, gives us peace, and provides us with a sense of worth and security.

Our society is bent on destroying our sense of contentment. All the advertising that bombards us from our television screens and radios and magazines is designed to disturb our sense of contentment. Advertisers want us to feel that our lives are not complete unless we are driving their car, drinking their beverage, or rolling on their deodorant. Nothing is more universal and inescapable than the propaganda that drives us to possess more things. If we are not aware of the goals of these media mindbenders, we may succumb to their pressure without even understanding why.

Paul gives us the key to resisting the pressure of media propaganda: "People who want to get rich fall into temptation and a trap and into many foolish and harmful desires that plunge men into ruin and destruction" (1 Timothy 6:9).

Here the apostle describes a subtle peril that endangers our hearts. First, temptation comes to us in a seemingly innocent form. We open a magazine and see a picture of a beautiful automobile. There is nothing wrong with owning an automobile. We all need transportation.

But the advertisers encourage us to see their automobile as something more than transportation. It is something mystical and magical. It's a symbol of having arrived. It expresses our personality. It is an extension of the self. Some advertisements even suggest that it enhances our status, the way people view us, and even our sexual attractiveness. It even becomes, for some, a kind of god to be worshiped, adored, and fed expensive fuels to be burned internally as incense.

Advertising stirs up a hunger in us to have one of these gods in our driveway. And when we see our neighbors driving around in a more beautiful god than ours, we feel cravings of envy and covetousness—the opposite of contentment.

The most misquoted verse

Paul tells us that the stages of discontentment grow progressively worse. Those who want to be rich fall into a trap from which it is difficult to escape. Note that Paul does not say it is a sin to have wealth. He says that the desire to have wealth is a trap. Think of it as a mouse trap or a bear trap. It clamps down on us and pins us in place. The desire for wealth is deadly to the soul.

Next, Paul tells us what happens to us when we fall into that trap: "For the love of money is a root of all kinds of evil. Some people, eager for money, have wandered from the faith and pierced themselves with many griefs" (1 Timothy 6:10).

This is probably the most misquoted verse in the Bible. People often say, "Money is the root of all evil." But that's not what Paul says. He writes, "The love of money is a root of all kinds of evil." In other words, when people desire wealth, when they crave riches, they easily rationalize all sorts of evil acts in order to obtain it. When the love of money takes root in the human heart, even an otherwise kind, gentle, and caring Christian becomes capable of astounding evil.

Money itself is not evil, nor is it the root of evil. Money is a necessary commodity of life. We can't get along without money in one form or another. When we earn our money by working hard and using our abilities to honor God with our labor, the money we earn is a fair and honorable recompense. No one who has amassed a fortune through honest labor should be accused of doing something evil.

What Paul is telling us is that we fall into a trap of temptation when we no longer possess our possessions but our possessions possess us. There are many ways in which we are possessed by our possessions. You may know the feeling of bringing home a shiny new car or an expensive new computer or television. Suddenly, you discover a whole set of anxieties and worries that you never considered before. What if someone breaks in and steals it? What if it gets damaged? Do we need to change our locks? Do we need to upgrade our insurance? Our possessions demand that we take care of them. That is how they begin to possess us.

Possessions also change our relationships with others. We discover that some of our possessions are status symbols. If we own certain possessions, such as a home in a certain part of town or a country club membership, people start to treat us differently. Our friends no longer treat us for who we are but for what we have. People start to approach us, offering friendship, and we wonder about their real motives. Could it be that they want something from us? In time, we no longer know who our true friends are.

Paul says that those who fall in love with money risk a destructive end. Some, he says, have "wandered from the faith and pierced themselves with many griefs." The love of money can seduce us away from the faith.

I can name a number of young men and women from my congregation who were once deeply committed to the Lord and eager to understand His Word. But somewhere along the line, perhaps in school or in their career, they began to absorb the values of the world. They became concerned about their prestige and status. They became obsessed with getting a well-paying career, and in the process they slowly turned away from the faith. They lost what had once been the center of their lives. They forgot that God is the source of all blessing, and they plunged into the pursuit of blessing themselves with material things. As Paul predicted, they wandered from the faith.

And Paul predicted that those who fall in love with money would pierce themselves with many griefs. During the late 1970s and 1980s, I continually heard about a prime-time television soap opera, *Dallas*. Finally, I decided to watch an episode and see what all the talk was about. From the one episode I saw, it seemed that the show revolved around the Ewing family, who had made millions in cattle and oil.

The most evil and cruel member of the Ewing family was J. R., played by Larry Hagman, who used financial manipulation to get his way. He would lure some with promises of money and threaten others with financial ruin. He would destroy relationships and drive people to murder or suicide. He would always get his way, but in the end he seemed bitter and dissatisfied with what he had accomplished. J. R. Ewing was only a fictional character, but he was an excellent symbol of what happens to those who fall in love with money.

The love of money generates cruelty, callousness, division, and shameful indulgence. Those who become possessed by the love of money eventually end up committing acts they would have once thought themselves incapable of. Amazingly, those who love money the most often find themselves betrayed and abandoned by money.

My friend and fellow pastor, Ron Ritchie, once told me of a man he knew who had been enormously rich, then lost it all. When Ron asked how it happened, the man replied, "Greed. I turned down the street called Greed, and I just kept right on going." This man had fallen in love with money, and he had pierced himself with many griefs.

Let's say you spend your life in the quest for riches. Finally you reach a point in life where you have achieved all of your goals. That is the moment I call destination sickness. It's a common illness in our day. Destination sickness is the feeling of arriving at your destination, possessing everything you always wanted to have, then realizing you don't want anything you've got. You have spent your entire life chasing things that mean nothing.

What an awful feeling that must be! How devastating it must be to realize that you have lived your entire life for nothing. Everything you have amassed now goes to relatives who will waste it as they please—and a huge chunk will go to the government in inheritance taxes. Now you must stand before God with nothing to show for the life you have lived.

That's the picture that Scripture paints for us of the life that is lived for the love of money.

The deceitfulness of wealth

Next, let's skip to verse 17, because the intervening paragraph is a personal word from Paul to Timothy, and we will examine that passage in the next chapter of this book. It appears that, having nearly closed this letter on a personal note to his spiritual son Timothy, Paul realized that perhaps he left a misimpression. He doesn't want Timothy to think that it is wrong to be rich, so he adds this postscript, verses 17 through 19, to answer the question: "How should a rich person in the church conduct himself?"

Paul answers this question in two realms, the realm of attitudes and the realm of actions. He writes, "Command those who are rich in this present world not to be arrogant nor to put their hope in wealth, which is so uncertain, but to put their hope in God, who richly provides us with everything for our enjoyment" (1 Timothy 6:17).

A rich person first must remember: Remain humble. Don't let your wealth go to your head. Do not credit your cleverness, your education, your investing wisdom as the reason for your riches. Everything you are and everything you have comes from God, so remember to put your hope in God, not in your wealth.

The Lord Jesus spoke about "the deceitfulness of wealth" (see Matthew 13:22; Mark 4:19). Riches can lie to you. A fat bank account can say, "You're better than other people." And you'll begin to believe it, because people will treat you as though you're better than other people.

That's why we have a so-called aristocracy. For centuries, such people have been referred to as bluebloods. That term comes from the fact that upper-class people used to live indoors and never had to work in the sun. As a result, their skin was pale and their blue veins could be easily seen, giving rise to the idea that their blood was blue. Their blood was no bluer than anyone else's, and they were no better than anyone else. But peopled treated them as superior because they had money—and many bluebloods started acting as if they were superior to everyone else.

That is the deceitfulness of wealth.

The uncertainty of wealth

Next, Paul tells Timothy, "Command those who are rich in this present world not to... put their hope in wealth, which is so uncertain." In other words, the rich must not count on their riches. Wealth can disappear overnight.

A stock portfolio can lose half its value overnight. Real estate doesn't always increase in value; sometimes it loses value, and in the event of an earthquake or flood, a piece of property loses a lot of value almost instantly. Even precious metals, such as gold and platinum, can lose value. And money, whether you store it electronically in a bank or you stuff it under your mattress, can be stolen by thieves.

Riches are uncertain. No one is more foolish than the person who counts on riches to provide a sense of security. That's why Jesus said, "Do not store up for yourselves treasures on earth, where moth and rust destroy, and where thieves break in and steal. But store up for yourselves treasures in heaven, where moth and rust do not destroy, and where thieves do not break in and steal" (Matthew 6:19–20).

Paul tells Timothy to command the rich "to put their hope in God, who richly provides us with everything for our enjoyment." We must never forget that God is the giver of all good gifts. God gave us the strength to work. He gave us good minds and educational opportunities. He gave us the economic environment in which we work. Yes, we work hard to make a living, but it is God who makes work possible.

Both the Old and New Testaments tell us clearly that it is not wrong to possess wealth. But those who spend all their God-given wealth upon themselves, heaping up luxury upon luxury, are misusing God's gift of wealth. The truth be known, they are probably not enjoying their riches. In fact, luxuries inevitably become commonplace and boring. And riches always come with an extra measure of anxiety and worry.

God intended the material things of this world to be enjoyed. If God gives you riches, how should you enjoy them? Well, that's easy! Use your riches to make someone happy. Use the blessings God has given you to bless someone else. When you live to bless others, you receive back a sense of joy and gladness that can't be attained in any other way. If God has given you riches, He has given you a unique privilege—the privilege of giving. Paul affirms this principle: "Command them to do good, to be rich in good deeds, and to be generous and willing to share. In this way they will lay up treasure for themselves as a firm foundation for the coming age, so that they may take hold of the life that is truly life" (1 Timothy 6:18–19).

There are three commands wrapped up in this passage.

First, "do good." Use your money to help people. In the Greek, the phrase "do good" implies an impersonal form of giving. In other words, you give money to an organization that uses that money to help other people. You never see the people who are helped, but you know that the money you donated has been used to meet human need. You can donate funds for a variety of causes, including famine relief, helping the homeless, supporting missionaries, and so forth. Before you give money to an organization, do your homework and make sure that the organization has a track record of using donated funds wisely and effectively to serve God and meet human needs.

Second, "be rich in good deeds." Good deeds are personal. They are things you do to help people you know, people you see. You can do good deeds for others in a personal way yet still keep your donation anonymous. You can find out who in your church has a financial need, and you can donate the needed funds anonymously through your pastor or deacons.

Third and finally, "be generous and willing to share." There is no worse testimony than a rich yet stingy Christian. Christians should be generous by nature, because we are to be like Christ, who generously gave up everything for our sakes. Jesus said, "Freely you have received, freely give" (see Matthew 10:8).

If the rich will follow these three commands, Paul says, two wonderful results will follow. "In this way they will lay up treasure for themselves as a firm foundation for the coming age, so that they may take hold of the life that is truly life."

When we die, what do we possess? What can we take from this life into the next? We can't take our money. We can't take our expensive homes and cars. We can't take any of our material possessions. We can take only the things we have done for others.

What is the greatest treasure you could possibly lay up in heaven? People! Think of all the people you meet every day. Think of your neighbors and co-workers, the people who check and bag your groceries at the store, the people on your campus. Wouldn't it be wonderful if you could continue seeing them and talking to them in heaven?

You could use your money to help win them to Christ. You could invite them out to a Christian concert, then take them out for dessert afterwards, and talk to them about Christ. You could share a Christian book with them. If they have a need, such as an unpaid bill or an empty pantry, you could meet that need—and then tell them about the love of Jesus.

Your money will never get to heaven, but you can use your money to help get people to heaven. That's what Jesus and Paul are saying to us when they tell us to lay up treasures in heaven.

Then Paul tells us the second result: "So that they may take hold of the life that is truly life." He is telling us that in this present age, we can use our wealth in such a way that we will be filled with the adventure and excitement of the Christian life, "a life that is truly life." If you use your wealth to bless others, you will experience one of the richest of all joys—the joy of allowing God to use you to transform lives.

When it's time for you to leave this earth, make sure you leave nothing behind. Live each day for God and others—and send your riches on ahead of you to heaven.

CHAPTER 19

O Man of God!

1 Timothy 6:11–16, 20–21

We have come to the end of 1 Timothy. In these closing verses, Paul addresses Timothy with an unusual title, which the King James Version translates "O man of God." The phrase "man of God" appears more than seventy times in the Old Testament but only twice in the New Testament—once in 1 Timothy and once in 2 Timothy. Later, in 2 Timothy, Paul will use that phrase in a general sense: "All Scripture is God-breathed and is useful for teaching, rebuking, correcting and training in righteousness, so that the man of God may be thoroughly equipped for every good work" (2 Timothy 3:16–17).

But here, near the end of Paul's first letter to Timothy, Paul applies these words to Timothy. He writes, "But you, man of God, flee from all this, and pursue righteousness, godliness, faith, love, endurance and gentleness. Fight the good fight of the faith. Take hold of the eternal life to which you were called when you made your good confession in the presence of many witnesses" (1 Timothy 6:11–12).

In the Old Testament, the title "man of God" was reserved for the prophets. In the New Testament, only Timothy is addressed this way. It must have meant a great deal to Timothy to know that his father in the faith saw him as a man of God.

This title combines two remarkable concepts: man and God. Man, in the sense of all humanity, is weak, blind, confused, and prone to sin and error. God is the epitome of majesty, power, and truth. To be called a "man of God" is the greatest honor that Timothy could receive. Every believer should want to live worthily of that title, to truly be a man or woman of God—not of the world, not of the flesh, but of God.

How should a man of God respond to this world in which we live? Paul gives Timothy three commands, expressed in three imperative verbs, instructing Timothy in exactly how a man of God can maintain his godliness while living in an atmosphere of utter worldliness.

First, Paul says, "flee from all this." Second, he says, "pursue righteousness, godliness, faith, love, endurance and gentleness." Third, he says, "fight the good fight of the faith." Flee, pursue, fight. Let's take a closer look at each of these three commands.

Flee from all this

The apostle Paul tells Timothy, "Flee from all this." Elsewhere in Scripture we are told to "flee immorality" or "flee youthful lusts." There are times in our Christian experience when the only defense we have is to get up and go. But that is not what Paul is talking about here.

Remember the context. In 1 Timothy 6:3–10, Paul has been talking about false teachers. He is telling Timothy to flee or shun the three characteristics of these false teachers.

The first characteristic is conceit—taking arrogant pride in one's knowledge. As followers of Christ, we are to live humbly. It is not Christlike to think ourselves superior to others because of our knowledge, even our knowledge of the Bible. That kind of smug superiority is the conceit of Pharisees and false teachers.

The second characteristic of false teachers is combativeness, the love of controversy. Some people enjoy stirring up conflict among the people. This is a mark of a false teacher: he wants to form a faction around some contrarian idea he has. He delights in the quarrels and heated atmosphere that always swirls around him. Paul says that Timothy should flee from this as well.

The third characteristic of false teachers is greed—the love of money, with all the luxury, status, and arrogance it brings. Paul warns Timothy to flee this as well.

Six things to pursue

Then Paul tells Timothy that he is not only to flee certain things but also to pursue certain things. In fact, Paul lists six traits or qualities that Timothy should pursue. The first set of three qualities relates to Timothy's relationship with God: righteousness, godliness, and faith. The second set of three qualities relates to Timothy's relationship with his fellow human beings: love, endurance, and gentleness.

The first trait on the list is righteousness. Paul wants Timothy to pursue righteousness in two ways. First, Timothy should pursue righteous behavior; he is to live a righteous life. Second, Timothy should pursue righteous belief. Righteous belief is the word of the gospel; when you come to know Jesus

Christ as Lord and Savior, He gives you His righteousness. As a follower of Christ, you understand that God sees you as no longer guilty, no longer powerless in the grip of sin. You have been made righteous by the sacrifice of His Son Jesus upon the cross.

If you focus only on righteous behavior and forget righteous belief, you will become a legalist, seeking to please God and make yourself acceptable to Him through your works. But if you focus on righteous belief, on the gospel of grace, you will understand that God has already made you acceptable in Jesus Christ. Your righteous belief gives you a sense of security and acceptance before God. That is the basis of a stable faith and a healthy Christian life. So Paul tells Timothy to remember that he is already righteous in Christ, and so avoid the trap of legalism.

The second trait Paul mentions is godliness. Paul has used this word many times throughout this letter. As we've seen, godliness refers to balanced wholeness—keeping the body, soul, and spirit healthy and stable.

These days, we see great emphasis on physical health. We can purchase everything from running shoes to home gym equipment to a weight loss plan with food delivered to our door. There is nothing wrong with keeping the body healthy. In fact, since the body is the temple of the Holy Spirit, we should pursue good health. But if we focus purely on physical health to the exclusion of a healthy soul and spirit, then our lives are out of balance.

We develop healthy souls by properly feeding our minds and emotions. We read good books, listen to good music, meditate on God's Word, and bring our emotions under the control of God's Spirit. The goal of the healthy soul is to become balanced and whole, not continually tossed from one emotional extreme to the other.

We develop healthy spirits by keeping in touch with the living God. This means that we seek to live in a continual awareness of God's presence, so that we are talking to God and listening for His voice within us at all times (see 1 Thessalonians 5:17). A believer with a healthy spirit views a relationship with God as the most crucial aspect of life. That is godliness and balanced wholeness.

The third trait Paul mentions is faith. In the Greek, the word Paul uses can be translated as "faith" or "belief," but it can also be translated as "faithfulness." I think it is this second sense, faithfulness (meaning fidelity or loyalty to God) that Paul means here. Timothy has already committed his life to Christ. Now that Timothy has made this basic commitment, Paul is urging him to never go back on his commitment but to always remain faithful.

Those first three traits deal with our relationship with God. Next, Paul charges Timothy to pursue three traits that have to do with how he treats other people. Those traits are love, endurance, and gentleness.

The first of these three traits is love. There are more than two hundred verses in the New Testament that speak of Christian love—what the Greek calls *agape* love. Near the beginning of this letter to Timothy, Paul says that the goal of all of these instructions to Timothy, especially the instructions to teach the truth and oppose falsehood, is "love, which comes from a pure heart and a good conscience and a sincere faith."

I don't think there is any more convicting and challenging question a Christian can ask himself than this: "Am I acting in love?" This is a question I often ask myself whenever I'm interacting with another human being. If I'm engaged in a conversation with someone, I often think, "What is my motive for saying these words? Is it a selfish motive, or am I acting in love with this person? Is my tone of voice loving and kind, or am I being caustic, hurtful, pompous, or self-important?"

One of the most profound verses of Scripture is only four words long. If I lived to be a thousand years old, I could never exhaust the depths of meaning embedded in these four words: "Do everything in love" (1 Corinthians 16:14).

What would our lives look like if we did *everything* in love? What if we carried out our household chores—washing the car, cleaning the toilets, taking out the trash—as acts of love? What if we made every interaction of our daily lives—greeting people on the street, talking to our neighbors, tipping the waitress—an act of love? What if we made sure that every word we spoke to our spouse, children, parents, co-workers, boss, employees, professors, students, and on and on, was an act of love? Wouldn't our lives be transformed? Wouldn't our testimony for Christ be powerful?

We know we are commanded to love. We know that Jesus said, "Love one another." We have had love preached to us thousands of times in sermon after sermon, and every time we heard those words, we nodded in agreement. Christian love makes perfect sense on Sunday mornings. But then we get up on Monday morning, and every other morning of the week, and we promptly forget to apply Christian love to our real-life problems and situations.

"Do everything in love." Once we have internalized to this truth, our lives and our witness will be transformed.

The second of these three traits is endurance. This means perseverance in the face of obstacles and opposition. It means refusing to give up.

Defeatism is contagious. It's amazing to see how, when one person says, "I can't go on anymore," everyone around him throws in the towel as well. But a mindset of endurance is also contagious. If one person says, "I refuse to quit; God will get us through this if we persevere," everyone around that person is suddenly inspired with the will to press on.

The willingness to persevere is the mark of true Christian faith. To give up and become discouraged is to let go of your faith in God. But pressing on in spite of problems is the mark of a Christian man or woman who truly believes, "I can do everything through him who gives me strength" (Philippians 4:13).

The third of these three traits is gentleness. To be gentle toward other people is to empathize with their feelings and to treat them with love and kindness. As Christians, we are called to exhibit the character qualities of our Lord, who said, "Take my yoke upon you and learn from me, for I am gentle and humble in heart" (see Matthew 11:29). Even in the midst of conflict and controversies, the Lord's servant must remain gentle and loving. He must never compromise the truth, but he must always speak the truth in love and gentleness.

Paul says, "Pursue righteousness, godliness, faith, love, endurance and gentleness." This is an excellent checklist for testing the validity of our Christian character. Paul said elsewhere: "Examine yourselves to see whether you are in the faith; test yourselves. Do you not realize that Christ Jesus is in you—unless, of course, you fail the test?" (2 Corinthians 13:5).

Every Christian should periodically take a quick mental checkup and ask, "How am I behaving? Does my life demonstrate these six qualities that Paul told Timothy to pursue? Does the conduct of my life prove that I'm truly a follower of Christ?"

Fight on!

Paul told Timothy to flee, to pursue, and finally to fight. He wrote, "Fight the good fight of the faith. Take hold of the eternal life to which you were called when you made your good confession in the presence of many witnesses."

In these words, the apostle recognizes the true nature of the Christian life: It is a battleground. In the thick of battle, it's hard to find rest. The enemy is constantly coming at you with everything he's got. We tend to engage in wishful thinking as the battle rages. We wish the enemy would give up and go home. We wish the battle would end.

That would be nice. But here in the trenches of spiritual warfare, the battle never ends. The enemy never gives up. There is never any truce, any letup. Our enemy is relentless. His strategy is to discourage us and make us quit or divide us and turn us against each other. Or seduce us and turn us against God. That's the battle we face.

So Paul tells us how to fight the good fight of faith. He says, "Take hold of the eternal life to which you were called when you made your good confession in the presence of many witnesses." This is a parallel passage to Paul's instruction to the Ephesians: "Put on the full armor of God so that you can take your stand against the devil's schemes" (Ephesians 6:11).

The armor Paul speaks of is Jesus Christ—His strength, His wisdom, His love, His gentleness, His peace. This means that we trust Jesus to be in charge of our lives, our battles, our offensive and defensive strategies. He is the armor we wear, the sword we wield. He is the strength in our arm. He is the mind that designs the plan of attack.

With Jesus going before us, we can fight the good fight of faith and lay hold of eternal life. Paul reminds Timothy that this was how he started in the faith when Timothy made his confession and profession of Christ in the presence of many witnesses. Paul is saying, in effect, "You have made a great start in fighting the good fight. Keep it up! Fight on! This is what God has called you to!"

So the man of God, the woman of God, is called to do three things in life: flee, pursue, and fight. And the Christian fights the good fight of faith by taking hold of the power and provision given to us by Jesus Christ our Lord.

Keep this command

Next, Paul takes us into the presence of a God we serve. It's as though he were taking us up in a cosmic elevator above the horizon of this world and revealing to our amazed eyes the mighty God before whom we stand. He writes:

> In the sight of God, who gives life to everything, and of Christ Jesus, who while testifying before Pontius Pilate made the good confession, I charge you to keep this command without spot or blame until the appearing of our Lord Jesus Christ, which God will bring about in his own time—God, the blessed and only Ruler, the King of kings and Lord of lords, who alone is immortal and who lives in unapproachable light, whom no one has seen or can see. To him be honor and might forever. Amen. (1 Timothy 6:13–16)

Paul wants us to have an exalted understanding of who God is. If we can begin to grasp even a fraction of the true nature of God, we will be emboldened for the battles of this life. Paul begins by telling us that the God we serve is the giver of life.

Do you ever feel beaten and dejected, buffeted by more things than you can handle? You need the renewed vitality that comes when you turn to God and see Him as the source of your power. That's where prayer comes in. We have all experienced the infusion of fresh strength and courage that comes when we seek God in times of pressure and fear. When you are tempted to lose heart, turn back to the Author of life.

Next, Paul points us to the example of Jesus before Pontius Pilate. Do you ever feel awkward or embarrassed about sharing your faith in Christ? Think of Jesus, "who while testifying before Pontius Pilate made the good confession."

Pilate examined Jesus and found no fault in Him. Then Pilate asked a question that would determine whether Jesus would live or die. Pilate wanted to set Jesus free, knowing he was an innocent man, so he gave Jesus a chance to free himself. "Are you the King of the Jews?" he asked. Jesus could have denied his messiahship and escaped the cross. Instead, he answered in a Hebrew idiom that is the strongest possible affirmation, translated into English as, "Yes, it is as you say" (see Matthew 27:11).

Paul reminds Timothy that there will be times when he must take a lonely and perilous stand against the crowd, even if it costs him everything. He must stand firm, as Jesus stood His ground before Pilate.

The apostle goes on to remind Timothy that, though Jesus was put to death in weakness, He is coming again in power as the Lord of life, the focus of history. Moreover, he says, "I charge you to keep this command without spot or blame until the appearing of our Lord Jesus Christ." What is this command Timothy must keep? There is only one possible answer. Paul refers to the Lord's command in the upper room: "A new command I give you: Love one another. As I have loved you, so you must love one another" (John 13:34).

Love is the central action of the Christian life. "Love does no harm to its neighbor," Paul wrote elsewhere. "Therefore love is the fulfillment of the law" (Romans 13:10). If you do everything in love, then you will keep the Ten Commandments.

But Paul does not simply tell Timothy to keep this commandment. He tells Timothy to keep this commandment "without spot or blame." In other words, he warns Timothy against the danger of turning Christian love into fleshly lust.

For example, a young and unwary pastor might seek to show Christian love and caring to a young widow in his congregation. But his spiritual motives can easily be contaminated by human sexual attraction, with the result that he no longer keeps the commandment "without spot or blame." In this way, Christian love can be polluted by fleshly sin. So Paul tells Timothy to keep this command without spot or blame.

Unapproachable light

Jesus is coming again. When will this happen? Will He come soon? Is the end of history at hand? We don't know. Paul says that God will bring this event about "in his own time." Regardless of when it takes place, Paul is certain that Jesus will return. At His return, history will be fulfilled. God and His saints will be vindicated. This is a great encouragement to our hearts.

Paul closes with a final word about the Lord's majesty: "God, the blessed and only Ruler, the King of kings and Lord of lords, who alone is immortal and who lives in unapproachable light, whom no one has seen or can see."

The arsenals of many nations bulge with weaponry, waiting to unleash Armageddon upon the earth. What is the solution to the global arms race? The solution is God, "the only Ruler, the King of kings and Lord of lords." All of the kings and lords, the presidents and prime ministers, the tyrants and dictators of the earth are subject to God's control. If we place our trust in Him, we will have peace while all others' hearts are failing them in fear.

Paul tells us that God "alone is immortal." Because He is the everlasting One, He is able to give everlasting life to all who believe in Him. Those who have joined their mortal lives to His eternal Life will conquer the darkness and corruption of death.

And, Paul tells us, God "lives in unapproachable light." What a picture of majesty! The sun is the brightest, most unapproachable manifestation of light we know. The closest approximation to the sun that we could create on earth would be the blinding fireball of a hydrogen bomb explosion. "Unapproachable light" suggests a glare of light that is dazzling, blinding, and even searing in its intensity. No one is remotely like this God who lives in unapproachable light.

The God we serve is beyond our ability to describe, and He dwells amid such glory that no mere human being could withstand it. The unapproachable God, however, has been made approachable. You and I can draw nearer to this light because of the provision that God has made through Jesus Christ.

Guard the truth!

Finally, God is an invisible Spirit, "whom no one has seen or can see." The most profound mystery of Christianity is the fact that the invisible God has become a visible human being, a baby born in a filthy stable in a cave in Bethlehem. When He was born, the angels announced His birth and called him Christ the Lord, Emmanuel, God with us. Jesus is God with us, God among us, God made like us.

The invisible God has become visible in a Man. We cannot see God, but we can see the Man, Jesus. In this way, the unknowable God has made himself known. He has placed himself on our level. That is why Paul closes with this shout of praise: "To him be honor and might forever. Amen."

These words strengthened the heart of Timothy immeasurably. After adding a postscript regarding the proper use of wealth (which we examined in the previous chapter), Paul ends his letter to Timothy with these two verses: "Timothy, guard what has been entrusted to your care. Turn away from godless chatter and the opposing ideas of what is falsely called knowledge, which some have professed and in so doing have wandered from the faith. Grace be with you" (1 Timothy 6:20–21).

What does Paul wish Timothy to guard? What has been entrusted to Timothy's care? Answer: The truth set forth in the Scriptures. Timothy is to guard the truth by using it wisely and defending it against error. Significantly, Paul addresses Timothy by name in these closing lines. The name Timothy means "he who honors God." So Paul is saying, "Timothy, you who honor God, guard the truth that has been entrusted to you."

This same body of truth that was entrusted to Timothy has also been entrusted to you and to me. Every Christian is a trustee of God's truth. It's a precious thing to know the difference between right and wrong, between error and truth, between the broad road and the narrow way. We guard the truth every day by studying it, applying it to our lives, and not allowing it to be watered down by falsehood.

Paul knew that counterfeits were crouching around the church, waiting to ambush the truth. By the first century, a fraudulent faith called Gnosticism was already seducing people away from the truth. Gnosticism encouraged people to worship angels and seek special revelations of hidden truth. There are many variations on Gnosticism still being proclaimed: New Ageism, Urantia, Scientology, Neopaganism, Wicca, humanism, militant atheism, and much more. Tendrils of fraudulent faith are constantly seeking new ways to invade the church and take root.

My friend, guard the truth that has been entrusted to your care. Turn away from the godless chatter that masquerades as hidden knowledge and special revelation. Don't fall for every new idea that comes along, posing as truth.

Remember those who once professed Jesus as Lord and then wandered from the faith. I've known such people, and I'm sure you have too. Pray for them, but always remember their tragic example. Don't end up as they did.

Friend in Christ, guard the truth.

Part II

Be Strong in the Lord

2 Timothy

CHAPTER 20

The Last Letter of All

Overview of 2 Timothy

I n the sixty-eighth year of the first century of the Christian era, an old man
sat in a prison cell in Rome. His underground cell was about twenty feet
in diameter. Seated on the stone floor of his cell, he dictated a letter. On the
other side of the bars, writing by torchlight, the old man's companion took
down the letter.

The letter was addressed to a young man in the distant city of Ephesus,
far across the Aegean and Adriatic seas. The subject of the old man's letter:
How to maintain your courage and strength while civilization is collapsing
all around you.

That's the theme of Paul's second letter to his son in the faith, Timothy.
It's an appropriate subject to study in this hour, when it seems that our civilization is teetering on the brink of collapse due to moral decay, ecological
peril, racial division, population pressure, terrorism, and the threat of nuclear
war. Like Timothy, we desperately need the courage and strength to face a
disintegrating world.

So we come to Paul's second letter to Timothy, the last words we have
from Paul before he was executed in Rome.

The gospel: the promise of life

Paul knew that Timothy was plagued by physical and emotional obstacles.
He had a weak physical constitution—literally, a weak stomach. He also had
a somewhat timid spirit. Paul knew that Timothy could be intimidated by
strong personalities and difficult situations, and this trait could cause him to
back away from tough decisions.

Timothy faced difficult challenges and persecution in his position at
Ephesus. He needed all the physical, spiritual, mental, and emotional strength
he could muster, and Paul knew Timothy could not find that strength within
himself. It could come only through faith in God.

Most important of all, Paul realized that his departure was at hand. He was going to be with his Lord, and he was passing the torch to this young man he had mentored. So this final word to Timothy, this last will and testament of the apostle Paul, is an especially important and poignant document for us. These are his final words of encouragement and exhortation, and they are directed not only to Timothy but also to all people who live in turbulent times.

The first verse is the key to the letter: "Paul, an apostle of Christ Jesus by the will of God, according to the promise of life that is in Christ Jesus" (2 Timothy 1:1).

The key phrase is this: "the promise of the life that is in Christ Jesus." This is an apt definition of the Christian gospel. The gospel is the promise of life, not merely of life to come but of the abundant life in the here and now.

Many people look at the Christian life as a sort of detour away from real life. They think that if you are a Christian, you have to give up all of the things about life that are truly enjoyable and exciting. But Christianity is not a detour. It is a highway through the center of reality. The gospel of Jesus Christ is the key to life, the fulfillment of the hunger and longing of human hearts. So, at the beginning of his second letter to Timothy, the apostle Paul gives us this key to life.

Paul has four charges or instructions for young Timothy. These four charges are as important today as they were two thousand years ago:

1. Guard the truth.
2. Be strong in the Lord.
3. Avoid traps and pitfalls.
4. Preach the Word.

Let's look at each of these themes in turn.

Guard the truth

First, guard the truth. God has committed to Timothy a deposit of truth. Timothy is responsible for protecting that truth and for shoring up the defenses of the church, which was under attack by a pagan and morally corrupt society. Paul's counsel to Timothy applies to our lives as well.

If you want to know why the world operates the way it does and why people do what they do, you find the answers in God's Word. Why does evil seem to reign unchallenged? Why do the righteous suffer unjustly? Why do we continually fall into temptation and sin when we want to do what is right?

The answers to these and so many other questions are found in the deposit of truth, the Scriptures. Like Timothy, we have a solemn responsibility to guard this truth.

How do we guard the truth? Paul suggests three specific actions we must take. First, we must exercise our spiritual gifts. Paul writes, "For this reason I remind you to fan into flame the gift of God, which is in you through the laying on of my hands. For God did not give us a spirit of timidity, but a spirit of power, of love and of self-discipline" (2 Timothy 1:6–7).

People often ask me, "What is going to happen in world events? Will there be war? Will there be nuclear terrorism in our country? Will events in the Middle East bring about Armageddon? Will there be another worldwide depression? Will the world be plunged into a famine? Are we approaching an ecological crisis?"

I don't know the answer to any of these questions. No one knows. But I do know this: God has not given us a spirit of timidity and fear. He has given us a spirit of power, of love, and of a sound, self-disciplined mind. So if we are anxious and troubled, we know that this spirit of fear does not come from God. The Spirit of God is a Spirit of power and love. He gives us a sound and disciplined mind with which to function amid frightening times.

The Spirit of God gives us spiritual gifts, and as the world grows dark and perilous, we are to use those gifts to minister to those around us. If you are a Christian, you have spiritual gifts, and you can do something for God. If you are not putting your gifts to work, you are wasting your God-given life. When you exercise your gifts, your faith and confidence grow as God's power is unleashed in your life.

Exercising our spiritual gifts is one of the most effective ways to guard the truth. The Christian faith is not a delicate, fragile flower that needs to be protected in a hothouse. Someone once said, "Lies need defending, but the truth defends itself." We do not need to guard the truth by shielding it or attacking its opponents. We have to exercise our gifts and proclaim God's truth. If we do that, God's truth will defend itself.

Next, Paul says we should guard the truth by suffering patiently: "So do not be ashamed to testify about our Lord, or ashamed of me his prisoner. But join with me in suffering for the gospel, by the power of God" (1 Timothy 1:8).

Paul reminds Timothy that every Christian, without exception, is called to suffer for the gospel's sake. You might say, "Oh, no! I don't want to suffer. If I had to go through suffering, I don't know if my faith would survive." We tend to think we are exempt from suffering—or should be.

Perhaps it's because we think of suffering as physical torture—being stretched on the rack or burned at the stake. It's true, Christians have suffered in this way in times past, and many Christians around the world still suffer physical torture for the sake of the gospel. In fact, in the past one hundred years, more Christians have suffered persecution, execution, and torture than in any other time in history, including the first century. Why should you and I be exempt from the suffering that so many other Christians have endured and still endure?

But the suffering Paul speaks of is not only physical in nature. There are many forms of suffering, including mental, emotional, and spiritual suffering. We suffer when we are ridiculed or shunned for our faith. The Christian employee suffers when he is denied a promotion because his employer only promotes people who will lie and cheat for the company. The valedictorian suffers when her school won't allow her to speak the Lord's name in her commencement speech. The young Christian convert suffers when he goes home to witness to his parents and siblings and they treat him like an outcast.

Paul tells us that we should endure suffering patiently. We are not to react with anger or vengeance but with Christlike patience and love. When we endure suffering this way, we validate the gospel and guard the truth.

One reason the gospel is widely scorned in our society is that Christians are not patient in suffering. When attacked, we become offended, we retaliate. We respond just as people of the world respond. There is no Christian witness in that.

We must challenge the world, but we must do so as Jesus did: with grace and truth. If we speak the truth in a gracious way and respond gently when attacked, the world will still hate us, because the world hates our Lord. But at least our Christlike response will be a witness to the world that the God we serve is a God of love.

If you challenge the world and its sin, expect to be attacked. Expect to be hated, defamed, and even physically attacked. Expect to suffer for the gospel's sake, because that is one of the ways we guard the truth.

Another way we guard the truth, Paul tells us, is by studying the Scriptures and applying its principles to our lives. Paul writes, "What you heard from me, keep as the pattern of sound teaching, with faith and love in Christ Jesus. Guard the good deposit that was entrusted to you—guard it with the help of the Holy Spirit who lives in us" (2 Timothy 1:13–14).

I love the phrase Paul uses: "the pattern of sound teaching." There are so many teachers today who have departed from that pattern. They follow this secular writer or that fraudulent religious leader because they have not studied the pattern of sound biblical teaching. They do not know what the Scriptures teach, so they are easy prey for any false teaching that comes their way.

If we are diligent to guard the truth, then God will be faithful in guarding us and securing our faith. As Paul writes, "That is why I am suffering as I am. Yet I am not ashamed, because I know whom I have believed, and am convinced that he is able to guard what I have entrusted to him for that day" (2 Timothy 1:12).

I believe that last phrase is a mistranslation. Paul is saying, "I am convinced that God is able to guard what he has entrusted to me for that day." This rendering is consistent with the original Greek and with the context of the surrounding verses. Paul is saying that if we are faithful in guarding the truth, then God will protect and defend the deposit of truth within us and keep us secure in the faith.

So Paul has instructed Timothy in three ways to guard the truth: exercise your spiritual gifts, endure suffering with patience, and follow the pattern of sound teaching. Do this, and you will stand firm. You have God's word on it.

Be strong in the Lord

Paul's second exhortation is, "Be strong in the Lord." You may think, "How can a person choose to be strong when he is weak?" But Paul knows that Timothy understands where his strength comes from. If Timothy is weak, he knows how to become strong. And so do we. Strength comes from the Scriptures. Timothy did not need instruction in how to become strong. He simply needed Paul's exhortation to do so. He needed to be reminded to go to the source and obtain that strength.

Someone once said, "When I *try,* I fail. When I *trust,* God succeeds." That is the way the Christian life is to be lived.

Paul uses three word pictures to describe what it means to be strong in the Lord. First, he tells us to be strong as soldiers: "Endure hardship with us like a good soldier of Christ Jesus. No one serving as a soldier gets involved in civilian affairs—he wants to please his commanding officer" (2 Timothy 2:3–4). A soldier must be utterly dedicated to his commander and his mission. How can you follow Christ if you are distracted by conflicting goals and interests? If you would be strong in the Lord, then be as dedicated as a soldier.

Second, be strong as an athlete: "Similarly, if anyone competes as an athlete, he does not receive the victor's crown unless he competes according to the rules" (2 Timothy 2:5). To be strong in the Lord, Paul says, a follower of Christ must be disciplined. You cannot take shortcuts or cut corners or break the rules. Just as an athlete cannot win the crown without observing the rules, so a Christian cannot experience victory by taking moral shortcuts. A Christian must follow Christ and follow the rules.

Third, be strong as a farmer: "The hardworking farmer should be the first to receive a share of the crops" (2 Timothy 2:6). To be strong in the Lord, Paul says, a Christian must be diligent. He must not slack off. Any farmer knows that if he expects to reap a crop in the fall, he must plant in the spring. In the same way, Christians cannot reap a spiritual harvest if they never toil and plant. To be strong in the Lord, the Christian must diligently study the Word, pray, serve others, and be a witness in the world. The Christian who drifts through life will reap nothing. The Christian who disciplines himself and works hard to produce a harvest will grow strong in the Lord.

Avoid traps and pitfalls

Paul's next charge to Timothy is to avoid the traps and pitfalls that can destroy our effectiveness for Christ. He outlines three pitfalls to avoid.

First are battles over words. Have you noticed that Christians often become embroiled in controversy over the tiniest snippets of Scripture? I have seen this tragedy played out many times: Christians divide into camps and battle it out over the most trivial of issues. Paul writes, "Keep reminding them of these things. Warn them before God against quarreling about words; it is of no value, and only ruins those who listen" (2 Timothy 2:14).

Paul warns against foolish and useless controversies that infect the church and spread like gangrene. This is not to say that theological questions are unimportant. Understanding the precise meaning of the Scriptures is extremely important. Bible scholars often differ on the meaning of this word or that verse. There is nothing wrong with exchanging views in an atmosphere of mutual respect. But divisions and controversies over interpretations have no place in the church. They only tear down; they never build up.

Second, Paul warns against the trap of dangerous desires. Timothy undoubtedly possesses a healthy sex drive. He lives in a sex-saturated society like ours. He is exposed to pagan propaganda and false moral doctrines, just as we are. So Paul says to Timothy, "In a large house there are articles not only of gold and silver, but also of wood and clay; some are for noble purposes and some for ignoble. If a man cleanses himself from the latter, he will be an instrument for noble purposes, made holy, useful to the Master and prepared to do any good work. Flee the evil desires of youth, and pursue righteousness, faith, love and peace, along with those who call on the Lord out of a pure heart" (2 Timothy 2:20–22).

Paul is talking about the whole world as a great house. He says that God has certain kinds of people in that great house. There are those he uses for base and ignoble purposes. History is filled with people whom God has used to accomplish His purpose, even though they were unwilling and unrighteous. But there are others whom God uses for noble purposes. These are righteous people who honor God and work in partnership with Him through faith. God will accomplish His purposes through us whether we are willing or not.

But for our own sakes, isn't it better that we be willing instruments in the Master's hands? If you want God to use your life for a noble purpose, then separate yourself from the sins and habits that would destroy your life. Flee the evil desires of youth, and pursue righteousness, faith, love, and peace.

Third, Paul warns against the trap of a rebellious attitude:

> But mark this: There will be terrible times in the last days. People will be lovers of themselves, lovers of money, boastful, proud, abusive, disobedient to their parents, ungrateful, unholy, without love, unforgiving, slanderous, without self-control, brutal, not lovers of the good, treacherous, rash, conceited, lovers of pleasure rather than lovers of God—having a form of godliness but denying its power. Have nothing to do with them. (2 Timothy 3:1–5)

When Paul speaks of the last days, he is not referring to the end times that are prophesied in the book of Revelation and elsewhere. The last days Paul speaks of include the entire span of time between the first and second comings of Christ. We are in the last days now.

The apostle tells us that in the last days, there will be recurrent cycles of turmoil and trouble. People will become unbelievably self-centered, cruel, and rebellious. Demonic forces will be at work in society, causing destruction and division. How do we respond to such lawlessness? How do we avoid falling into this trap?

Paul's answer: Avoid such people. Have nothing to do with them. Do not join them, and do not allow yourself to be infected by their way of life.

We often wonder how far such evil will go. When will God step in and say, "Enough is enough"? Paul cites the example of Jannes and Jambres, two magicians who opposed Moses before the court of Pharaoh (see Exodus 7:11). He concludes that men of depraved minds will not get far because God will see to it that their foolishness is made plain to everyone. In an age when it seems that evil men get away with murder while good people suffer, Paul's conclusion gives us comfort.

Preach the Word

Paul's final charge to Timothy is a clear, strong, bold challenge: Preach the Word. Paul writes:

> In the presence of God and of Christ Jesus, who will judge the living and the dead, and in view of his appearing and his kingdom, I give you this charge: Preach the Word; be prepared in season and out of season; correct, rebuke and encourage—with great patience and careful instruction. (2 Timothy 4:1–2)

Note, first, the solemnity of Paul's charge to Timothy. Paul gives this word to Timothy in the presence of God and the Lord Jesus, the judge of the living and the dead. Paul adds that the entire universe is watching. So Timothy has a solemn responsibility to carry out this charge.

Timothy is a preacher, and it seems superfluous for Paul to tell a preacher to preach. But if you examine this passage closely, you see that Paul does more than merely challenge Timothy to do his job. He breaks down the preacher's calling into three distinct parts. Let's look at each part.

First, correct. The Greek word Paul uses here is *elegcho*, which means to convict or convince. In other words, Paul tells Timothy that he should correct those who are straying and convince those who are doubting.

Second, rebuke. When Timothy encounters people who are living in rebellion or sin, he is to confront their behavior and call them to repentance. He is to rebuke them.

Third, exhort. Paul uses the Greek word *parakaleo*, meaning to comfort, encourage, console, or exhort. Paul is telling Timothy to comfort and encourage people who are fearful.

So Timothy is called to proclaim the Word and to declare the great truth God has given him. And Paul goes on to impress upon Timothy the urgency of this charge: "For the time will come when men will not put up with sound doctrine. Instead, to suit their own desires, they will gather around them a great number of teachers to say what their itching ears want to hear" (2 Timothy 4:3). So, Paul says, preach the Word with intensity and urgency, because the day is coming when people will stop listening. Now is the time. Do not delay.

Paul's last will and testament

Paul closes with a profoundly moving testimony as his journey through this life nears its completion:

> For I am already being poured out like a drink offering, and the time has come for my departure. I have fought the good fight, I have finished the race, I have kept the faith. Now there is in store for me the crown of righteousness, which the Lord, the righteous Judge, will award to me on that day—and not only to me, but also to all who have longed for his appearing. (2 Timothy 4:6–8)

Sitting in a tiny cell, cramped and cold, the apostle Paul has just written his own epitaph. Once, he traveled the world, spreading the gospel and planting new churches. Now his world has shrunk down to a darkened chamber, twenty feet by twenty feet. His circle of companions has shrunk to one: Luke the physician, the author of the gospel of Luke and Acts. Luke probably serves as Paul's amanuensis, his secretary, writing down this letter as Paul dictates it.

Paul knows his fate is sealed. He has already appeared once before Nero, that monster in human form who rules the Roman Empire. He knows he must appear before Nero once more—and he does not doubt what the result will be. He will be condemned and then executed. "I am already being poured out like a drink offering," he wrote.

But that is not the end. Paul already looks beyond the end of his life to future glory. For the believer, death is merely an incident. It is not the end of anything. Paul looks forward to the day when he appears before the Lord. He is confident, and he is eager to see his Lord face to face. And yet—

We also see a human mixture of emotions in Paul's closing words. He writes:

> Do your best to come to me quickly, for Demas, because he loved this world, has deserted me and has gone to Thessalonica. Crescens has gone to Galatia, and Titus to Dalmatia. Only Luke is with me. Get Mark and bring him with you, because he is helpful to me in my ministry. I sent Tychicus to Ephesus. When you come, bring the cloak that I left with Carpus at Troas, and my scrolls, especially the parchments. (2 Timothy 4:9–13)

Paul is cold in body, lonely in spirit, bored in mind. Paul is no super saint. He's a lonely man, forsaken by Demas, lonely for his friends Crescens,

Titus, Mark, and Timothy, and longing for the mental stimulation of his books. It is no sin to experience normal human emotions in circumstances of suffering. Paul is not ashamed to admit his feelings—and I'm grateful that he reveals his inner self in such a vulnerable way.

Here we see the balanced Christian life: Paul shows us the depth of his humanity and the depth of his faith. And it is his faith that enables him to transcend the weakness of his humanity. Because he is confident of the reality of the unseen world to come, he is able to endure the misery of his prison. Moreover, he is able to continue preaching the Word, even before the murderous emperor Nero. He recalls:

> At my first defense [before Nero], no one came to my support, but everyone deserted me. May it not be held against them. But the Lord stood at my side and gave me strength, so that through me the message might be fully proclaimed and all the Gentiles might hear it. And I was delivered from the lion's mouth. The Lord will rescue me from every evil attack and will bring me safely to his heavenly kingdom. To him be glory for ever and ever. Amen. (2 Timothy 4:16–18)

Tradition tells us that on an April morning, shortly after Paul wrote his second letter to Timothy, he was taken out on the Via Ostiensis (the Ostian Way), outside the city of Rome, and was executed at Aquae Salviae. His fellow apostle, Peter, was crucified upside down in Rome, but Paul, being a Roman citizen, was permitted a swift and merciful death by beheading. We know that Paul expected Timothy to visit him. It may well be that Luke and Timothy were with Paul at his execution. Both tradition and Scripture are silent on the precise details of Paul's death.

At the time Paul wrote those final words to Timothy, the name Nero was honored among men and known throughout the empire. Who was Paul? A despised Jewish preacher from Tarsus, a prisoner whose days were numbered. Yet today, two thousand years later, we name our sons Paul and our dogs Nero.

What a tremendous letter this is—and how Timothy's heart must have been challenged and encouraged but also broken to read of Paul's lonely suffering. God made certain that this wonderful letter not only reached Timothy but also was preserved for generations of believers.

So turn the page with me, and let's plunge into the depths of this letter, Paul's last will and testament for the church.

CHAPTER 21

The Promise of Life

2 Timothy 1:1–7

The historical and biblical record is incomplete, but it appears that Paul was imprisoned in Rome on two separate occasions. After his release from his first imprisonment, he continued traveling around the Roman Empire accompanied by Timothy and Titus.

He went to the island of Crete, where he left Titus in charge of the growing church there. With Timothy, he went to Ephesus. There he left Timothy in charge so that the growing church in that city could be firmly established under his leadership. Paul then proceeded up into Macedonia, where he wrote his first letter to Timothy.

There is some evidence that Paul probably journeyed west into Spain. Some historians believe he may have gone as far as the British Isles, which were under Roman rule. If so, he certainly returned to the eastern Mediterranean region, where he was arrested once more. His arrest probably took place in the Troas region of Asia Minor, north of Ephesus.

The arrest and imprisonment of the apostle Paul probably took place as part of the great persecution of Christians by Nero, beginning around A.D. 64. This persecution followed the great fire in Rome (July 64), which started in the shops of the Circus Maximus and which Nero blamed on the Christians.

Though Christians had been persecuted by the religious authorities in Judea for decades (Paul had once been a ringleader of that persecution), this was the first time that Christians had been officially persecuted by the Roman Empire. At Nero's orders, hundreds of Christians were covered with pitch and burned as living torches to light the emperor's gardens. They were thrown to lions and slaughtered by gladiators. They were slandered and called cannibals because they claimed to eat the body and blood of Christ. Because they shunned the worship of pagan gods, they were derided as atheists. They were hated as revolutionaries because they denied the authority of Caesar and called Jesus their Lord.

After his second arrest, Paul was taken to Rome and imprisoned in a dungeon, the Mamertine Prison, across the street from the old Senate building in the Roman forum. You can visit Paul's tiny cell by descending a narrow flight of steps. The only light in the cell is a small hole in the ceiling. The place is dark, cold, and claustrophobic.

There, about four or five years after writing his first letter to Timothy, Paul likely composed his second letter to Timothy. The apostle knew his life was nearly over. His race was nearly over. It was time for Paul to pass the torch to his spiritual son Timothy.

The promise of life

Despite the darkness of his circumstances, Paul greets Timothy with his usual air of calm, confident faith: "Paul, an apostle of Christ Jesus by the will of God, according to the promise of life that is in Christ Jesus, to Timothy, my dear son: Grace, mercy and peace from God the Father and Christ Jesus our Lord" (2 Timothy 1:1–2).

Paul's greatest boast was that he was called to be an apostle of Jesus the Messiah, not of his own choosing but "by the will of God." That is a remarkable claim. Here Paul raises himself to the level of the twelve apostles, whom Jesus had chosen and sent out into the world with the Great Commission: "Go into all the world and preach the good news to all creation" (see Mark 16:15). To add his own name to that list would be an act of presumption, if it were not true.

The Lord Jesus appeared to Paul, not only on the Damascus Road when he was first converted, but many times afterwards. During these appearances, Jesus imparted to Paul the same truths he had taught the Twelve when He was with them in the flesh. The fact that Paul knew that same apostolic body of truth convinced the other apostles that he was indeed a chosen apostle of the Lord. So Paul reminds Timothy of his apostleship to underscore his position as an authentic spokesman for the Lord.

Paul opens this letter with a description of the gospel that appears nowhere else in the New Testament: "the promise of life that is in Christ Jesus." Paul gloried in the message he proclaimed. The gospel transforms lives, sets captives free, and heals people whose lives are ridden with sin.

Elsewhere, Paul has described the gospel in many other ways. In Corinthians, Paul describes the gospel in these words: "We have this treasure in jars of clay" (see 2 Corinthians 4:7); that is, an infinitely valuable message contained within weak creatures, made of human clay. Writing to the Ephesians, he calls the gospel "the unsearchable riches of Christ" (see Ephesians 3:8). Writing to the Colossians, he calls the gospel "Christ in you, the hope of glory" (see Colossians 1:27). These phrases amplify Paul's meaning when he calls the gospel "the promise of life that is in Christ Jesus."

Everyone hungers for life. Not just existence—life! Abundant life. Meaningful life. A life that is exciting and filled with adventure.

I once watched a television interview with some punk rockers in Goth makeup. Their skin was as white as the pallor of death, and with black eye makeup, black lipstick, and black clothing, they looked like walking corpses. The interviewer asked, "Why do you dress this way? Why do you live a violent and dangerous lifestyle?" Their honest reply: "What else is there?"

Their existence was a silent protest against the emptiness of life. They felt cheated by life, by the world, and by society. Why? Because they want to truly live! They want a life that is abundant and meaningful—and they have concluded that they are living pointless lives in a meaningless universe.

Contrast the meaninglessness of so many lives today with the meaningful life that Paul writes of in this letter, written in the closing days of his life. He writes about life as God intended it to be lived—not the old stereotypical idea of "pie in the sky, when you die, by and by," but an adventurous, exciting life in the here and now. It is a life that has richness and meaning even when the world is falling apart, even when you are facing your own death.

Paul opens his letter to this introverted, sometimes timid young man with a description of the gospel as the promise of life in Jesus Christ. Paul immediately adds these words, "Grace, mercy and peace from God the Father and Christ Jesus our Lord." We often read these words as if they are a perfunctory greeting. But these are not throwaway words to Paul. He wants Timothy to remember that Jesus truly supplies grace, mercy, and peace to us every day.

Grace is the goodness and kindness of God that we do not deserve. His grace brings us life, food, shelter, material blessings, and the forgiveness of sin. The grace of God enables us to overcome our weaknesses and destructive habits, so we can truly live for Him.

Then there is mercy. Whereas grace is a gift we do not deserve, mercy is the withholding of punishment we do deserve. God's mercy tempers His justice. As the Old Testament tells us, "It is of the LORD's mercies that we are not consumed, because his compassions fail not" (Lamentations 3:22 KJV).

I am amazed at how many people, even Christians, feel entitled to a life of ease; the fact that we have life at all is a gift of God's mercy. Are we grateful for the mercies of God?

Finally, there is peace—that inner sense of well-being you experience in a turbulent world. True peace does not come from our circumstances; it comes from God alone. As Jesus told His disciples, "Peace I leave with you; my peace I give you. I do not give to you as the world gives. Do not let your hearts be troubled and do not be afraid" (John 14:27). As my friend and fellow pastor Steve Zeisler so aptly put it, "This is the great 'shalom' of God, the inner calm that keeps you panic-proof."

Are you panic-proof? Have you learned to leave God in charge of your circumstances? Paul did. That's why he was able to face the end of his life with confidence in the grace, mercy, and peace of God. Those are the ingredients of the "promise of life in Christ Jesus"—abundant grace, mercy beyond measure, and the peace of God that surpasses human understanding.

Joy and tears

Alone in his prison cell, Paul misses Timothy and is concerned that he remain faithful and fruitful in his ministry at Ephesus. Paul knows he is about to leave this world, so he writes:

> I thank God, whom I serve, as my forefathers did, with a clear conscience, as night and day I constantly remember you in my prayers. Recalling your tears, I long to see you, so that I may be filled with joy. I have been reminded of your sincere faith, which first lived in your grandmother Lois and in your mother Eunice and, I am persuaded, now lives in you also. For this reason I remind you to fan into flame the gift of God, which is in you through the laying on of my hands. For God did not give us a spirit of timidity, but a spirit of power, of love and of self-discipline. (2 Timothy 1:3–7)

Those words "I thank God" are a weak translation of the Greek. A more accurate translation might be, "I have joy in God." When Paul remembers Timothy, he experiences transcendent joy because of Timothy's service to God.

Note also the phrase "with a clear conscience." It would be more accurate to say that Paul prayed with a cleansed conscience. Paul is not claiming that his record of behavior is perfect. He is expressing gratitude to God for forgiveness and the cleansing of his conscience. Whatever Paul has done wrong, God has washed it away.

Why does Paul open his letter to Timothy this way? It's because Paul knows what Timothy needs to hear. Timothy is a young man, relatively new in the ministry, and new ministers make mistakes. Timothy knows Paul has made his share of mistakes. But just as God has cleansed Paul's conscience, he can cleanse Timothy's conscience, too.

Paul adds that even before he became a Christian, he learned this principle from his Jewish ancestors. Before Jesus came as the perfect sacrifice, when a Jew had sinned, he would bring a sacrifice and God would cleanse his conscience. Paul had learned that the Old Testament system of sacrifices was a symbolic picture of the perfect sacrifice that was to come, the death of God's Son on the cross.

Paul stated that he prayed constantly for Timothy because of four unforgettable aspects of Timothy's life and character. First, Paul recalled Timothy's tears of love. "Recalling your tears," he writes, "I long to see you, so that I may be filled with joy."

We don't know when Timothy wept with Paul. Some Bible scholars suggest that this probably occurred when Paul was arrested the second time. If Paul was arrested in Troas, as tradition suggests, Timothy may have been with Paul at the time. Troas is not far from Ephesus, and Timothy may have been with Paul when the soldiers came for him and dragged him away. The experience was probably traumatic for Timothy.

As he was led away, Paul probably saw Timothy's anguished face, with tears running down his cheeks. So here Paul writes, in effect, "I can't forget that. Every time I think of you, Timothy, I see the tears running down your face, and the memory prompts me to pray for you."

I think I have an inkling of what Paul felt because of an experience I had when I was twenty-one. I taught a Sunday school class for high school boys in Chicago. These teens were not much younger than I was. I became especially good friends with two boys, Archie and Lloyd. We studied the Word, prayed, and hung out together.

When the time came for me to leave Chicago and move to Denver, I realized I would probably not see Archie and Lloyd again. They went with me to the train station where we said goodbye. As I stepped aboard the train I saw the tears running down their faces. That image stuck with me, and I can see their faces to this day. Whenever I thought back to that day, I was moved to pray for Archie and Lloyd.

That's what the apostle Paul says here: "I remember you in my prayers whenever I think of your tears of love."

Sincere faith

The second unforgettable aspect of Timothy's life and character Paul refers to is this young pastor's sincere faith. "I have been reminded of your sincere faith," he writes, "which first lived in your grandmother Lois and in your mother Eunice and, I am persuaded, now lives in you also."

Paul reminds Timothy of the genuine faith he exhibited even as a young man in his teens, when he came to Christ under Paul's ministry in Lystra. It's hard to know what the apostle means when he speaks of the "sincere faith" of his grandmother and mother. Was Paul referring to the Christian faith or to a devout Jewish faith? We don't know.

When my wife and I visited Israel, we traveled with a devout Jewish couple whose faith was strongly fixed on the messianic promises of the Old Testament. They knew that Elaine and I believed in Jesus as the Messiah, but they had not yet come to that conviction. They had an unshakable faith, however, that the coming Messiah would fulfill the promises of the prophets.

Paul may have meant that Timothy's Jewish grandmother and mother were godly Jews. Or these two women might have converted to Christ before Timothy did. On the day of Pentecost, when three thousand Jews were converted on one day, Timothy's grandmother Lois may have been among that throng. And when Eunice later married a Greek and gave birth to Timothy, they may have brought him up in the knowledge of the Scriptures.

But it was not until Paul came to Lystra and preached the gospel with great power that Timothy committed his life to Jesus Christ. Remembering Timothy's sincere faith, Paul was encouraged to pray for him.

Timothy's gifts

The third unforgettable aspect of Timothy's life and character was Timothy's spiritual gift. Paul writes, "For this reason I remind you to fan into flame the gift of God, which is in you through the laying on of my hands." Some commentators refer to this laying on of hands as Timothy's ordination for ministry, occurring a year or so after his conversion. I disagree with this view.

The Scriptures teach that the gifts of the Spirit are imparted to us at the moment of our new birth in Christ. If that is so, then Paul could not be referring to Timothy's ordination. He could only be referring to Timothy's conversion. Timothy probably came to Christ at a public meeting where Paul preached. When Timothy expressed his faith in Jesus, the elders laid hands on him and Paul prayed for him. As we learned in 1 Timothy 1:18, a prophetic utterance was made, indicating that this young man would be greatly used by God. Here, Paul reminds Timothy of the imparting of the gift of the Spirit.

What gift or gifts did Timothy receive? I believe it was the gifts of a pastor-teacher. But whatever Timothy's gifts might have been, he needed to exercise them and "fan them into flame" to keep those gifts alive and functioning properly.

The indwelling Spirit

The fourth unforgettable aspect of Timothy's character was the evidence of the indwelling Spirit of God in his life. Notice the contrasts Paul notes for us: "For God did not give us a spirit of timidity, but a spirit of power, of love and of self-discipline." Paul says two fascinating things about Timothy, one negative and one positive.

First, Paul says that the Spirit within us is not the spirit of fear. This is one of the most powerful statements in all of Scripture: "For God did not give us a spirit of timidity, but a spirit of power, of love and of self-discipline." Anytime you feel anxious or fearful, repeat those words to yourself. If you are worried about finances, or your family's safety, or some difficult challenge, or the state of the world, remember: Fear doesn't come from God. He wants us to experience his power, his love, and a calm, steady, disciplined mind.

Did you know that Christians are forbidden to fear? Jesus told us, 'Do not let your hearts be troubled. Trust in God; trust also in me . . . Peace I leave with you; my peace I give you. I do not give to you as the world gives. Do not let your hearts be troubled and do not be afraid" (John 14:1, 27).

That's not a suggestion; that's a command. So, the moment you feel your emotions tilting toward fear—stop! Remember that God has not given us a spirit of fear. He commands us to release our fears to Him and to not let our hearts be troubled.

So the first fascinating thing that Paul says about Timothy is that God has not given him a spirit of fear. That's the negative. The second thing Paul says is the positive: God has positively given us three things: a spirit of power, of love, and of self-discipline (or, as the King James Version puts it, "a sound mind").

The power of the Lord shatters the power of Satan. God's power has been released in our hearts, giving us the ability to refuse the wrong and obey the right. This power is released in us when we choose to obey. We may not feel powerful, but God's strength is imparted to us, enabling us to maintain our walk with Him.

Next, God gives us the spirit of love, which overcomes our fears. It's the spirit of love for God, which motivates us to trust Him and attempt great (and even scary) things for Him. It's the spirit of love for others, which enables us to overcome our fear of what people think of us, so we can truly reach out with the message of Christ. And it's an awareness of God's love for us, so that no matter what perils we face, we know that nothing can ever separate us from God's all-encompassing love.

Finally, God gives us the spirit of self-discipline and sound judgment. Many people are subject to fear because their thinking is unsound. They constantly think about their fears and blow their worries out of proportion. Paul says that we have been given the spirit of rational, disciplined thinking that is able to assess reality clearly, taking God's power into account. A sound mind keeps our fears in check.

As Paul reflected on all of these memories of Timothy, he was continually moved to pray for him. Paul knew that this young pastor, his spiritual son Timothy, would stand strong in the faith, no matter how difficult the circumstances may be. If he stumbled, God would set him back on his feet. If he sinned, God would forgive and restore him.

Paul wrote these words from a prison cell and directed them to a young man who faced intense opposition in a hostile world. These inspired words crackled with the power to strengthen Timothy for opposition and persecution. And these words have power for you and me as we face our own trials and uncertainties in the days ahead.

CHAPTER 22

The Call to Courage

2 Timothy 1:8–13

The sixteenth-century English preacher Hugh Latimer stood in the pulpit of Westminster Abbey, preaching to a congregation that included the notorious King Henry VIII. Afterwards, the king was unhappy with Latimer's preaching and sent the preacher a message: Next Sunday, begin by apologizing to the king.

The following Sunday, Latimer stepped into the pulpit and said, "I have asked myself, 'Hugh Latimer, do you know before whom you speak? His Majesty, the king, has power to take your life! Do not displease him!' Then I thought to myself, 'Hugh Latimer, do you know whose message is entrusted to your care? The message of almighty God, who knows all your ways and is able to cast your soul into hell! Therefore, take care that you deliver God's message faithfully!'"

Then he proceeded to preach God's truth with even more vehemence than he had the previous Sunday—as King Henry VIII sat glaring and fuming. The king of England did not punish Latimer immediately, but over the years of his reign, Henry twice imprisoned Latimer in the Tower of London.

Eventually, Henry VIII died, and his daughter, Mary I, became queen of England. She became known as Bloody Mary for ordering three hundred Protestants burned at the stake. In October 1555, Hugh Latimer joined that procession of martyrs. Along with fellow clergyman Nicholas Ridley, Latimer was led onto the grounds of Oxford University. The two men were tied to a wooden stake, and the fire was lit. As the flames raged, Latimer shouted, "Be of good comfort, Master Ridley! Let's die like men! Today, we shall light such a candle in England that, by God's grace, shall never be put out!"

Here in 2 Timothy, we see the apostle Paul awaiting his own execution. As death approaches, he calls out to his spiritual son Timothy and says, in effect, "The time of my departure is at hand—but be of good comfort, Master Timothy! Preach the message boldly! And when your time comes, die like a man! In life and in death, light such a candle that, by God's grace, shall never be put out!"

Don't be ashamed of the gospel

Paul knows that Timothy has a problem with timidity. He had undoubtedly seen Timothy in situations where he faced opposition or ridicule and had probably seen the young preacher yield to intimidation and pressure. Perhaps you identify with Timothy's shyness and timidity. You may work or go to school in a hostile environment. You may fear that people will find out you're a Christian, so you keep your faith to yourself. You make sure no one finds out that you attend church, pray, and read the Bible. Perhaps you even compromise your moral principles in order to fit in.

If you've ever experienced that kind of timidity in the face of pressure to conform to this world, then Paul is speaking directly to you in this passage. Like Timothy in ancient Ephesus, you are living in a hostile, pagan culture. Paul's message to you is the same as his message to Timothy: Do not be ashamed of the gospel of Jesus Christ.

In these verses, the apostle Paul will show his struggling young son in the faith how to overcome his tendency toward shyness. Paul addresses three specific issues that probably inhibited Timothy in his proclamation of the good news. Paul writes, "So do not be ashamed to testify about our Lord, or ashamed of me his prisoner. But join with me in suffering for the gospel, by the power of God" (2 Timothy 1:8).

The first issue is that Jesus is invisible. Paul doesn't say so directly, but I think he is suggesting that the entire subject of an invisible Lord made Timothy a bit reluctant to share Christ with others. It's not easy to tell people, "I serve a Lord who died and rose again and is now in heaven, and He also lives within me. He's the most important person in my life, though I can't see Him. I talk to Him every day, though I can't hear Him." To say that is to expose yourself to ridicule.

The second issue is that Paul is a prisoner. He says, "Do not be... ashamed of me his prisoner." Perhaps Timothy is tempted to be ashamed because Paul is a political prisoner, held in a Roman prison, viewed as an outcast and an enemy of the emperor. Paul urges Timothy to overcome these feelings of shame.

The third issue is that the gospel stirs up opposition. Paul says, "Join with me in suffering for the gospel, by the power of God." Timothy knows that if he preaches the gospel to the pagan culture around him, he will stir up a hornet's nest of opposition. The gospel insults human pride. People love to imagine themselves as powerful and adequate to solve their own problems. The message of the gospel punctures the balloon of human self-sufficiency and says, "You cannot save yourself. You are lost in your sin. You need a savior." Paul acknowledges that this message angers people and generates opposition, yet he urges Timothy to preach the gospel anyway. "Join with me in suffering for the gospel," he says.

I once heard evangelist Luis Palau speak at a conference in San Diego. He told a story about two people he had led to the Lord. One was the president of a South American nation, the other a janitor in Atlanta. His point: Both the president and the janitor came to Christ in exactly the same way. They both had to admit that they were lost in sin and incapable of saving themselves. And both experienced a radical transformation through faith in Jesus Christ.

The ground is level at the foot of the cross. Rich and poor, powerful and powerless all come to Jesus Christ in exactly the same way. The gospel shatters human pride and self-sufficiency. That's why we often feel intimidated at the thought of sharing the gospel with powerful people. We know they will likely say, "How dare you suggest that I'm lost in sin? Don't you know who I am? Who do you think you are, preaching to me? Save your Bible thumping for someone who really needs it!"

Results belong to God. Our responsibility is to be faithful and obedient.

The power of God

So how does Paul help this introverted man overcome his tendency to be ashamed of the gospel? He does so by underscoring Timothy's spiritual resources. First, Paul says that Timothy needs to realize that the gospel is "the power of God." He writes, "But join with me in suffering for the gospel, by the power of God, who has saved us and called us to a holy life—not because of anything we have done but because of his own purpose and grace" (2 Timothy 1:8b–9a).

The gospel is the power of God. You never need to be ashamed of power. Who could be ashamed of the power that created the universe, the power that controls human destiny? In fact, let me tell you a story about the power of the gospel message.

I once received a letter from a man in prison at the state correctional institution in Tracy, California. It's a long letter, so I have edited and condensed it.

I'm sixty-six years old, and this is my third time in prison. After my third conviction, I decided that life was no longer worth living. Soon after I arrived here, I was called out of my cell for a meeting with my attorney. As I walked past a trash can in the hall, I saw some papers lying on top. Wanting something to read, I grabbed the papers out of the trash can. They were the printed sermon transcripts from your church.

I started reading, and the first message was called "How to Be Saved." It had never occurred to me that I needed to be saved from anything in my life. But after I read it, I realized my life was a mess and I needed to be saved. I thought, "If I want God to accept me, I need to clean up my life first. I need to get rid of my bad habits so God will accept me."

Then I read the second message. It was called "Who Chose Whom." When I finished reading that message, I knew I was going about it the wrong way. I thought I could get rid of my sins, do some good deeds, and then God would accept me. But I was not letting God save me; I was trying to save myself.

That night in my bunk, I woke up and couldn't get back to sleep. I couldn't think of anything but those messages and what I needed to do to be saved. I felt God in the cell with me, and I couldn't keep from crying. I opened my heart to Jesus and asked Him to come into my life and save me. And that's what He did. I didn't feel different except that, for the first time in years, I was able to sleep through the night.

In the morning, everything seemed different. The cell looked different; the prisoners around me looked different; the food I had been complaining about tasted good. One of the other prisoners said, "You look different. What's happened to you?"

A little voice inside me said, "Tell him." So I told this guy the whole story. And there were about twenty-five other guys all around me, listening in. Eleven of them asked Jesus to come into their lives.

Now, that's the power of the gospel! A prisoner happened to pull some papers out of a trash can, and God used those papers to show him how to have a personal relationship with Jesus Christ. There was no power in those papers, no power in the man who preached those messages, but there is amazing power in the gospel message. There was so much power in that message that this prisoner, who had been a Christian for less than a day, led eleven fellow prisoners to Christ just by telling his story.

There is no power on earth that compares with the power of the gospel.

A holy life

Next, Paul tells us that God has "saved us and called us to a holy life." What is this holy life Paul speaks of? He refers to a process theologians call sanctification, by which we are not merely saved but gradually conformed into Christlikeness. Salvation is an instantaneous miracle of regeneration. But sanctification is a gradual process of growth and change.

Day by day and year by year, a Christian should display increasing evidence of the power of God in his or her life. If a Christian is not growing, there is something desperately wrong. The saving power of God, which prompts a believer to turn away from sin, should now motivate the believer to grow toward spiritual wholeness. After all, that is what holiness means: wholeness in Christ.

The work of becoming whole and sanctified in Christ does not originate with us. The apostle Paul tells us clearly that it is the work of God, "who has saved us and called us to a holy life—not because of anything we have done but because of his own purpose and grace. This grace was given us in Christ Jesus before the beginning of time" (2 Timothy 1:9).

This is an amazing statement. Paul says that though we have free will and must choose to follow Christ, God determined before the world began that He would graciously draw us to himself.

Imagine that you arrive in a big city. There's a convention going on, and you know that all the hotels will be sold out. Still, you go to the nearest hotel, hoping against hope that they might have a room. To your amazement, the clerk says, "We have a reservation for you. We've been expecting you. Go right on up."

That is the feeling we get when we read this passage. We think that we have chosen God. We think that we have made the decision to receive Christ and follow Him. But the moment we set foot in the kingdom of God, we discover that He knew we were coming all along. Our reservation in heaven has been waiting for us since the beginning of time. God graciously arranged our circumstances so that we would be drawn to Him.

Isn't that amazing? Yet that is the powerful God we serve. He works out His plans and purposes in ways that are beyond our understanding. He is a God who calls us to himself by His infinite grace.

Life and immortality

God's grace and power are demonstrated, Paul says, through the Lord's sacrifice upon the cross. Paul writes, "This grace was given us in Christ Jesus before the beginning of time but it has now been revealed through the appearing of our Savior, Christ Jesus, who has destroyed death and has brought life and immortality to light through the gospel" (2 Timothy 1:9b–10).

Here, Paul expresses the heart of the Christian faith: Our Savior poured out His blood upon the cross, and through His death He destroyed death. Through His resurrection, He showed the world what eternal life looks like. He brought immortality to light. His death and resurrection affected our existence in two important ways:

First, Jesus destroyed death. This doesn't mean that biological death has been eliminated from the human race. Human beings, including Christians, die. When Paul says Jesus destroyed death, he uses a Greek word that means to nullify or bring to nothing. That's why he is able to write:

> "Where, O death, is your victory?
> Where, O death, is your sting?" (1 Corinthians 15:55)

The film *On Golden Pond,* starring Henry Fonda, Jane Fonda, and Katherine Hepburn, tells the story of an aging professor who faces the relentless approach of death. Though the film is a moving portrait of the human spirit, a sense of dread hangs over its characters. In the background of every scene, we sense the cold, clammy shadow of death. All the characters feel it, and so does the audience. The film ends with a sense of tragedy, and the audience leaves the theater in a somber mood.

I don't say this to criticize the film. It truly captures, as few films do, the dread that fills the hearts of millions as they contemplate death. If you face death without the hope of salvation, then the bleak despondency of *On Golden Pond* is all that remains.

I have sat at the bedside of many Christians who faced the end of their lives. What a difference between the mood of these believers and the mood one feels while watching *On Golden Pond.* In almost every case of the Christians I sat with, I saw a sense of joy and hope in the hour of death. That is what the resurrection of Jesus has accomplished: It has nullified the fear of death.

Paul goes on to say that Jesus "has destroyed death and has brought life and immortality to light through the gospel." The Old Testament does not tell us much about what lies beyond the grave. But when Jesus came, He revealed to us what eternal life looks like. His glorified body gives us a glimpse of what our bodies will be like in glory. He also told us what to expect in the life to come: "In my Father's house are many rooms; if it were not so, I would have told you. I am going there to prepare a place for you. And if I go and prepare a place for you, I will come back and take you to be with me that you also may be where I am" (John 14:2–3).

The New Testament is filled with descriptions of our heavenly home. So when Jesus came, He opened the windows of heaven and allowed us to look inside. He has truly "brought life and immortality to light through the gospel."

I recall when my wife's mother was in her nineties and becoming quite frail. Gram would spend most of her time sitting, sometimes watching television or visiting with the people around her. She had reached a point in life where, physically, she was unable to do much more than that. One day, when Elaine was visiting with her, Gram talked about heaven. She asked, "What will heaven be like? Will we just sit around? I'm so tired of sitting around."

Elaine assured her, "Absolutely not! The Bible says we will leap and run and enjoy our new bodies. Our resurrection bodies will respond to every desire of the spirit."

The glorious expectation of the Christian life is immortality. Our present bodies are subject to weariness and death. "The spirit is willing," we say, "but the flesh is ready for a nap." In our new bodies, however, the spirit will say, "Do this," and our bodies will joyfully obey.

That's the promise of eternal life that Jesus has revealed to us. That's the power of the gospel, and we need not be ashamed of it. It's the answer to the deepest longings of men and women everywhere.

Success and suffering

Timothy faces great pressure and opposition, but Paul has been there too, and he now offers himself as a role model:

> That is why I am suffering as I am. Yet I am not ashamed, because I know whom I have believed, and am convinced that he is able to guard what I have entrusted to him for that day.
>
> What you heard from me, keep as the pattern of sound teaching, with faith and love in Christ Jesus. (2 Timothy 1:12–13)

Paul says, in effect, "Timothy, you don't need to be ashamed. I'm not ashamed, and I've been through everything you're going through. I know that the resources that were available to me are available to you, and they are sufficient for the challenge."

Notice Paul's statement, "That is why I am suffering as I am." In preaching the gospel, Paul has challenged the powers and philosophies of this dark world—and the world has lashed back at him. Because of Paul's bold stand for Jesus Christ, he has been beaten, assaulted, flogged, stoned, and now arrested and sentenced to death. If he had been content to keep his mouth shut and quietly enjoy life, he could have avoided all the persecution he has suffered.

Paul wants Timothy—and us—to know that every person who lives a godly life in Christ Jesus will suffer persecution. That's not one of the more pleasant promises of Scripture, but it is definitely true. If you are faithful in speaking God's truth, you will suffer.

Adoniram Judson was a nineteenth-century Baptist missionary who took the gospel into Burma. He endured great suffering, laboring in that land for almost four decades with only one furlough trip home. As a young Christian, I read the story of his life and was greatly challenged in my faith.

Soon after the beginning of the Anglo-Burmese war in 1824, soldiers burst into Judson's home, tied him with torture thongs, and dragged him off to one of the most wretched, vermin-infested prisons in the world. It was known as a death prison because few who went there survived more than a few weeks or months. After surviving twelve months there, Judson was marched barefoot to a primitive village where he was kept for days at a time, manacled and suspended by his feet.

Finally, after seventeen months of captivity and torture, Judson was released to his family. Only a few months later, his wife, Ann, died, a victim of stress and illness. Six months after Ann died, the youngest of Judson's three children also died.

Reflecting on the losses and suffering he endured to bring the gospel to Burma, Adoniram Judson reflected, "Success and suffering are vitally and organically linked. If you succeed without suffering, it is because someone else has suffered for you without succeeding; and if you suffer without succeeding, it is so that someone else may succeed after you."

Success and suffering are intertwined. Paul, having experienced both, says to Timothy that he has been down that road.

The pattern of sound teaching

The gospel of Jesus Christ has been entrusted to the apostle Paul. Now he hands that responsibility to the next generation. Paul wants Timothy to know where to find the strength to carry that burden: God.

In verse 12, Paul writes, "Yet I am not ashamed, because I know whom I have believed, and am convinced that he is able to guard what I have entrusted to him for that day." As I've previously noted, I believe that last phrase is a mistranslation. I believe Paul is saying, "I am convinced that God is able to guard what he has entrusted to me for that day."

God has entrusted the deposit of apostolic truth to Paul, and Paul now passes the torch to Timothy. Paul wants Timothy to know that God will guard that truth that now is entrusted to Timothy. God is faithful and will keep Timothy secure in the faith.

A young man once asked Dr. Donald Grey Barnhouse, "How could two million Israelites wander in the barren wilderness for forty years, and at the end of that time emerge from the wilderness with their clothing showing no signs of wear?"

Dr. Barnhouse replied with a single word: "God!" Yes, God is our resource—the only resource we need.

Finally, Paul encourages Timothy with these words: "What you heard from me, keep as the pattern of sound teaching, with faith and love in Christ Jesus" (2 Timothy 1:13).

The pattern of sound teaching Paul speaks of is the Word of God. It's our roadmap, our instruction book, our blueprint for living. We are under assault by the god of this world, Satan. The satanic mindset continually bombards us from our popular media, trying to make us question God's moral standards in the Bible. At times, we may even wonder if the standards of our fallen world are so bad after all. But the Bible tells us, "There is a way that seems right to a man, but in the end it leads to death" (Proverbs 14:12).

We ask ourselves, "What's wrong with sex outside of marriage? Is it really so wrong? Who would I be hurting?" But God's Word says, "Abstain from sinful desires, which war against your soul" (see 1 Peter 2:11).

We may ask, "Is divorce so wrong? I've fallen out of love with my spouse. Why should I remain stuck in a marriage that makes me unhappy?" Yet the Bible tells us, "'I hate divorce,' says the LORD God of Israel" (Malachi 2:16).

Or we may ask, "Is it so wrong to steal music or movies via the Internet? The corporations and producers don't need my money. If I can download entertainment for free, why should I have to pay? Is that so wrong?" Yet God's Word is clear: "He who has been stealing must steal no longer" (see Ephesians 4:28).

Let us not be ashamed of the gospel of Jesus Christ. Rather, let us pray for the strength and boldness to stand, to endure, to be tested—and to keep the pattern of sound teaching that has been entrusted to us.

CHAPTER 23

How to Defend a Lion

2 Timothy 1:14–2:2

The English evangelist Charles Haddon Spurgeon (1834–1892) was known as the prince of preachers. He once said, "Scripture is like a lion. Who ever heard of defending a lion? Just turn God's Word loose; it will defend itself."

Paul, in his second letter to Timothy, commends a similar approach. Writing from his prison cell in Rome, Paul reaches out to Timothy, who undoubtedly feels alone in that great pagan city of Ephesus. He writes, "Guard the good deposit that was entrusted to you—guard it with the help of the Holy Spirit who lives in us" (2 Timothy 1:14).

The world calls Christianity a religion. But the great claim of Christianity is not that it is a religion, but that it is the truth. The Christian Scriptures and the Christian gospel describe reality as it truly is. Dorothy Sayers put it this way: "The test of any religion is not that it pleases us, but that it is true."

This is why, when Jesus taught the people on the hills of Galilee and in the towns of Judea, they responded by saying, "Yes! Of course!" They followed Him and hung on His words because His words rang true. His message had the ring of truth. It freed the people from the religious lies and dead traditions that had kept them bound in darkness.

When you get a new washing machine or computer or camcorder, you get an instruction book that tells you how to operate it. People, too, have an instruction book. We are complicated beings, and we need instructions in how to operate our lives. So God gave us an instruction book, the Bible. Here, Paul tells Timothy to protect that instruction book from being lost. He says, "Guard the good deposit that was entrusted to you—guard it with the help of the Holy Spirit who lives in us."

Notice, it is not merely the words of the Book that make it powerful. Rather, the Holy Spirit infuses the words of the Book with power, life, and eternal significance. The Spirit illuminates the Book and brings it home to the heart. He transforms lifeless ink on dead paper into living, penetrating words that pierce the heart and enlighten the mind. While it's true that the words themselves are God's revelation of himself to humanity, it's the Spirit who transforms this book into a powerful lion, fully capable of defending itself.

Deserted in Asia

How do you turn the lion loose? That's what Paul reveals in the verses that follow: "You know that everyone in the province of Asia has deserted me, including Phygelus and Hermogenes" (2 Timothy 1:15).

Here, Paul reminds Timothy of news that the young pastor has undoubtedly heard: There had been a great defection away from Paul and his apostolic authority. And because Timothy is well known as Paul's protégé, the opposition against Paul was also directed at Timothy. This does not mean there was a widespread defection from Christianity. Rather, these defectors were Christians who were turning away from Paul's teaching. They were denying Paul's apostolic authority.

Paul faced this criticism wherever he went. He was not one of the original Twelve. He had not walked with Jesus during the Lord's earthly ministry. He had met Jesus only after the Lord's resurrection. Many criticized Paul on this point and accused him of appointing himself an apostle without true authority from the Lord.

We still hear such criticism of Paul. Some Bible scholars claim that Paul's teachings should not be taken seriously. Some advocate a view of Scripture called red-letter Christianity, a term that comes from the fact that some Bibles print the words of Jesus in red ink. These teachers say that we should build our theology only on the words of Christ. They claim that we should feel free to pick and choose among Paul's words and disregard any of Paul's teachings we find disagreeable.

Who were Phygelus and Hermogenes? We don't know for sure, but they were evidently prominent church leaders who had once supported Paul. We know that many in the province of Asia were converted by Paul's preaching. Luke records that, years earlier, Paul had rented a lecture hall in Ephesus where he taught and preached for five hours every day. "This went on for two years," Luke writes, "so that all the Jews and Greeks who lived in the province of Asia heard the word of the Lord" (Acts 19:10).

What an exciting time that must have been! From that lecture hall, the gospel went out with power for two years, and thousands of people came to Christ. But that was years earlier. Now Paul languishes in a prison cell in

Rome, and he writes these heartbreaking words: "Everyone in the province of Asia has deserted me."

Bringer of help

Paul employs a touch of hyperbole when he says everyone in that province has deserted him. Certainly, there are a few who still support Paul. One is Timothy. Another is a man named Onesiphorus. Paul writes:

> May the Lord show mercy to the household of Onesiphorus, because he often refreshed me and was not ashamed of my chains. On the contrary, when he was in Rome, he searched hard for me until he found me. May the Lord grant that he will find mercy from the Lord on that day! You know very well in how many ways he helped me in Ephesus. (2 Timothy 1:16–18)

The name Onesiphorus means "bringer of help," and this man lived up to his name. He was evidently a businessman. Paul had known Onesiphorus and his family when he lived in Ephesus. In his business travels, Onesiphorus went to Rome. While there, he searched for Paul and eventually found him in the Mamertine dungeon. Once he found Paul, Onesiphorus was not ashamed of Paul's chains. He took a great risk in identifying himself as Paul's friend, because to befriend an enemy of the emperor was to put one's own life at risk.

Onesiphorus ministered to Paul in prison and refreshed his spirit. He didn't wring his hands and complain about the terrible state of events. He came with confidence that God was sovereign over all of Paul's circumstances. He came to pray with Paul and sing hymns with him. During his visit with Paul, he blessed the old apostle to the depths of his soul.

In return, Paul asked God to bless the family of Onesiphorus and to be merciful to him "on that day," the day of the Lord's judgment of believers. By the actions of his life, Onesiphorus had turned loose the lion of truth in his own time. He reminds me of my favorite definition of what a Christian is supposed to be:

Completely fearless,
Continually cheerful, and
Constantly in trouble.

The zing in "Amazing Grace"

Next, Paul returns to the task of giving Timothy step-by-step instructions on how to guard the truth of the gospel and set loose the lion of truth in the world: "You then, my son, be strong in the grace that is in Christ Jesus. And the things you have heard me say in the presence of many witnesses entrust to reliable men who will also be qualified to teach others" (2 Timothy 2:1–2).

When the world is falling down around your ears, the first thing you must do is to remain strong in the grace of Jesus Christ. The first principle of helping others is that you can pass on to others only what you have received. Unless the grace and truth of Jesus Christ have infused and transformed your life, you will never be able to help others stand strong in the hour of danger.

That's why Paul says, "Be strong in the grace that is in Christ Jesus." That is how we guard the truth. That is what Onesiphorus has done. Because he was strong in the grace of the Lord, he could withstand the fear and pressure of his day. He was not afraid to enter that prison and identify with Paul.

It is grace that strengthens us, Paul says—"the grace that is in Christ Jesus." Now here is the paradoxical thing about grace: It's never available to the strong. Grace is for the weak. To be strong in the Lord, you must first admit your weakness.

I love to hear the hymn "Amazing Grace," especially when the singers put the emphasis upon the "zing"! That's what grace does: it puts zing into life. "Amazing grace, how sweet the sound that saved a wretch like me!" That is the grace that Paul describes to Timothy.

Pass it on!

Paul goes on to the next step: "And the things you have heard me say in the presence of many witnesses entrust to reliable men who will also be qualified to teach others." In other words, pass it on! And please understand, this instruction from Paul is not addressed to pastors only. God, through Paul, is speaking to all Christians everywhere. He expects all believers to be communicators of His truth. He has given each of us as Christians this precious deposit of His truth, and He expects us to transmit this truth to the next generation.

So, whether you are a preacher or a teacher, a stockbroker or a stocking clerk, a corporate CEO or a stay-at-home mom, be a communicator of God's truth. Mentor and disciple others by word and example. Pour your life into other faithful people and entrust this deposit of truth to their care. And as you speak about grace, let people see grace lived out in your life, giving you victory over your hurts, struggles, and failures.

Timothy must have seen Paul in times of discouragement and times of rejoicing. Through it all, Timothy had seen the blessings of the gospel spread throughout the world. He had seen lives changed and entire communities transformed. So Paul reminds Timothy of what he has witnessed: "And the things you have heard me say in the presence of many witnesses entrust to reliable men who will also be qualified to teach others."

How do you know if a person is reliable and faithful? Let me suggest to you four qualities I always look for when I seek to mentor and disciple a believer in the truths of the gospel.

First, I look for a person with a teachable mind, ready and willing to learn. I look for people who are hungry for truth and serious about following Jesus Christ.

Second, I look for a person with a humble heart, someone who is more concerned for God and others than for building up his own reputation.

Third, I look for a person with an identifiable spiritual gift. Paul mentions this qualification when he says to entrust these truths "to reliable men who will also be qualified to teach others." He is speaking here of the spiritual gift of teaching. Spiritual gifts enable Christians to minister to others, so that the gospel will spread from one person to another, and the church will grow.

Fourth, I look for a faithful spirit. I look for a person who has demonstrated a willingness to keep going even when the going gets tough. I look for someone who is reliable, dependable, and loyal—someone who can be counted on to keep commitments.

A searching mind, a humble heart, an evident gift, a faithful spirit: When you find a Christian with these qualifications, then pour your knowledge, faith, insight, and experience into that person. Mentor that person, just as Jesus mentored the Twelve, just as Paul mentored Timothy. That is how the truth of the gospel spreads from person to person, from generation to generation.

Lock up all the preachers!

I once visited a church that, years ago, had a vibrant and exciting ministry. For a while, that church had an astounding influence on the surrounding community. Then, calamity: The church was rocked by a dispute. The congregation split, many people left, and the church never regained its former vitality and influence. During my visit to that church, I asked one of the elders what went wrong.

He replied, "It was our fault as elders. We assumed that the younger generation had the same understanding of the Scriptures that we did. We were mistaken. We had failed to disciple the next generation of elders. As a result, we ordained elders who did not understand and respect the authority of Scripture."

In short, this church had failed to entrust the truth of God's Word "to reliable men who will also be qualified to teach others."

Every church is just one generation away from apostasy. The work of a church can fall apart in a single generation if the leaders fail to pass on God's truth to the next generation. Our faith is not passed down through our DNA. It is not absorbed by osmosis. It must be faithfully taught, parents to children, leaders to followers, mentors to disciples. Those who are old and wise in the faith must entrust their wisdom to the young. If we fail to transmit God's truth to the next generation, we should not be surprised if that generation falters in the hour of crisis.

When Mao Zedong and his Communist forces took over China in 1949, all of the Western missionaries were forced to leave the Chinese mainland. Christians around the world wrung their hands and said, "This is a disaster! The church will never survive under the Communist heel. The Chinese Christian movement is doomed!"

After the death of Mao, the door to China opened again. Western Christians were amazed to discover that the Chinese church had multiplied sevenfold during the years of persecution and oppression. Why? It turned out that the church in China had stood strong because, prior to the Communist takeover, the missionaries had entrusted God's truth to reliable people who are qualified to teach others. Even during times of opposition, God's truth spread. The church in China endured.

One of God's most effective ways of evangelizing is to lock up all the preachers. Paul stated this principle when he wrote from prison, "Because of my chains, most of the brothers in the Lord have been encouraged to speak the word of God more courageously and fearlessly" (Philippians 1:14). As we see apostasy spreading in many parts of Christendom, we must remember, as the poet James Russell Lowell put it:

> Though the cause of evil prosper,
> Yet 'tis truth alone that's strong.
> Truth forever on the scaffold,
> Wrong forever on the throne.
> Yet that scaffold sways the future,
> And behind the dim unknown,
> Standeth God within the shadows
> Keeping watch above his own.

How shall we respond when the truth is under attack and people all around us seek to water down the Christian faith? Turn loose the lion of truth! Turn it loose in our own lives, in our churches, and in the world around us. If we are faithful to do so, the church will not only stand. It will advance against the enemy with power and might!

CHAPTER 24

Soldiers, Athletes, and Farmers

2 Timothy 2:3–13

One of the most famous heroes of World War I was an Irish-American named Duffy. He wore a soldier's uniform, was a member of the famed Fighting 69th Infantry Regiment, yet he never carried a weapon or fired a shot in battle. He was a chaplain, Father Francis P. Duffy. Though he was a man of faith rather than a man of war, he was awarded the Distinguished Service Cross, the Distinguished Service Medal, and the Croix de Guerre. Today, a statue of Father Duffy stands in Times Square.

Whenever his unit went up to the front, Father Duffy was with them. He counseled the men, calmed their fears, and prayed with them when they were wounded or dying. He was always in the thick of battle, exposed to machine-gun fire and the threat of mustard gas, praying for the safety of his men and lifting their morale. It was often said that his greatest ministry was his ministry of presence.

In mid-July 1918, Father Duffy's unit withstood two straight days of continuous machine-gun fire and shelling. Going without sleep, Father Duffy dedicated himself to rescuing the wounded and ministering to the dying. When it seemed that the enemy was about to overtake their position, a major offered Father Duffy a sack of grenades and a gun. "Here, Father," he said. "You'll need these to make a last stand."

"Thank you," the chaplain replied, "but I've decided to stick to my own trade."

Father Duffy survived that battle and returned home to the streets of New York. He served as pastor of the Holy Cross Church in the roughest section of New York City, a place known as Hell's Kitchen. The streets of Hell's Kitchen were owned by street gangs and organized crime, but Father Duffy ministered there with the same serene courage he demonstrated on the battlefield in France. Though he never fired a shot, Father Duffy was a true hero and a good soldier of Jesus Christ.

We now come to the section where Paul uses this imagery: Stay focused on your mission as a member of the Lord's infantry. Paul writes:

Endure hardship with us like a good soldier of Christ Jesus. No one serving as a soldier gets involved in civilian affairs—he wants to please his commanding officer. Similarly, if anyone competes as an athlete, he does not receive the victor's crown unless he competes according to the rules. The hardworking farmer should be the first to receive a share of the crops. (2 Timothy 2:3–6)

The image of a "good soldier of Christ Jesus" is the first of three metaphors Paul uses to express a powerful theme: When the world is falling apart, Christians must commit themselves to the Lord Jesus Christ. In short, surrender your options, give up all other objectives, and burn your bridges behind you. Follow the Lord.

The soldier's life is hardship

Paul says that the Christian life demands the dedication of a soldier, the discipline of an athlete, and the diligence of a farmer. Why is this message necessary? It's because in every generation there are Christian hangers-on, people who adopt the superficial guise of Christianity but who are not true Christians. They like hanging around Christian people, but they are not willing to endure hardship as a good soldier of Jesus Christ.

Paul brings out two facets of the Christian life that parallel the life of a soldier.

First, the authentic Christian life involves suffering. "Endure hardship with us," Paul says, "like a good soldier of Christ Jesus."

Union General William Tecumseh Sherman famously said, "War is hell." Though General Sherman undoubtedly underestimated hell, it is true that war is the closest thing to hell anyone can experience in this life: the terror, the pain, the screams, the awful suffering of war is beyond the imagination of anyone who hasn't experienced it. War is madness. Sometimes war is necessary, but it is never glorious.

The military recruitment posters will never tell you this, but the essence of a soldier's life is hardship. A soldier is expected to suffer. That's his duty. Soldiers spend months and even years away from home and family. They live under arduous conditions.

Paul says that Christians face a life of hardship as well. The Christian life is not a vacation from reality. It's a battle that we fight every day. We face a relentless enemy who is bent on our destruction. Many Christians have suffered incredible hardships for the sake of the gospel. Some have been martyred. Others have been wounded and carried off the field of battle. Spiritual warfare is not a metaphor. It's the real thing.

Paul says that to be a soldier for Christ, we must be willing to endure hardship and suffering. We must be willing to march into the thick of battle, where the bullets are flying, where our friends are falling and dying. We must be willing to take the gospel message into the mean streets of our inner cities, into the jails and prisons, into the shelters and rescue missions, wherever sin is rampant and human need is great.

"Endure hardship with us," the apostle says, "like a good soldier of Christ Jesus."

The single-mindedness of a soldier

But the life of a soldier not only entails hardship and suffering. It also demands single-mindedness. Paul says that a solder must be dedicated to a single objective: "No one serving as a soldier gets involved in civilian affairs—he wants to please his commanding officer."

Paul's words are particularly true for soldiers in the Roman army. A Roman commander would recruit soldiers who knew him, loved him, and would follow him anywhere. This intense devotion to duty and commanders enabled Rome to conquer much of the known world.

So the apostle Paul picked up on that theme and said, in effect, "This is how Christians should be. This is what Christian devotion should look like. As Christians, we are not serving ourselves. We are committed to serving and pleasing our Lord, our heavenly commander."

Paul makes it clear that we are not to have divided loyalties. We cannot serve our heavenly commanding officer and also serve money. We cannot serve our Commander and also serve fame or pleasure or power. If we try to serve God and serve some idol of our own desires, then we no longer exhibit the single-mindedness of a soldier. Instead, we have become double-minded. And the Scriptures tell us that to be double-minded is to be unstable in all our ways (see James 1:8).

To be single-minded does not mean that we must pursue a full-time ministry career. There is nothing wrong with having a secular job. Paul, for example, was a tentmaker by trade. But Paul did not define himself as a tentmaker; he defined himself as the apostle and a follower of Jesus Christ. He was a Christian, a minister of the gospel, who happened to make tents for a living.

Paul's instruction to be single-minded and dedicated to pleasing our Commander underscores an important principle of the Christian life: Christianity is not a way of doing special things; it's a special way of doing everything. And whatever we do, regardless of our line of work, our objective is clear: We are to manifest the character of Jesus Christ. We are to seek to please Him in everything we do.

The Christian's sole objective should be to follow wherever the Lord Jesus leads. Our motive should be love. The Lord of heaven and earth has done so much for us. How can we ever repay Him? Answer: We can't. But we can serve Him. We can obey Him. We can follow Him to the gates of hell—and those gates cannot prevail against us.

What is our motivation? Our Lord's amazing love. In the words of Charles Wesley's magnificent hymn:

> And can it be that I should gain
> An interest in the Savior's blood?
> Died he for me, who caused his pain—
> For me, who him to death pursued?
> Amazing love! How can it be,
> That thou, my God, shouldst die for me?

Amazing love. That is the motivation of a Christian soldier.

Our noble ambition

Next, the apostle Paul says that the Christian lifestyle requires the discipline of an athlete: "Similarly, if anyone competes as an athlete, he does not receive the victor's crown unless he competes according to the rules."

Here, Paul supplies a different motivation. This motivation is a form of ambition, but a noble ambition. Every athlete learns that he must deny himself certain things if he wants to win. He cannot eat whatever he pleases. He must consume foods that are high in protein and low in fat. That means he must give up chocolate sundaes in favor of low-fat cottage cheese. He must give up smoking, drinking, and wild night life, and he must discipline himself for the competition ahead.

Why does he sacrifice so much for the sake of victory? It's because he wants to win the victor's crown. The crown is nothing but a sprig of laurel leaves plaited in a circle to wear upon the head. But that crown represents an achievement. It tells the world that this athlete was victorious on the field of competition.

One of my favorite motion pictures is *Chariots of Fire*. It's the true story of an athlete who prepares to compete in the 1924 Summer Olympics. The athlete, Eric Liddell, is a Scotsman who was born in China and plans to return there as a missionary after the Olympics. He wants to win, but he wants to win with honor and remain true to his Christian principles. In one of the most memorable scenes in the film, Liddell tells his sister, "I believe that God made me for a purpose, but he also made me fast, and when I run, I feel his pleasure."

In the film, Liddell must say no to a number of things in order to win the victor's crown—and in order to remain true to his Lord. The same is true for you and me as we run the race of the Christian life. We Christians are called to say no to many things the world offers. We are surrounded by temptations and seductive messages, urging us to yield and compromise.

Paul wants us to see ourselves as athletes, as competitors, willing to discipline ourselves for the sake of the victor's crown. He wants us to say no to the things that would cause us to lose our focus. If we are to carry out the mission God has given us, if we are to win the victor's crown, then we must learn the discipline of an athlete. We must compete to win. That is our noble ambition.

Being a Christian is hard work

Next, the apostle Paul tells us that the Christian needs the diligence of a farmer. "The hardworking farmer should be the first to receive a share of the crops."

The emphasis there is upon the word *hardworking*. To some Christians, this is an alien concept. There are all too many Christians who think that the Christian life is focused totally on them. It's all about what God can do for them, not what they should do for God. They have a sense of spiritual entitlement. They think they should be able to pray for a big house with a Mercedes in the garage, and a life of ease, devoid of any major problems. A number of preachers encourage this kind of self-centered Christianity.

Those who adopt this attitude of Christian entitlement have a weak faith that is easily shattered. They think, "I became a Christian so God would bless me. God works for me. His job is to answer my prayers. If He doesn't serve me the way that I expect, then I'm quitting. I will be a Christian only as long as it works for me. If the going gets tough, I'm out of here."

You won't find this kind of Christianity in the Bible. Salvation is a free gift, but it isn't a free ride. Now that we have received the gift of salvation, shouldn't we be grateful? Shouldn't we be willing to demonstrate our gratitude to God by eagerly, joyfully serving Him? There is no greater privilege than that of being a servant of the Lord Jesus, working in partnership with almighty God.

So Paul warns us in this passage against the assumption that we are entitled to a life of ease. The Christian life takes work. To be effective as a Christian requires hours spent studying the Bible, reading books about the Bible, praying and meditating upon the Bible, until you are able to see life the way the Bible depicts it. This is diligent labor. Maturity in Christ doesn't come automatically just because you happen to be a Christian.

Like a farmer, we might have to rise up early and work hard in expectation of a harvest. We may experience a portion of that harvest in this life. But much of the harvest that we labor for will not be ours until we step out of time and into eternity. That is the day for which we labor.

Five motivations

You may say, "If that's what the Christian life consists of, count me out! Why should I trade a life of pleasure for a life of sacrifice and self-discipline?"

Paul has an answer for that question. He supplies five motivations for maintaining our diligence in following Christ. Here is the first one: "Reflect on what I am saying, for the Lord will give you insight into all this" (2 Timothy 2:7).

Paul is telling us to meditate upon his words, to think about the Scriptures and how they apply to our lives. As we reflect on God's message to us, He will give us insight into how these biblical principles make practical sense for our everyday experience. The Scriptures explain the pressures and problems that we face. They give us insight into the spiritual and emotional issues we deal with on a daily basis. They offer sound, practical solutions for our troubled relationships.

God's Word is a mirror that reflects who we truly are with unerring accuracy. In its pages, we discover previously unknown facets of ourselves. The mysteries of life that have baffled us for so long are answered, at least in part, in God's Word. The more we study and meditate in its truths, the better we understand our lives.

The second motivation Paul supplies for being diligent in following Christ is this: "Remember Jesus Christ, raised from the dead, descended from David. This is my gospel" (2 Timothy 2:8).

Here, Paul tells us that he is sustained through his ordeals by the thought of the resurrected Lord Jesus. Because Jesus became human, made like us in His life and death, we shall be made like Him in His resurrection. The resurrection of Jesus is the source of Paul's hope of resurrection. Paul knows it won't be long before he is beheaded and sent to the cemetery. But he also knows that resurrection power shines brightest in the cemetery.

And Paul observes that Jesus was not only resurrected but also was fully human. This same Jesus who was raised from the dead was descended from David. He is one of us. He knows what we are going through. That knowledge sustains Paul through his ordeal of imprisonment. It will sustain him until the moment of his death.

The third motivation for being diligent in following Christ is: "This is my gospel, for which I am suffering even to the point of being chained like a criminal. But God's word is not chained" (2 Timothy 2:8b–9).

Nero could chain Paul like a criminal and confine him to a dungeon cell. But Nero could not chain the gospel. Nero could execute Paul, but he couldn't kill God's Word. Even while the apostle Paul was bound and imprisoned, God's Word was on the loose, being passed from person to person, spreading from city to city, being carried across seas and over mountains, permeating culture after culture across the face of the Roman Empire. No matter what happened to Paul, God's Word was not chained and could not be stopped.

The fourth motivation for being diligent in following Christ is this: "Therefore I endure everything for the sake of the elect, that they too may obtain the salvation that is in Christ Jesus, with eternal glory" (2 Timothy 2:10).

Paul was willing to suffer in order that others would be saved. He was willing to endure the deprivation, discomfort, anxiety, loneliness, boredom, wretched food, and insults of being a prisoner, because he knew his suffering would produce blessing and salvation in the lives of others.

German pastor Dietrich Bonhoeffer was martyred by Hitler during World War II. As he often pointed out, God does not dispense "cheap grace." Grace is free to all who receive it, but grace is costly to those who dispense it. Grace is made possible only by suffering.

The next time you open your Bible, remember: The Bible comes to us soaked in the blood and tears of men and women of generations past. God's people have been chained, tortured, and burned at the stake so that we might have this book. We must never forget that in a fallen world, some must suffer so that others may be blessed. You and I have reaped the rewards of the sufferings of other people. If we are called upon to suffer, then we can be comforted to know that someone else will be blessed.

The fifth and final motivation for being diligent in following Christ is this:

Here is a trustworthy saying:
If we died with him,
we will also live with him;
if we endure,
we will also reign with him.
If we disown him,
he will also disown us;
if we are faithless,
he will remain faithful,
for he cannot disown himself. (2 Timothy 2:11–13)

Again, Paul underscores a message of special importance with the phrase "Here is a trustworthy saying." These lines were undoubtedly part of an early Christian hymn, quoted by the apostle Paul to encourage Timothy. There are four pairs of thoughts in these lines, and the first two pairs connect the trials of this life with the glories of the life to come. If we die with Christ, we will be resurrected and live with Him. If we endure our present trials, we will one day reign with Him.

The apostle is not saying that we earn rewards from God by suffering hardship in this life. We do not serve God to earn favor from Him. We serve Him out of gratitude for His grace and mercy. If we could earn blessings from God, then our service to God would put Him in debt to us. God does not owe anything to anyone.

Next, Paul says, "If we disown him, he will also disown us." God knows if we are genuine or not. He knows if our faith is sincere or not. If we have accepted Christ, in the sense of aligning ourselves with the Christian faith in order to get God to serve us, God knows that our conversion is not authentic. The moment things don't go our way, we will fall away and disown Him. That's what Jesus means when He says, "Many will say to me on that day, 'Lord, Lord, did we not prophesy in your name, and in your name drive out demons and perform many miracles?' Then I will tell them plainly, 'I never knew you. Away from me, you evildoers!'" (Matthew 7:22–23).

Tragically, some people receive Christ as Savior, but they never receive Him as Lord. They may call Him Lord, but they do not obey Him as the Lord and Master of their lives. Instead, they treat Him as a genie in a bottle and demand to be served. If you would have Jesus as your Savior, you must receive Him as Lord.

Next, Paul says, "If we are faithless, he will remain faithful, for he cannot disown himself." Here, Paul recognizes that we, as human beings, will fail from time to time. If we are genuine Christians, if Jesus Christ is the Lord of our lives, there will be times when we stumble. Like Peter, when he denied his Lord, we may prove faithless. Yet God will remain faithful, because we belong to Him, He lives in us, and He will not deny himself. We are sealed by His Holy Spirit, and the Spirit keeps us secure until the end. If we stray, He will bring us back. If we fail, He will restore us.

God has placed us here in front of a watching creation. The universe is observing, waiting to see if our faith is genuine. Will we stand or fall? The answer depends on whether we have truly received the grace of Jesus Christ. If we dedicate ourselves like soldiers, if we discipline ourselves like athletes, if we are diligent like a farmer, then we will experience victory and an abundant harvest to the glory of God.

That is the Christian life to which we are called.

CHAPTER 25

Congregational Gangrene

2 Timothy 2:14–19

Every soldier in training is required to study the strategy and weapons the enemy will use against him. This requirement is all the more urgent for us as Christian soldiers, who face an inhumanly fierce enemy. Satan is a crafty and cunning strategist. Martin Luther correctly described him in the hymn "A Mighty Fortress Is Our God":

> For still our ancient foe
> Doth seek to work us woe;
> His craft and power are great,
> And, armed with cruel hate,
> On earth is not his equal.

Read through the Old Testament and you'll see that every saint, prophet, patriarch, and king of Israel, without exception, suffered at least one major defeat or setback at the hands of the devil. The wisest and greatest of men are helpless to outwit the devil in their own wisdom and strength.

But we are not doomed to defeat. Satan's attacks are devious, yet the Bible clearly shows us how to have victory over Satan. The apostle James writes, "Submit yourselves, then, to God. Resist the devil, and he will flee from you" (James 4:7).

Imagine that! This scheming strategist who has held the world in bondage for centuries will flee if we learn how to resist his devices. As the apostle Paul wrote to the Corinthians, we do not have to be defeated by Satan, because "we are not unaware of his schemes" (2 Corinthians 2:11).

In 2 Timothy, Paul has been addressing the question of how to stand firm and guard the truth in a world that is collapsing around us. This is a relevant issue for our times because we live in a post-Christian age. The pagan and secular culture around us regards the Christian faith as irrelevant and foolish. Now Paul introduces the issue of Satan's tactics and shows us how to prevail over the devil's schemes.

Word battles

Satan will attack the truth of the gospel in any way he can. He may even attack the gospel by making Christians popular and successful, by feeding their egos and diverting them from their real mission of serving God and advancing His agenda. Satan has destroyed many Christian witnesses this way.

Sometimes Satan's attacks are brutal and obvious, involving intense persecution. At such times, he tries to paralyze us with fear and blunt our effectiveness by inciting opposition. At other times, his attacks are more insidious, using clever strategies of pitting one Christian against another—a devilish divide-and-conquer strategy.

But as we are about to see, the apostle Paul is deeply concerned for Timothy and the Ephesian Christians because they are facing a two-front war. Satan is attacking the church in Ephesus from both directions at once. He has stirred up persecution from the outside and polarization within. Paul writes:

> Keep reminding them of these things. Warn them before God against quarreling about words; it is of no value, and only ruins those who listen. Do your best to present yourself to God as one approved, a workman who does not need to be ashamed and who correctly handles the word of truth. Avoid godless chatter, because those who indulge in it will become more and more ungodly. Their teaching will spread like gangrene. (2 Timothy 2:14–17a)

Paul employs strong metaphors to describe the behavior that threatens the ministry of the church at Ephesus. The Ephesian Christians are disputing about words and dividing into factions because of what the apostle calls "word battles" (the literal meaning of the phrase "quarreling about words").

We easily fall into the same trap. Of course, when Christians quarrel over words, those words represent doctrinal viewpoints. Sound doctrine is important, but we often forget that Christian love is at least as important as Christian truth.

An example of the kind of word battles Paul warns against occurred during the Protestant Reformation. In 1529, the founder of the Reformation, Martin Luther, became embroiled in a controversy with the Swiss Protestants over the meaning of the Lord's words, "This is my body," which Jesus spoke when He instituted the Lord's Supper. Luther said that these words should be taken literally. He insisted on the "real presence" of the Lord's body and blood in the consecrated bread and wine. The Swiss Protestants believed that the bread and wine were symbols of the body and blood of Jesus.

Huldrych Zwingli, pastor of the Grossmünster in Zürich and the leader of the Swiss delegation, went to Germany to meet with Luther. He hoped a dialogue with Luther would resolve the controversy. When Luther entered the room for the meeting, he strode to the meeting table with a piece of chalk in his hand and wrote across the length of the table *Hoc est corpus meum,* Latin for "This is my body." Whenever Zwingli tried to speak, Luther would point to those words. He would not hear Zwingli out, or reason with him, or entertain any compromise.

The Reformation was nearly shattered by the controversy and by Luther's intransigence. It's ironic that Luther, who penned the words, "For still our ancient foe / Doth seek to work us woe," played into Satan's scheme of dividing the church.

Such word battles have raged from the early days of the church till this day. After the Council of Nicea in the fifth century, Christians debated the nature of Jesus: Was He of the same substance as God the Father, or was He of like substance as God the Father? The quarrel raged over two nearly identical Greek words: *homoiousious* ("like substance") and *homoosious* ("of the same substance"). This word battle divided Christendom into two camps, and the effects of that controversy are still felt.

I have seen Christians battle one another over such matters as the proper mode of baptism, the proper interpretation of Bible prophecy, styles of worship music, and on and on. Is it right to split the church over such matters? Or should we be more concerned to show love for one another, whatever our differences?

Today, one word that divides many churches is *inerrancy.* This is a good word. It means that the Scriptures were given to us by God through the Bible writers without scientific, historical, or theological error. This is a good doctrine, and I believe it. But people in the church sometimes get so caught up defending the Bible that they forget to practice the essence of Christianity, which is love. They forget that the best way to defend Scripture is to proclaim it.

That's Paul's counsel to Timothy: Avoid word battles. Share the truth of the gospel, and let God's Word defend itself.

Four guidelines

Paul suggests four guiding principles to resolve the quarreling in Ephesus, and they are just as valid for us as they were in Timothy's day.

The first guideline: Avoid quarrels over words. Paul writes, "Keep reminding them of these things. Warn them before God against quarreling about words; it is of no value, and only ruins those who listen."

Paul told Timothy to instruct the Ephesian believers to maintain peace. One of Satan's most brilliant strategies is to divide and conquer. If he can get us to turn our weapons on each other, then he has succeeded in getting us to do his fighting for him.

At the battle of Trafalgar, Admiral Nelson saw two officers of his flagship engaged in a heated argument. When they drew their swords, the admiral stepped between them and pointed to the approaching French fleet. "Gentlemen," he said, "*there* is the enemy!"

We Christians need to remember that our brothers and sisters in Christ are not the enemy. Let's attack Satan, not one another. As Paul tells us, quarreling in the church "is of no value, and only ruins those who listen." The truth of Paul's warning has been demonstrated in church after church down through the centuries.

I once heard of a church that divided over whether or not to have a Christmas tree inside the church building. One faction claimed that Christmas trees, being of pagan origin, defile the church. The other faction believed Christmas trees are a meaningful Christian tradition. The pro-tree faction decorated a tree in the church basement. When the anti-tree faction showed up, they dragged the tree, ornaments and all, into the parking lot. The pro-tree people dragged it back inside. At that point, a fistfight broke out, and someone called the police. The next day, the whole sorry incident was spread across the local newspaper. The witness of that church never recovered.

This is what Paul means when he says that such quarrels only ruin those who listen. Whatever principle was at stake in the quarrel was lost when the community saw a church divided over a ridiculous controversy.

The second guideline: Lead by example. Paul writes, "Do your best to present yourself to God as one approved, a workman who does not need to be ashamed and who correctly handles the word of truth." In other words, be a role model. Set a good example of how to properly handle the Scriptures. Seek the approval of God, not the approval of people.

Many church quarrels are caused by people trying to win the favor of this or that group in the church. Some church leaders succumb to this temptation. They see a controversy growing in the church, and they side with one group or another, often the one that wields the most power. This temptation is especially strong for those who tend to be easily intimidated, as Timothy evidently was. Paul wants Timothy to focus on being a God pleaser, not a people pleaser.

Timothy's response to controversy in the church must reflect the truth of God and the love of God. If his response comes from timidity or a desire to please some faction in the church, that response is not of God.

The third guideline: Do your homework. Paul writes that Timothy is to be "a workman who does not need to be ashamed." Paul urges Timothy to be diligent and thorough when he studies the Scriptures. He is not to impose his biases and preconceived notions on the Scriptures. Instead, he is to teach the whole counsel of God.

I have found that it takes a minimum of ten to twelve hours to prepare a message for a Sunday morning service. When I study a passage of Scripture, I have to look up each word in the Scripture text and find out what it means in the Greek or Hebrew. I have to understand each verse in comparison with other passages of Scripture. I have to understand the culture and customs of that era. It's not easy, but I have a responsibility to correctly handle the Word of truth.

Paul urges Timothy to be a workman who has no need to be ashamed, a workman who has done his homework.

The fourth guideline: Handle God's Word correctly. Paul writes that Timothy is to be a workman "who correctly handles the word of truth." This statement has been widely misunderstood in our day.

I grew up on the Scofield Reference Bible, an extensively annotated Bible that uses the King James Version text. In the KJV, verse 15 reads, "Study to shew thyself approved unto God, a workman that needeth not to be ashamed, rightly dividing the word of truth." As a young Christian, I was told that "rightly dividing" means you must divide the Word according to which part is addressed to the Jews, which to the Gentiles, and which to the church. Then you must divide it according to which part deals with the church versus which deals with the kingdom. Then you must divide it according to which part deals with those under the law and which deals with those under grace.

This approach gave rise to a theological approach called dispensationalism. The dispensationalists teach that you must understand to whom God is speaking in order to properly interpret Scripture. While there is some truth to that view, that's not what Paul is saying here. The text translated "rightly handling" (NIV) or "rightly dividing" (KJV) is a single word in the Greek. That word means "to cut straight." So Paul literally says that the workman of God should "cut straight the Word of truth."

Down through the ages, Bible scholars have struggled to understand what Paul's metaphor means. Some have suggested that he is envisioning a farmer plowing a field. The farmer sets his eye on a landmark at the far end of the field and plows a straight course to that landmark. According to this view, Paul is telling Timothy that as he reads the Scriptures, he is to lay hold of God's truth and not deviate from that. He is to plow a straight course through the Word of truth.

Other commentators have suggested that Paul envisioned a stone mason building a wall. The stone mason drops a plumb line and is careful to cut the stone straight according to that line.

However, I think Paul is probably drawing upon his experience as a tentmaker. Timothy had traveled with Paul and had watched him cut and sew material to make tents. This is a metaphor Timothy would grasp. Paul says, in effect, "When you handle the Scriptures, Timothy, be sure to cut a straight line. Don't try to pull or stretch the fabric of Scripture to make it fit some notion. If you cut a straight line, everything in Scripture fits together naturally."

Paul tells Timothy that all Scripture must be understood in the light of the rest of Scripture. We don't understand a single passage until we have placed it in context with the entire Word of God. If we pull a passage out of context and try to interpret it in isolation from the rest of Scripture, we will end up in error.

So this is Paul's fourfold counsel to Timothy: Avoid quarrels over words. Lead by example. Do your homework. Handle God's Word correctly. If Timothy will do these four things, then he will be a workman of the Word, unashamed and approved by God.

The stench of gangrene

Next, Paul warns Timothy about a special danger in the church: "Avoid godless chatter, because those who indulge in it will become more and more ungodly. Their teaching will spread like gangrene" (2 Timothy 2:16–17a).

Note that first word *avoid.* In the Greek, this word means "take a detour around." In other words, keep your distance and do not get involved. Do not let yourself get drawn into these kinds of word battles and godless talk. The term "godless chatter" literally means "empty babblings" in the Greek. This refers to people who talk without thinking. Paul says Timothy should avoid people who engage in such talk because their "godless chatter" only escalates into greater and greater unwholesomeness.

Godless teaching, Paul says, spreads like gangrene. Because of modern medical care, few of us are acquainted with gangrene, but it was a familiar medical issue in Paul's day. Gangrene occurs when the soft body tissues die and decay due to insufficient blood supply. The dead flesh turns black, becomes putrid, and begins to stink. Once gangrene sets in, it is difficult to treat. It spreads rapidly in the flesh and can kill the patient. Often, the only solution is amputation of the affected area.

Paul tells Timothy that godless chatter is like a gangrenous infection in the church. It spreads, it smells foul, and it threatens the church with death. Once godless chatter sets in, the whole congregation quickly becomes infected. And Paul has an example ready to support his case: "Among them are Hymenaeus and Philetus, who have wandered away from the truth. They say that the resurrection has already taken place, and they destroy the faith of some" (2 Timothy 2:17b–18).

We have already encountered Hymenaeus in Paul's first letter to Timothy, where Paul wrote, "Among them are Hymenaeus and Alexander, whom I have handed over to Satan to be taught not to blaspheme" (1 Timothy 1:20). Some time has passed—probably five years or so—since that first letter was written. Paul has handed Hymenaeus over to Satan in order to teach him a lesson, but Hymenaeus is unteachable. He continues spreading false doctrine in the church at Ephesus, teaching that the resurrection has already taken place.

Apparently, Hymenaeus decided that there would be no bodily resurrection and that when we die we only rise in spirit. Perhaps Hymenaeus was accommodating Christianity to Greek philosophy. According to the Greeks, the physical body is evil, so it's unthinkable that God would resurrect the body. Clearly, Hymenaeus was not rightly dividing the Word of truth. He was compromising God's Word to make it fit worldly doctrines. That's how heresy begins. In spreading this gangrenous doctrine, Hymenaeus ignored the Lord's words: "Do not be amazed at this, for a time is coming when all who are in their graves will hear his voice and come out—those who have done good will rise to live, and those who have done evil will rise to be condemned" (John 5:28–29).

Hymenaeus was a false teacher who denied the truth of the literal resurrection of the body. He upset the faith of many people in the Ephesian church. His words spread the stench of death throughout the congregation—a deadly serious matter. In his first letter to the Corinthians, Paul said that if we have lost the doctrine of the resurrection, we have lost our faith. The weight of Christian truth rests upon whether or not Jesus was bodily raised from the dead—and whether or not we will be raised with Him. If we lose that central truth, then our faith is in vain (see 1 Corinthians 15:17).

A solid foundation

Paul concludes this section of the letter by reminding Timothy of the firm foundation of our salvation and our faith: "Nevertheless, God's solid foundation stands firm, sealed with this inscription: 'The Lord knows those who are his,' and, 'Everyone who confesses the name of the Lord must turn away from wickedness'" (2 Timothy 2:19).

In other words, "Timothy, don't panic over the dissension in your church. Yes, there may be heresy and controversy. You may have to do battle against it, but remember, 'God's solid foundation stands firm in you.'"

Then Paul quotes two statements from Numbers 16 that are opposite sides of the same coin: "The Lord knows those who are his," and, "Everyone who confesses the name of the Lord must turn away from wickedness." Here is an amazing thought: Jesus knew that Judas Iscariot was a traitor from the beginning. The Scriptures tell us that even before Jesus chose him, He knew that Judas would betray Him.

The same principle holds true in the church. Even though there are false teachers in the church, even though heresies rage among us, God's church will not be shaken. His foundation stands firm. The Lord knows who are His and who are not.

The other side of the coin is that we can know those who belong to God when we see them repent of their false teaching and turn back to God. Sometimes, genuine Christians are led astray for a while. They get caught up in false ideas. But those who truly belong to the Lord will eventually see their error and turn back to God.

These two quotations from Numbers 16 deal with the rebellion of Korah, Dathan, and Abiram. During Israel's wandering in the wilderness, these men jealously challenged the authority of Moses and Aaron, saying in effect, "You're no more holy than the rest of us. Why do you think you can tell the rest of us what to do?" So Moses took the problem to the Lord, and the Lord told Moses to separate the rest of Israel from Korah, Dathan, and Abiram. When this was done, the ground opened and swallowed up the three rebellious men, along with everything they owned.

Yes, God knows who are His. Imposters and pretenders should tremble in their boots. Genuine believers cannot compromise with sin and evil forever. They will undergo a struggle, possibly for months or even years. But if they truly belong to God, He will not let them go on in sin. He will draw them back to himself.

Paul's message to Timothy is to avoid quarrels over words. Lead by example. Do your homework. Handle God's Word correctly. Urge those in the congregation to stop quarreling. Do not try to please people by taking sides, but seek to unify the church in a spirit of Christian love. No matter what happens, don't panic. God is in control. His solid foundation will stand firm because God knows those who belong to Him.

That was sound advice for the first-century church in Ephesus. Twenty centuries have come and gone, and Paul's words are no less true today.

CHAPTER 26

Fit for His Use

2 Timothy 2:20–22

If you genuinely belong to Jesus Christ, you will want to be used by God. There is no thrill on earth like that of knowing God has used you to serve others to bring glory to himself. This experience is not just for pastors or evangelists. Any willing follower of Christ can be used as an instrument in the hands of almighty God.

In this next section of Paul's second letter to Timothy, the apostle describes what it means to be fit for God's use:

> In a large house there are articles not only of gold and silver, but also of wood and clay; some are for noble purposes and some for ignoble. If a man cleanses himself from the latter, he will be an instrument for noble purposes, made holy, useful to the Master and prepared to do any good work. (2 Timothy 2:20–21)

Most Bible commentators interpret "a large house" as a reference to the whole professing church. They see the church as the house of God. In fact, Paul did refer to the church as "God's household" in 1 Timothy 3:15. But if we compare this passage to other portions of Scripture, we are forced to extend this analogy not only to the church, but to the whole world. Every person in the world is a possible vessel for God to use, regardless of whether he or she belongs to God or not.

The Scriptures reveal that God, in His sovereignty, can use anyone— even His enemies, even the devil—to accomplish His purposes. In the Old Testament, we are told that Nebuchadnezzar was the servant of God (see Jeremiah 27:6), even though he was a Babylonian pagan. Cyrus the Persian king is called "God's anointed one" (see Isaiah 45:1), even though he too was an unbeliever. If we understand life from the biblical point of view, we must acknowledge that all people can be used of God.

In Exodus, we learn that not only was Moses used as God's instrument, but so was Pharaoh. Paul, in Romans 9, says that Pharaoh was used of God to resist the departure from Egypt so that the greatness of God might be manifest. God raised up Pharaoh, set him on his throne, and used him for His purposes. Paul continues:

> Does not the potter have the right to make out of the same lump of clay some pottery for noble purposes and some for common use?
>
> What if God, choosing to show his wrath and make his power known, bore with great patience the objects of his wrath—prepared for destruction? What if he did this to make the riches of his glory known to the objects of his mercy, whom he prepared in advance for glory—even us, whom he also called, not only from the Jews but also from the Gentiles? (Romans 9:21–24)

So Paul supports the idea that God can use anybody, believer or nonbeliever. The real question is not, "Can God use me?" The question is, "How does God plan to use me? Will he use me for a noble purpose? Or will I be put to common use? Will he use me for blessing—or judgment?"

I once saw a sign on a businessman's desk that read: "My purpose in life is to serve as a warning to others." On the surface, that's an amusing statement, but it is the tragic reality of many human lives. God can use anyone for His purposes, even if only to serve as a warning for others.

God used Judas Iscariot, giving him a place among the Twelve, knowing all along that Judas would betray his Lord. By his act of betrayal, Judas volunteered for the role of fulfilling the Scriptures, which predicted that a friend would lift up his heel against the Messiah and betray Him. Woe to anyone whom God uses as He used Judas Iscariot.

Noble and ignoble

So the great question that confronts us is: "For what purpose is God using me?" Paul says God will use everyone for one of two purposes. "In a large house," he writes, "there are articles not only of gold and silver, but also of wood and clay; some are for noble purposes and some for ignoble."

This is true of every home. Today, as in Paul's time, we have vessels for honorable, noble purposes. We have the dishes we use for dining and entertaining and decorating our homes. These are the noble vessels.

But we also have common vessels for ignoble purposes. We have wastebaskets, mop pails, paint cans, and toilets. These are necessary and useful, but they are not presentable. We do not display them with pride. We keep them out of view.

That's how God sees humanity. Some people are fit for noble purposes while others are Judas-like people, given over to sin and corruption, fit only for ignoble use. At this point, you may ask the question Paul raises: "One of you will say to me: 'Then why does God still blame us? For who resists his will?'" (Romans 9:19).

In other words, if God uses everybody to serve His purposes, why does He then blame people for doing what He intended to accomplish? Isn't God being unjust in judging such people? Many nonbelievers raise this question about God's sovereign justice. In Romans 9, Paul replies with a fourfold answer:

First, he says that humanity, being a finite creation, has no right to judge the wisdom and righteousness of the infinite Creator. The clay has no right to talk back to the Potter. Because we are finite, our understanding is limited, our logic is flawed, and we lack the ability to see reality from God's perspective.

Second, God does not force people to sin in order to accomplish His purpose. Human beings have free will. God did not force Judas to betray Jesus. Rather, in His foreknowledge, He knew that Judas would play the traitor. But Judas made his own choices. God folded the actions of Judas into His eternal plan. God is patient with the human race, showing grace and mercy, and no one who calls out to God is refused.

Third, God is patient and gives people time to repent. Even Judas could have repented of his betrayal, just as Peter repented of his denial, and he would have been saved. It's paradoxical and difficult to understand: The election of God does not cancel out human free will, nor does human free will cancel out God's election. In some mysterious calculus beyond human comprehension, predestination and free will operate in a complementary fashion. We cannot understand it, so we must simply accept it.

Fourth, the objection to God's justice begins from the wrong premise. It assumes that human beings stand in a place of moral neutrality. It assumes that if God did not use this or that person as a vessel for an ignoble purpose, then that person would have remained morally neutral and escaped judgment. That's a false assumption.

No human being is morally neutral. Every human being is born lost. We are victims of Adam's original sin. As Paul wrote, "There is no one righteous, not even one; there is no one who understands, no one who seeks God" (see Romans 3:10–11). Without God's grace, no one would ever be saved. The door of His mercy stands open to all without distinction.

If... then

I hope that this brief detour through Romans 9 will help us to better understand what Paul is saying in 2 Timothy 2. Paul is making a similar analogy in both passages, and it's clear that the analogy of a house and its vessels breaks down at a certain point when it is applied to human beings. In our homes, pots and pans have no choice as to what they will be used for. Unlike pots and pans, human beings have free will.

As Paul states in verse 21, "If a man cleanses himself from the [ignoble purpose], he will be an instrument for noble purposes, made holy, useful to the Master and prepared to do any good work." So we have a choice about whether we will be used by God as a beautiful decorative vase or as a lowly trash can. God is sovereign over the household of humanity, but every member of humanity has free will. If you go through life as a trash can, you have no one to blame but yourself.

Paul's statement "If a man cleanses himself" does not mean that we have the power to redeem ourselves from sin; only Jesus Christ can do that, and He did so on the cross. When Paul speaks of cleansing ourselves in this sense, he refers to the process of repentance and confession by which we are restored to a right relationship with God. This is consistent with what the apostle John writes: "If we confess our sins, he is faithful and just to forgive us our sins, and to cleanse us from all unrighteousness" (1 John 1:9 KJV).

Paul makes it clear that cleansing precedes consecration for use. It is never the other way around. Paul uses a classic logical argument—a conditional statement—to make this point. A conditional statement uses the form "if A, then B." Paul tells us that *if* we cleanse our way and live obediently before God, *then* we will become instruments for noble purposes, made holy and useful to God, prepared for any good work.

What is the condition that determines whether we will be used for noble purposes? Our choice—our willingness to cleanse ourselves and align ourselves with God's plan. That is the only condition. But cleansing must come first, then the consecration for use.

Suppose you go to a rummage sale and find an antique tea cup. It's so encrusted with filth that you can't even see its pattern. You rub it with your thumb, and you see, underneath the grime, a beautiful pattern. You ask the owner, "How did this cup get so filthy?" The owner says, "I kept it in a bag of steer manure, and I used it to spread fertilizer on my lawn."

You purchase the filthy cup, take it home, and cleanse it. You lovingly wash away all the filth with soap and water, and you disinfect it with bleach.

Now you have a beautiful, clean cup. Even though it was once used to scoop manure, you would not hesitate to serve tea in that cup.

But you would never reverse the order of those steps. You would not bring it home, drink tea from it, then cleanse and disinfect it. Cleansing precedes the consecration for use.

To be cleansed means more than saying yes to God. We must also say no to sin and the world. You have to reject the self-centered and sinful philosophies of this world. You have to reject friendship with this world.

Once we have cleansed ourselves from ignoble purposes, Paul says we become a vessel for noble purposes, prepared to do any good work. There is a sense of permanence in this statement. We are permanently set aside in God's mind for useful purposes, for the adventure of being used by God to accomplish great things.

And Paul says we are prepared to do any good work. God can use us in a variety of innovative, unexpected ways. That's why life with God is so interesting. He is endlessly creative, and a life of service to Him is filled with joyful surprises. But it all hinges on our willingness to turn away from sinful habits and rebellious attitudes.

Righteousness, faith, love, and peace

This is the correct interpretation of this passage, as demonstrated by the way Paul specifically applies this principle to Timothy's life. Paul writes: "Flee the evil desires of youth, and pursue righteousness, faith, love and peace, along with those who call on the Lord out of a pure heart" (2 Timothy 2:22).

This is the way to cleanse ourselves from ignoble uses and turn ourselves toward a noble way of life. Paul says, "Flee! Run away as quickly as you can!"

When we hear the phrase "the evil desires of youth," we immediately think of sexual urges, and the phrase Paul uses does include sexual sins. Youth is the time when sexual drives are the strongest. In a sex-drenched society like ours, these passions can become powerful, occupying our minds, becoming an obsession. This verse does include sexual passions, but it means more than that.

Sexual urges aren't the only "evil desires of youth." Young people also desire to be right. They are tempted to be prideful and rebellious. They desire to be contentious and show off how much smarter they are than the gray-haired old fogeys around them.

Remember, the congregation at Ephesus had erupted with controversy. False teachers were spreading lies there, and some in the congregation were ready to follow them. Timothy might have been tempted to argue in a dogmatic way. So Paul warned Timothy about all the various "evil desires of youth," from sexual urges to prideful urges.

It is not wrong for Timothy to defend the faith and stand up for the truth of Scripture. Paul has urged him to do so. But Paul also warns Timothy to beware the sin of pride, the selfish pleasure of putting other people in their place, the adrenaline-laced excitement of getting into shouting matches with opponents. Paul calls Timothy to cleanse himself of everything ignoble, including the evil passions of youth, so God can put him to a noble use.

The first step in cleansing oneself: Flee that which is evil. The second step in cleansing oneself: Pursue that which is good.

Paul goes on to say, "And pursue righteousness, faith, love and peace, along with those who call on the Lord out of a pure heart." Notice those four things that Paul says Timothy is to pursue: righteousness, faith, love, and peace. Each of those positive qualities is presented in Scripture as a gift from God. These are qualities that only God can give, yet God will not give them to you unless you pursue them. You must make a positive, deliberate choice to go after righteousness, faith, love, and peace.

Righteousness means right behavior. Every day as Christians, we are called upon to choose between wrong and right. We have to say no to what is wrong and yes to what is right. We have to say no to unbelief and yes to obedient faith. If you have not learned to say no, if you drift along with whatever the crowd is doing, you will never be an instrument for noble purposes.

Faith means belief that goes beyond mere agreement, belief expressed in action. The Scriptures tell us that "faith comes from hearing the message, and the message is heard through the word of Christ" (see Romans 10:17). The more conscious you are of God's Word, the more you will be stirred up to lay hold of what God says. God will not force himself on those who have no time for His Word. He will use you only when you are ready to seek Him and lay hold of His Word.

Love—genuine, Christlike love—is not an emotion, not a feeling, not an affection. It's a deliberate decision of the will. That's why we can choose to love people who are not loving, lovable, or lovely. That is why Jesus commands us to love our enemies. Love is an action we can choose to perform. Our feelings and emotions may say, "Strike back! Get even!" But we can still choose to obey God and love those who have hurt us, offended us, and treated us as enemies.

Peace means having whole relationships with the people around you. Peace doesn't just happen. We must seek peace; sometimes we must initiate reconciliation. The responsibility for peace is always on each individual believer. If you have been grievously offended by another believer, you are responsible to go to that person in a spirit of love and forgiveness and seek peace. If you know you have offended another believer, you are responsible to go to that person in a spirit of repentance and contrition and seek to make peace.

Surround yourself with Christian fellowship

Paul says, "Pursue righteousness, faith, love and peace, along with those who call on the Lord out of a pure heart." What does Paul mean? Who are these pure-hearted people he speaks of? Understand, Paul is not speaking of "Holy Joes" who have never done anything wrong. A better translation of the word *pure* would be "cleansed." Paul is speaking of people who have been cleansed by repentance and forgiveness.

Along with my friend and fellow pastor, Steve Zeisler, I once visited the California State Prison, Solano, in Vacaville, California. We spent the day there, and it was the most remarkable experience to have fellowship with Christian brothers in a place so filled with hate, corruption, and, at times, violence. It was a rainy day, so no one went out in the prison yard. The halls were crowded with people who stood talking or staring at the two preachers who had invaded their turf.

In the chapel, I sat next to a gang member who had been convicted of multiple murders. While in prison, he had stabbed several people. Though he had once been one of the most vicious killers in the prison, God had reached him, saved him, and transformed him into one of the gentlest people in the prison population. He witnessed to the other prisoners and had led a number of them to Christ.

I asked one of the Christian leaders in the prison what was the most difficult aspect of prison ministry. He said, "The hardest thing is seeing so many lives dramatically changed—but when they get out, many go back to their old lives."

"Why?" I asked. "Why would they go back to sin and crime after they have found Jesus Christ in prison?"

He said, "Because they go back to the same old crowd. Their old friends drag them back into their old life."

We were not made to live alone. God created us to live in community with others. We become like the people we associate with. This doesn't mean that we should avoid contact with non-Christians. But we need to soak up the fellowship of other believers. We need to immerse ourselves in an atmosphere of Christian community. If we fail to do so, if we spend most of our time with people whose hearts are turned away from God, then it won't be long before we are just like them.

Paul tells Timothy, "If you want to be used as a noble instrument of God, then cleanse yourself. Say no to sin and worldliness. Say yes to righteousness, faith, love, and peace. Seek fellowship with people who call upon the Lord with a cleansed and purified heart.

Then live the adventure of being used in a mighty way by almighty God.

CHAPTER 27

Guidelines for Controversies

2 Timothy 2:23–26

The nineteenth-century evangelist Charles Haddon Spurgeon used to speak of those who "go about with theological revolvers in their ecclesiastical trousers." The theological gunslingers Spurgeon warned about are still with us—and there were a few in the Ephesian church in Timothy's day.

When Paul wrote his second letter to Timothy, he knew the church in Ephesus was rocked by theological arguments and divisions. Here the apostle tells Timothy—and us—how to handle conflict and controversy in the church. He writes:

> Don't have anything to do with foolish and stupid arguments, because you know they produce quarrels. And the Lord's servant must not quarrel; instead, he must be kind to everyone, able to teach, not resentful. Those who oppose him he must gently instruct, in the hope that God will grant them repentance leading them to a knowledge of the truth. (2 Timothy 2:23–25)

Some people misinterpret these words of Paul. They think he is saying, "Never get involved with any kind of controversy. Don't ever take sides or argue any issue." But that's not what Paul is saying.

While it's unhealthy for a church to be rocked by conflict, it can be equally unhealthy for a church to sweep serious issues under the rug. When there are differences of opinion about ministry and doctrinal issues, we need to find positive, loving ways to discuss those issues and resolve them. Unresolved problems have a way of festering until they explode, suddenly and catastrophically. But creative tensions and differing points of view, when discussed in a Christlike spirit, can be healthy for a church.

Foolish and stupid controversies

We can be grateful that past controversies have helped to clarify God's truth. The great hymn, "A Mighty Fortress Is Our God," resulted from the controversy that raged around Martin Luther over the doctrine of justification by faith. That controversy, as painful as it was for the church in that era, cleared the air on an important doctrinal issue.

Paul wants Timothy to know that there are certain kinds of controversies that he must never get involved in. "Don't have anything to do with" such controversies, Paul says. Paul mentions the kind of controversies that Timothy should avoid. In English translations, it seems that Paul is being redundant, because he speaks of "foolish" and "stupid arguments." What's the difference between "foolish" and "stupid"?

In the Greek, there is a distinction. The word the NIV translates *foolish* is, in the Greek, *moros,* from which we get our English word *moron.* Paul is warning against moronic controversies over trivial matters that make us look foolish. Such controversies do not advance the Christian cause.

An excellent example of a foolish argument occurred in the Middle Ages, when scholars of the church had lengthy, heated debates over such matters as how many angels can dance on the head of a pin. We have equally foolish arguments in the church today. I've heard people debate at length whether this or that prominent world figure has a name that can be numerically reduced to the numbers 666. For hundreds of years, people have played this game, trying to deduce the identity of the Antichrist, based on a numerical code from the book of Revelation. This is utter foolishness.

The second form of controversy involves what Paul calls "stupid arguments." The word the NIV translates *stupid* is, in the Greek, *apaideutos.* This word literally means "unlearned" or "uninstructed." This refers to arguments that arise out of ignorance—questions that are essentially insoluble because we will never have enough information to arrive at an answer. Down through the centuries, there have been many controversies over *apaideutos* issues. Christians have angrily debated matters that cannot be resolved with certainty.

An excellent example is the issue of baptism. Some Christians argue over what mode of baptism the early church must have used. The reason for this argument is obvious: If we can establish the original mode of baptism, we can demonstrate what the mode of baptism ought to be for the church today. One side will claim that the early church immersed; another side claims the early church sprinkled; another claims the early church poured water over the believer's head. The controversy can be carried to even finer distinctions: Were early believers baptized face forward or face backward? And on and on, ad infinitum.

The fact is, we don't know the answers to any of these questions—so why argue? I think one reason the New Testament text is vague on these issues is that they are not important. Like the Pharisees, we easily get obsessed with symbols and rituals, and we forget that God cares about the reality of the heart. It doesn't matter how we get wet. The only thing that matters is that baptism is an outward expression of an inward change.

I have heard people have angry debates over the question of human free will versus God's sovereign election. According to human logic, this question is a paradox. It would seem that either human beings have free will or are predestined by God's sovereign election. It is hard to understand how both can be true. So people argue the issue, and churches and denominations have split over the question. The cause of Christ is hindered by these conflicts that have no clear resolution.

Five guidelines

It's healthy to have a number of viewpoints in the church. Wouldn't it be boring if everyone thought alike? Who wants to worship in a church full of robots?

But as followers of Christ, we need to deal with our differences in a Christlike way. Can we discuss our differences? Of course. We can and we should. But when our "discussions" breed quarrels, then we have sinned and dishonored God. When we push our own viewpoint to the extent that we disparage others and treat our brothers and sisters with disrespect, then we are engendering division in the body of Christ. That is sin, and it's the kind of foolishness Paul says we must avoid.

What, then, is a fit and proper issue to discuss? What about some of the vital and central doctrines of the Christian faith, such as the inspiration of Scripture, the virgin birth, or the miracles in the Old and New Testaments? What about some of the burning social issues of our day, such as poverty, the environment, and abortion? These are important issues, and people feel strongly about them. Some Christians are so invested in these issues that they cannot compromise an inch without feeling they've betrayed the cause. How are we to discuss such issues in the church?

The apostle Paul gives us five clear guidelines to follow. If we obey his teaching, we will be able to discuss even difficult theological and social questions and still maintain the unity of the body of Christ.

As we examine these five guidelines, note, first, that one is stated in the negative while four are stated in the positive. Let's look at Paul's negative guideline first: "The Lord's servant must not quarrel." What does Paul mean by "the Lord's servant"? In the broadest sense, he is referring to any Christian. All believers are servants of the Lord. All believers are expected to exhibit a Christlike spirit.

A Christian leader like Timothy should be especially conscious of the example he sets before the congregation. A leader is a role model. But those of us in the church who are followers rather than leaders should not think that this command excludes us.

Christians should not quarrel. We should not be theological gunslingers who shoot from the lip. Every Christian should demonstrate Christlike love and humility. When there is controversy in the church, we should not set out to win arguments, squash the opposition, or silence dissent. We should encourage discussion, listen to all sides, practice patience and caring, and seek a godly resolution to the disagreement.

Next, Paul offers four positive guidelines, four descriptions of what the Lord's servant should be like. The first of these four guidelines is that "he must be kind to everyone." Everyone? Yes, everyone! Even if our opponent is angry, unreasonable, or has an ax to grind, we are to be kind to everyone. The Greek word here is *epios*, meaning "gentle and affable"; the best English translation might be "approachable."

When I was a student at Dallas Seminary, I had a Bible teacher who was a godly, gifted man. I had great respect for his Bible knowledge. I went to see him about a Bible question, and he was so stern and harsh that I never asked him another question. I listened to him teach, but I never went to speak with him again. He was not approachable. The Lord's servant, Paul says, must be kind and approachable.

The second positive guideline is that the Lord's servant must be "able to teach." In other words, he or she must deal realistically with biblical facts, not whims, wishes, or feelings. The Lord's servant must be able to call people to a recognition of the truth.

A friend and I once had a discussion about some biblical issue, and he pointed out some facts about the Scripture passage that I wasn't aware of. The moment he brought out those facts, the discussion was settled. He was right, and I was wrong. So I said, "The trouble with you is that you don't know how to argue. You just deal with facts. We can't get a good argument going if you insist on sticking to the facts." We both laughed, but it's true: A lot of arguments can be settled if the Lord's servant is able to teach from God's Word.

The third positive guideline is that the Lord's servant must be patient. I know, the NIV text says "not resentful," and that sounds like a negative guideline. But in the Greek text, the word Paul uses is *anexikakos,* which is a positive term meaning "patient" or "forbearing." Paul is telling us that the Lord's servant must remain cool, calm, and unruffled. When people become angry and contentious, the Lord's servant does not strike back. Instead, he or she responds in the same way Jesus responded: "When they hurled their insults at him, he did not retaliate" (see 1 Peter 2:23).

Understand, willpower alone will not help you to handle the pressure of being attacked and insulted. The Lord's servant must rely upon the Lord's power and the Lord's Spirit in order to respond in a Christlike way. When attacked, we must pray for God's strength to respond as Jesus would respond. That's where true forbearance and patience come from in times of conflict.

The fourth positive guideline is that "those who oppose him he must gently instruct, in the hope that God will grant them repentance leading them to a knowledge of the truth." Here, Paul sums up all the qualities he has just mentioned. When the Lord's servant gets caught up in a controversy, he or she must not quarrel but must be kind and gentle, able to teach, patient and forbearing, continually praying that God will use this controversy to produce peace, understanding, and Christlike character.

Three outcomes

There is an old saying, "A man convinced against his will is of the same opinion still." It's like the story of the defiant little boy whose mother ordered him to sit down. At first he refused, but when the mother threatened to impose punishment, the boy sat. Then he said, "I may be sitting on the outside, but I'm standing on the inside!" That's not the kind of resolution we seek to the controversies in the church. Our goal is not to force people to sit down but to enable us all to stand together.

Paul concludes with these words:

> Those who oppose him he must gently instruct, in the hope that God will grant them repentance leading them to a knowledge of the truth, and that they will come to their senses and escape from the trap of the devil, who has taken them captive to do his will. (2 Timothy 2:25–26)

Sometimes a conflict that seems utterly hopeless is a golden opportunity for deeper understanding. Paul suggests three positive outcomes that can flow from controversy when we follow God's guidelines for resolving conflict.

First, God may enable our opponent to come to a place of repentance. Paul writes that we should gently instruct others "in the hope that God will grant them repentance." That's a remarkable statement. Paul says that repentance is not something a person chooses; it is something God enables a person to do.

What does repentance mean? It doesn't merely mean to feel sorry, although sorrow is a first step toward repentance. Repentance means to change your attitude and your heart. The ability to experience such change is a gift of God. According to our own understanding, most of us are too stubborn to choose repentance. In order for us to experience repentance, God must open our eyes to the truth we are unable to see in our own limited wisdom.

So we must ask the great Mediator, the Prince of Peace, to break down the middle wall of partition that separates us from others. We are not responsible for any particular resolution to the controversy. We are only responsible to obey God's Word and conduct ourselves in a Christlike way. As Paul wrote elsewhere, "If it is possible, as far as it depends on you, live at peace with everyone" (Romans 12:18).

The second outcome we should pray for, Paul says, is that our opponent would come "to a knowledge of the truth." The truth Paul speaks of is scriptural truth. We can truly know that repentance has been granted if our opponent comes to a place where he or she agrees with Scripture. If this person accepts what the Bible says and knows it to be true, then the person has been granted repentance by God.

The third outcome we should pray for, Paul says, is that our opponent may "escape from the trap of the devil." Satan's goal is to destroy Christians and ruin their effectiveness for God. He seeks to take away their joy and peace by trapping Christians in confusion and deception.

A young man once drove five and a half hours to talk with me about a problem in his marriage. He and his wife were Christians and had been married for a dozen years. Lately, he had fallen in love with another woman.

He said, "A woman has come into my life, and she meets my needs, she turns me on, she makes me feel fulfilled! But I'm conflicted. I've always believed it's a sin to betray my wedding vows, but I think God may want me to leave my wife and marry this other woman."

I asked, "What makes you think God would want you to do that?"

"Well," he said, "the other night, I had a dream that the Lord came and told me it was the right thing to do."

This man had come to me, hoping I would tell him that God would bless him if he divorced his wife and married the woman he was having an affair with! I wondered if this dream came from his subconscious—or if it was sent by Satan to deceive him.

I knew God's Spirit would never tell a Christian to do what God's Word condemns as sin. But I listened to him patiently and didn't treat him harshly. I explained to him, as gently as I could, that no matter how pleasurable his experience with the other woman might be, God would not bless him if he betrayed his marriage vows. I pointed out that from God's point of view, this situation came under the heading of an ugly word.

"I know the word you mean," he said. "*Adultery*. And I know you're right."

At that moment, I knew God had granted this man repentance. That was the moment he made the decision to leave the other woman, renew his marriage vows, and begin rebuilding his marriage. He thanked me for leading him back to the Word of truth.

I am still learning what it means to be the Lord's servant in times of conflict and controversy. I have made more than my share of mistakes. But I am discovering that when we faithfully conduct ourselves according to the guidelines Paul gave to Timothy in this passage, we can have a hand in releasing God's power to grant repentance to others, so that they can escape the trap of the devil and come to a knowledge of the truth.

In times of controversy and conflict, that is the ministry we've been given by the Prince of Peace.

CHAPTER 28

Dangerous Times

2 Timothy 3:1–9

In April 1982, a full-page ad ran in *The Los Angeles Times* and eighteen other newspapers around the world. The headline announced, "Christ Is Already Here." The ad went on to say that Christ was living in a secret location and that on June 21 of that year he would be revealed to the human race on every television channel throughout the world. Not only was this soon-to-be-revealed person the second coming of Christ but also the second coming of Buddha (Maitreya), the Jewish Messiah, the Imam Mahdi of the Muslims, and the Kalki avatar of the Hindu god Vishnu.

June 21 came. *Monday Night Football* and the *Monday Night Movie* ran as scheduled on television, uninterrupted by any appearance by Christ-Buddha-Messiah-Mahdi-Kalki. I later learned that the advertisements had been placed by an eccentric British Theosophist named Benjamin Creme, who writes and lectures extensively on Eastern religion, UFOs, crop circles, and other exotic lore. Over the years, Mr. Creme has repeatedly announced the revelation of a New Age messiah who would unite all nations, religions, and peoples as one, ushering in a new millennium of global peace.

Yet the world keeps turning, with its wars, racism, poverty, crime, nuclear threat, and environmental problems. Decades after Mr. Creme announced that "Christ Is Already Here," the supposed messiah remains in hiding.

There's no shortage of would-be messiahs in our society. Some seek fame via the global media. Others lead their cults into the desert or the jungle. Whatever form these false christs take, they provoke speculation among Christians: "Are we living in the last days? Does the proliferation of false messiahs signal that the world is preparing itself for the greatest false messiah of all, the Antichrist?"

The last days

We now come to a discussion many Christians interpret as a reference to the last days before the return of our Lord Jesus Christ. Paul writes:

But mark this: There will be terrible times in the last days. People will be lovers of themselves, lovers of money, boastful, proud, abusive, disobedient to their parents, ungrateful, unholy, without love, unforgiving, slanderous, without self-control, brutal, not lovers of the good, treacherous, rash, conceited, lovers of pleasure rather than lovers of God. (2 Timothy 3:1–4)

This passage reads like a summary of the evening news, doesn't it?

I recall reading this passage when I was in elementary school. I remember being filled with a sense that the end of the world was just around the corner. After all, the world at that time was filled with self-centered, greedy, arrogant, abusive, unforgiving, brutal people. The world was in the grip of the Great Depression, and the storm clouds of approaching global war were on the horizon. I heard adult Christians speculating that we were in the last days and could expect the Lord's return at any moment.

So I was aware, even as a boy, that this passage was viewed by many as a prediction of the last days of the church, shortly before the return of Christ. But I believe that if you understand what this passage is truly saying, it becomes clear that Paul's phrase "the last days" refers to the entire period of time between the first appearance of Jesus on earth and His return. We have been living in the last days for two thousand years.

This interpretation is affirmed in Acts 2. There, on the day of Pentecost, Peter quoted the Old Testament prophet Joel:

"'And it shall come to pass in the last days, says God,
That I will pour out of my Spirit on all flesh;
Your sons and your daughters shall prophesy,
Your young men shall see visions,
Your old men shall dream dreams.'" (Acts 2:17)

After reciting that prophecy about the last days, Peter said that the prophecy was being fulfilled that day. And in the New Testament book of Hebrews, we read, "God... has in these last days spoken to us by his Son" (see Hebrews 1:1–2). So it is clear that in the New Testament, this phrase "the last days" refers to a time that began immediately after the resurrection and ascension of the Lord Jesus Christ. That period continues to this day. We now live in the last days.

Again and again over the past two millennia, our world has experienced stretches of relative peace and prosperity, interrupted at intervals by terrible times of agony and catastrophe. So these words from Paul to Timothy are not necessarily a prediction of the last days for the church. Rather, they are a recognition of the cycles the world undergoes on a periodic basis. And Paul wants us to know that these times of stress will be accompanied by false teachers, and we need to be careful not to be misled by them. He describes those false teachers as "having a form of godliness but denying its power. Have nothing to do with them" (2 Timothy 3:5).

In other words, Paul tells us that the primary cause of these repetitive cycles of stress and danger is the hypocritical lives of people who profess to be Christians. They outwardly seem pious and religious but inwardly do not have the power of God in their lives. Hypocritical Christianity is the reason for these recurring cycles of upheaval.

I'm convinced that few of us truly grasp what the Scriptures are saying to us about the nature of the church. God tells us throughout the New Testament that the church is the most important body in the world. God has built all of society and all of history around what happens in the church. The church controls history. And when the church ceases to be what God has commanded it to be, the world suffers.

"You are the salt of the earth," Jesus tells us. "But if the salt loses its flavor, how shall it be seasoned? It is then good for nothing but to be thrown out and trampled underfoot by men" (see Matthew 5:13 NKJV). When Christians lose their saltiness, the whole world goes to pot. "You are the light of the world," the Lord says (see Matthew 5:14). When our light dims, the whole world sinks deeper into darkness.

Lovers of themselves

Everywhere I go, I'm saddened to see the level of biblical ignorance among church members. Again and again, I talk to Christians and discover that they have only the most superficial knowledge of the Scriptures. As one man said to me, "I thought Dan and Beersheba were husband and wife, like Sodom and Gomorrah."

But the problem goes much deeper than a mere lack of Bible knowledge. Christians everywhere seem to have little understanding of the deep truths that the Bible reveals. They do not seem to understand how to apply Scripture to their lives and how to use God's Word to better understand human nature and human events. This kind of ignorance results in a manifestation of godless attitudes among people in the church.

In Romans 1, there's a passage that begins, "For the wrath of God is revealed from heaven against all ungodliness and unrighteousness of men."

And Paul goes on to list dozens of horrible sins and vices. Do not make the mistake of thinking that Paul is making the same point here in 2 Timothy 3 that he makes in Romans 1. The list of sins and vices in Romans 1 describes conditions in the world. The list of sins and vices in 2 Timothy describes conditions within the church, among people who profess to be Christians, who have a form of religion but lack the power of God within. Let's take a closer look at Paul's four-point analysis of the problem in the church.

The first section flows from that first term, "lovers of themselves." This is the basic sin of humanity. Self-love is the vilest form of idolatry because it is the worship of oneself as a god. It deprives God of the worship we owe Him, and it sets a rival god, the self, upon the throne of our lives. Paul tells us that many professing Christians, though they attend church, partake of the sacraments, and sing hymns, are lovers of themselves.

The first and primary expression of self-centeredness is that people become "lovers of money." Why are many Christian people so materialistic? If you look at the lives of Christians, you often find it hard to tell their values from the values of the world. They seek a constantly increasing standard of living, an ever more luxurious lifestyle, and a lack of generosity toward God's work and the poor. They use their money to indulge themselves, and though they claim to love God, they have truly become lovers of money.

People often point to the persecuted church in places like Communist China, and they wonder how the church can survive under such difficult conditions. But history shows that it is not persecution that destroys the church; it is prosperity, which often leads to love of money.

The next expression of self-centeredness is that people become boastful and proud. It troubles me to hear churches brag about their multimillion-dollar budgets, or how many thousands of worshipers attend, or the beautiful new buildings they have just constructed. It sometimes seems that these churches love to draw attention to themselves rather than to their Lord. This, too, is result of self-love.

Boastful pride can also take the form of contempt for others. Many Christians seem to have a self-righteous attitude toward the sins of others. They look down their noses at others who have been caught in an open, blatant sin, especially sexual sin. They use derisive terms for homosexuals, prostitutes, people who visit prostitutes, pornographers, and on and on. They are quick to pronounce judgment on sinners with the same scorn practiced by the Pharisees in our Lord's day. That's why Jesus spoke so sharply to the Pharisees and so kindly to prostitutes and sinners.

The next expression of self-centeredness is that people become "abusive." This word describes people who are insulting and deliberately hurtful toward others. This is a manifestation of an unhealthy, unwholesome, unchristian spirit within the Christian church.

The breakdown of the home

The next section flows from the term "disobedient to their parents," and it refers to the breakdown of the home that we see taking place within the Christian church. This section is addressed primarily to younger Christians.

We have become accustomed to horrific crimes in the news, but here is a crime that shocked even the most jaded news watchers: Fourteen-year-old Kara and eighteen-year-old David both came from Christian homes. They became infatuated with each other and, in defiance of their parents' wishes, began spending all their spare time together.

One night, Kara told her parents she was spending the night with a girlfriend, but instead she spent the night with David. When David brought Kara home early the next morning, her parents were waiting. Aware of Kara's deception, they decided to confront her and David. They had no way of knowing that the duffel bag in David's hand contained several guns.

In the front yard of Kara's home, while her father had his back turned, David pulled a handgun from the bag and shot Kara's father in the head, killing him in cold blood. Then he went into the house and shot Kara's mother dead in front of the girl's eleven- and fifteen-year-old siblings.

David grabbed his now-orphaned girlfriend by the arm, and they fled in his car. Police caught up with them thirty hours later, two states away. Just days before, David had bragged to friends that he could "kill someone and get away with it."

Paul said that in the last days, young people in Christian homes would become disobedient to parents. Here was a young man from a Christian home who murderously fulfilled Paul's prediction.

Following "disobedient to parents," Paul links the word *ungrateful*. He refers to young people in Christian homes who are uncaring about the labor and sacrifice their parents have expended to provide for them.

The next word is *unholy*. This suggests an unwillingness to observe even the basic decencies of life. Such people seem to take pride in ungodly behavior. They are shameless. They enjoy shocking people and provoking disgusted reactions.

Next, Paul speaks of people who are "without love." They lack normal human affections. They are brutish, beastly, and cruel. Next is "unforgiving." Such people are relentlessly bitter. You can't reason with them, you can't appease them, you can't soften their response no matter how you try. Even if you apologize to them, they throw your apology back in your face.

And we must remember that these attitudes all are to be found among people professing to be Christians. They go to church on Sunday, and they go through all the Christian motions. But during the week, at home and in the office, they are self-centered, cruel, and implacable.

Interpersonal relationships

The next section of Paul's list deals with the area we would call interpersonal relationships. The next word Paul chooses is *slanderous.* The Greek word is *diabolos,* meaning "devil" or "false accuser." It is the word from which we get our English word *diabolical,* meaning "devilish" or "fiendish."

The next term Paul uses is "without self-control." The Greek word literally means "incontinent," that is, lacking the ability to control one's bodily functions. It speaks of people who refuse to govern their own behavior and who satisfy their lusts without conscience.

The next word, *brutal,* means "savage" or "fierce." Paul is suggesting someone who is animalistic in nature, a brute.

Next, Paul speaks of those who are "not lovers of the good." In the Greek, this is a single word with a much stronger meaning. Paul is speaking of people who are aggressively hostile toward good people and good things. Such people do not simply not love the good; they despise and hate that which is good.

This was the charge the Lord Jesus leveled against the Pharisees. The Pharisees loved to be seen as morally respectable, but deep within, they opposed God and hated what was good. The Lord's accusation was proven when the Pharisees plotted the death of Jesus, a man in whom there was no fault.

Paul's next word is *treacherous.* This word speaks of a traitor, a betrayer who would hand his friends or his cause over to an enemy. This same Greek word is used in Luke 6:16 to refer to Judas Iscariot, who betrayed Jesus.

The next word, *rash,* means "reckless and careless." This is the kind of person who would drive seventy miles an hour through a school zone, not caring who might get hurt. Rash people act impulsively and don't think about the consequences.

Then there is "conceited." The Greek word means inflated or swollen with arrogance. Today, we would say that such a person has a swelled head.

All of these sins and vices create damage, dysfunction, and pain in relationships. If you know a person who has one or two of these traits, he can be difficult to live with. If he has a cluster of these traits, then he probably makes your life miserable.

Religious pretensions

The final section deals with the religious pretensions of such people. They are, Paul says, "lovers of pleasure rather than lovers of God, having a form of godliness but denying its power." We have to ask ourselves: Why? Why would people who profess the truth, who sing the hymns, who observe the sacraments and religious rituals—why would such people display the sins, vices, and brutal attitudes Paul describes?

Answer: They have a form of godliness but deny its power. They wish to be seen as good, religious people, but they deny the very power that makes Christians different from the rest of the human race.

What is the power they deny? Elsewhere in the New Testament, the apostle Paul tells us plainly: "For the message of the cross is foolishness to those who are perishing, but to us who are being saved it is the power of God" (1 Corinthians 1:18). The message of the cross is the power of God. When you let the cross have its effect upon you, then you experience the release of God's power in your life.

When people who profess to be Christians deny the word of the cross, they practice a kind of institutional religion, a Christianity without Christ, a semblance of godliness without God, a spirituality without the Spirit. The word of the cross is that which puts the life of the self to death. Jesus said it plainly: "If anyone would come after me, he must deny himself and take up his cross daily and follow me" (see Luke 9:23; see also Matthew 16:24, Mark 8:34). The cross is an instrument of death, and it exists to put sin to death within us, so that we can enter into eternal life. If we are unwilling to deny the self and crucify the sin, then we are unable to experience new life in Christ.

That's why we must consistently practice what we preach. We must say no to all the rebellious uprisings of the flesh within us so that we can lay hold of God's supply of power and life that enables us to walk with Him in righteousness and truth. If we do not say no to the flesh, then we contribute to these terrible cycles of tragedy and devastation that repeatedly come upon humanity.

Satan's two-pronged strategy

In the next three verses, Paul goes on to describe another form of religious pretension: pseudo-Christian cults. The many cults that abound today were begun, for the most part, by people who proclaimed themselves to be Christians but were utterly hypocritical—people of corrupt mind and counterfeit faith. Paul writes:

> They are the kind who worm their way into homes and gain control over weak-willed women, who are loaded down with sins and are swayed by all kinds of evil desires, always learning but never able to acknowledge the truth. Just as Jannes and Jambres opposed Moses, so also these men oppose the truth—men of depraved minds, who, as far as the faith is concerned, are rejected. (2 Timothy 3:6–8)

Here Paul reveals two favorite strategies of the devil: infiltration and imitation. Satan uses morally corrupt and hypocritical Christians, people who profess to be Christians, who talk like Christians but who do not live like Christians. They will either infiltrate the church or they will go out into the world, imitating genuine Christians. In these two ways, Satan generates cults that have church-like features but are not the true church of Jesus Christ.

As we have noted earlier, there have been two major waves of this kind of activity in the world. One occurred in the nineteenth century, when cults like the Jehovah's Witnesses, Christian Science, Theosophy, Mormonism, and other groups arose. It happened again with the explosion of cults in the mid-twentieth century—Scientology, the Moonies, the Eastern-related cults, metaphysical groups, EST, and other mind-bending pseudo-religious cults. Let's take a closer look at Satan's two-pronged strategy to seduce human beings ever deeper into error.

Satan's first tactic is infiltration. The devil works through certain misguided people, whom Paul calls "men of depraved minds, who, as far as the faith is concerned, are rejected"—that is, they are rejected by God because their faith is counterfeit and hypocritical. For their own benefit and advancement, they make their way into households and take captive gullible people whom Paul calls "weak-willed women, who are loaded down with sins and are swayed by all kinds of evil desires." These are people who believe anything they are told.

You might object that Paul is being sexist in singling out weak-willed women. Does this mean that women who work at home are morally weak and intellectually gullible? Obviously not. That's not Paul's point. So let's not get off on a tangent about Paul being sexist. He is speaking of a certain kind of person, and we know that this type of fleshly, weak-willed, easily swayed person can be found in either gender. Such people do not like to apply their God-given reasoning abilities and sift through ideas to determine which are true and which are false. In short, they do not like to think. Such people never arrive at the truth, because they swallow error and truth indiscriminately. When Satan uses tactics of infiltration against them, they are defenseless. They are easy pickings for any cult that comes their way.

The second tactic Satan employs is imitation—that is, counterfeit faith. Paul writes, "Just as Jannes and Jambres opposed Moses, so also these men oppose the truth." In Exodus, we read that when Moses was sent by God to Pharaoh's court, his brother, Aaron, did miraculous signs to prove to Pharaoh that Moses and Aaron acted under the power of the living God. Without such miraculous demonstrations, Moses and Aaron might just as well have been a couple of Hebrew shepherds who had been out in the desert too long.

There were two magicians in Pharaoh's court, Jannes and Jambres, who were able to do miracles like those of Aaron. (It's interesting that their names are given here though they are not named in the Old Testament accounts. The early Christian scholar Origen cites an apocryphal book, The Book of Jannes and Jambres, which relates their story; no copies of the book survive today. Jannes and Jambres are also mentioned by name in ancient Greek and Roman sources. Paul apparently took their names from one of these sources.)

When Aaron cast down the staff of Moses and it became a snake, Jannes and Jambres imitated this miracle using sleight of hand. This kind of counterfeit religion is all around us. The cults claim to do what only God in Christ can do: provide peace of mind to a troubled heart, provide meaning for a purposeless life, and provide forgiveness of sin for the heart that is riddled with guilt and shame. Many people fall for the promises of the cults. For a while, a counterfeit faith can seem to be the real thing, but it does not last.

How to live in the last days

Next, Paul brings this section of his argument to a strong conclusion: "But they will not get very far because, as in the case of those men, their folly will be clear to everyone" (2 Timothy 3:9).

Though Paul does not tell us, we know from the book of Exodus what happened to Jannes and Jambres. When the serpent made from Aaron's rod saw the two serpents of Jannes and Jambres, it swallowed them both. This was a visible sign that God's power is always more powerful than Satan's.

Paul says that this is the inevitable fate of the cults. In other words, don't panic—evil has its limits. Satan always overreaches, and God always has the last word. The cults inevitably leave people so hungry of heart that they are left wide open to the appeal of the gospel.

When you read the stories of the Great Awakening during the eighteenth century, you see that men like George Whitefield and the Wesley brothers sometimes preached to great crowds, but they also went out to street corners, shops, and even open fields. There they talked to individuals or small groups of people about the gospel. The entire English nation was so spiritually empty and hungry that they flocked to hear these men. The word of them spread so that whenever they began preaching, people would run to hear them.

It was not unusual for John Wesley or George Whitefield to begin speaking to a small handful of people and soon find that a crowd of thousands had gathered. I believe we are headed toward a similar situation in the future. The pop spirituality we see in the media and the false spirituality of the cults are leaving gaping voids in the souls of the men and women all around us. God is preparing hearts for an outpouring of the gospel.

Hypocrisy and insincerity within the church are producing a crisis like that which Paul describes here. The church has been infiltrated by people who profess Christianity while denying its power. God is not fooled by people who sit in the pews, singing hymns, hearing the message week after week, and even attending Bible studies, yet never allowing God's Word to produce real change.

May we awaken to God's grace and truth. May we stop fooling ourselves, today, right this moment. May we truly hear what the apostle Paul is saying to us through these strong words, so that we will know how to truly live for Jesus Christ in these last days.

CHAPTER 29

Be All You Can Be

2 Timothy 3:10–13

I was once asked to deliver the commencement speech at the Big Sky Bible College in central Montana, about forty miles from the tiny Montana town where I grew up. I arrived a day early so that I could take a sentimental journey to my old hometown. I saw many of my old high school classmates and was amazed to see how much of the old town was still standing as I remembered it.

The most nostalgic experience of the trip was driving past the acreage, about a mile outside of town, where a rancher and his wife had once lived. I had spent several years there working as a ranch hand. In fact, this couple had practically adopted me as a son while I was in high school.

My own father, a railroad man, had abandoned my mother and me when I was small. Since I was growing up without a father, this rancher became like a father to me. He mentored me, encouraged me, and instilled in me the virtues and values of manhood. All those memories came flooding back as I visited the place where I spent so many happy hours.

As we come to this section of Paul's letter to Timothy, I believe Paul seeks to stir up similar warm memories in Timothy. The essence of Paul's message to Timothy is, "Do what I did—and be the best that you can be." Paul writes, "You, however, know all about my teaching, my way of life, my purpose, faith, patience, love, endurance, persecutions, sufferings—what kinds of things happened to me in Antioch, Iconium and Lystra, the persecutions I endured. Yet the Lord rescued me from all of them" (2 Timothy 3:10–11).

When Paul says, "You, however, know all about my teaching," he uses a strong word in the Greek: *parakoloutheo*. This word does not merely mean "you know" or "you have seen." It means "you have come right alongside me." Paul is reminding Timothy of how closely they have worked together.

And what did Timothy see and hear as he worked so closely with Paul? The apostle says, "My teaching, my way of life, my purpose, faith, patience, love, endurance, persecutions, sufferings." How did Paul respond as the world was collapsing all around him? He continued to teach the truth. He exposed the illusions and delusions of his day, contending with the pagan world, urging his hearers to examine God's Word and learn to think rightly and realistically about life.

Paul's example is instructive. We live in a world that is crumbling under the pressure of false ideologies, social chaos, and global terrorism. In the midst of all this upheaval, we still need to teach the truth about life from the Word of God.

God does not want us to be paralyzed by fear. No matter how chaotic this world becomes, you and I have a job to do. We must never lose heart; we must never lose hope in God. We must proclaim the kingdom of heaven even as all hell breaks loose around us.

Paul's example of faith and courage

Paul spoke not only of his teaching but also of his conduct: "my way of life." When he faced danger, persecution, and opposition, Paul conducted himself in a way that was an example of faith and courage to Timothy. He practiced what he preached. He controlled his temper. He mastered his passions, conquered his fears, and forgave his enemies.

Not only did Paul model Christian conduct for Timothy, but also he modeled Christian attitudes. He says, "You, however, know all about... my purpose, faith, patience, love, endurance." Those are the great qualities and attitudes that the apostle demonstrated as an example for Timothy.

The most important of these attitudes is the first one: Paul's purpose, his aim in life. Everything Paul did was organized around his purpose for living. What was that purpose? To serve and please the Lord Jesus Christ. Elsewhere, Paul wrote, "So we make it our goal to please him, whether we are at home in the body or away from it" (2 Corinthians 5:9).

What a simple principle that is, yet what a profound effect it had on his life. Imagine how your life would change if you asked yourself, dozens of times every day, "Are my attitude and my conduct at this very moment pleasing to my Lord? Does my way of life reflect His beauty and character—or am I grieving Him?"

Next, Paul speaks of his faith, because it is faith that gives him his purpose in life. Faith is the confidence that certain invisible realities are true—and the conviction to live in light of those realities. Faith is believing that God is at work in human affairs and that He will give us the power to live out our faith in the midst of the pressures, perils, and opposition of this world.

Then Paul speaks of his patience. He speaks here regarding his patience toward other people. If you have been a Christian for any length of time, then you know that people are not always easy to get along with. We wonder, "Why aren't other people as sweet and gracious and easygoing as I am?" And we also wonder why other people don't realize how sweet and gracious and easygoing we are.

In our families and in the church, we desperately need patience with one another. I certainly need people to be patient with me, and in return, I need to learn patience toward others. Paul demonstrated patience toward other people many times in Timothy's presence, and Timothy undoubtedly learned from Paul's example.

Next, Paul speaks of love. This word, above all others, should characterize our lives. Love means accepting everyone as being a valuable human being, made in God's image. Authentic, Christlike love is indiscriminate and unconditional, treating all people equally. At times, love must be tough, and it must confront sin, but love is always accepting of the sinner, even as Jesus was always accepting.

Finally, Paul speaks of endurance. This means perseverance—refusing to quit when opposition and pressure get tough. Genuine endurance is not a stoic, grin-and-bear-it attitude. Rather, it is a faith-based confidence that God will work all events out for good if we keep trusting in Him.

Paul makes a point of reviewing for Timothy certain experiences he underwent that demanded endurance. He reminded Timothy of the persecutions and sufferings he underwent at Antioch, Iconium, and Timothy's hometown of Lystra. If you want to truly know someone, you have to see them when they are going through tough times.

The greatest failure in Christendom?

D. Elton Trueblood was a Quaker author and theologian who served as chaplain to Harvard and Stanford universities. The author of thirty-three books, Trueblood wrote a profoundly revealing biography called *Abraham Lincoln: Theologian of American Anguish*. The book traces the years of Lincoln's presidency, a time when Lincoln was growing mightily in stature as a mature believer in Christ.

The key to Lincoln's Christian growth was the personal anguish he suffered. He keenly felt the immense tragedy of the War Between the States—a horrible bloodbath that took the lives of tens of thousands of young men from both the North and the South. During those years, Lincoln suffered constant opposition from political opponents and the newspapers. Also, his beloved twelve-year-old son, Willie, died of typhoid fever. After the boy's untimely death, Lincoln said in his grief, "My poor boy. He was too good for this earth, and God has called him home."

Some people would have been crushed by everything Lincoln went through. But he learned to respond with grace and forgiveness instead of bitterness. As he put it, "I was often driven to my knees with the overwhelming conviction that I had nowhere else to go."

Here Paul reminds Timothy, in effect, "You were with me during many of those times of persecution. You remember how at Antioch I had to leave town lest my life be taken. You remember how at Iconium I was driven out by a lynch mob. You remember how at Lystra, your hometown, I was stoned and left for dead outside the city walls." Then Paul adds, "Yet the Lord rescued me from all of them."

Timothy was with Paul in many other times of trouble, but these early experiences were undoubtedly burned into Paul's mind—and Timothy's. There are few experiences stronger and more memorable than the shock of the first discovery of truth.

Paul wants to remind Timothy of the emotionally intense and surprising experiences he had as he watched God work in the life of the apostle. Timothy must have been truly amazed to see an apostle of the Lord Jesus Christ suffer so profoundly, and yet it was clear that God was at work in Paul's life even through his sufferings.

Here is an answer, if any answer is needed, to some of the false doctrines that are widespread in the church today. Some preachers teach that when you become a Christian, God will protect you from all kinds of danger and illness. He will bring you peace and prosperity. These preachers claimed that if you are suffering, then it must be because your faith is weak or there is hidden sin in your life.

Either there is something wrong with that kind of preaching or there was something seriously wrong with Paul's faith! He was constantly in trouble. He faced countless obstacles and suffered intense opposition. If the peace and prosperity gospel is true, then how do the preachers of that gospel account for the life of the apostle Paul? Indeed, how do they account for all the sufferings experienced by all the saints and martyrs down through the ages?

If peace and prosperity are signs of successful Christianity, then the apostle Paul was the greatest failure in all of Christendom. It's hard to imagine anyone who suffered more trials and persecution than Paul.

A countercultural movement

Next, Paul reveals another quality he modeled for Timothy, and it is undoubtedly the most important quality of all. Paul writes, "Yet the Lord rescued me from all of them. In fact, everyone who wants to live a godly life in Christ Jesus will be persecuted, while evil men and impostors will go from bad to worse, deceiving and being deceived" (2 Timothy 3:11b–13).

Paul knew how to stand in times of pressure. He knew that the secret of his strength was the presence of God. The Lord Jesus Christ was with him, working through all the events of his life, giving him the strength and perseverance to complete the mission God had given him.

As you read through Paul's letters, you can't help being struck by this theme: God was with him. We need to rediscover this secret for our lives. Paul saw Jesus as the Lord of every event of his life, the one of whom the apostle John said, "What he opens no one can shut, and what he shuts no one can open" (see Revelation 3:7).

Paul has been beaten, flogged, stoned, imprisoned, and more—but the Lord Jesus, the divine Presence, was always with him, restraining the evil of this world. The attacks of his opponents could go so far, but no further. If you think Christianity is a creed you believe in or doctrines you subscribe to or a church you attend, then you have missed the essence of Christianity. Christianity is a Person. He is not someone far away, up in the sky. He is the divine Presence. He is with you, in you, around you, and He walks with you day by day. He never leaves you. He never forsakes you.

Paul says, "Everyone who wants to live a godly life in Christ Jesus will be persecuted, while evil men and impostors will go from bad to worse, deceiving and being deceived." In other words, authentic Christianity is always a countercultural movement. Genuine followers of Jesus Christ always subvert the status quo. If you stand up and speak God's truth, you will not always be popular. In fact, you will likely be ridiculed, rejected, or even physically attacked. That's an essential part of being a Christian.

All who want to live a godly life in Christ Jesus will be persecuted. If you are not being persecuted and never have been, then you are doing something wrong. If you feel entitled to an easy life, then you want a Christianity that is not truly Christian. You want a form of godliness while denying its power.

Decades ago, a preacher named Wilbur Reese penned these lines about the difference between the hypocritical Christianity that is so common in our society and the authentic Christianity of Jesus Christ:

I would like to buy three dollars worth of God, please.
Not enough to explode my soul or disturb my sleep,
But just enough to equal a cup of warm milk,
Or a snooze in the sunshine...
I want ecstasy, not transformation.
I want the warmth of the womb, not a new birth.
I want a pound of the eternal in a paper sack.
I would like to buy three dollars worth of God, please.

That kind of Christianity isn't even worth three dollars. It does nothing to stem the tide of corruption and disaster toward which the human race is headed. If we want to be men and women of God, we must follow the example of the apostle Paul. It is an example of suffering, persecuted Christianity. Paul's brand of Christianity has a job to do and no time to waste.

God is searching this world, looking for men and women willing to risk everything for His sake. He is looking for men and women who will plant their feet on the bloody crossroads of history and stand firm against the approaching enemy. He is looking for more men and women like the apostle Paul.

If you want your life to count, then do what Paul did. Draw daily upon the Lord's presence in your life. Live righteously and courageously. Take bold risks for the gospel. Speak the truth, even if it costs you everything you have. Then thank God for the privilege of suffering for His sake.

CHAPTER 30

How to Think Christianly

2 Timothy 3:14–16

Someone once said, "Let the mind of the Master be the master of your mind." That is a good summation of Paul's counsel to Timothy in the next section of this letter.

We are bombarded by a worldly mindset through the electronic media that constantly clamor for our attention. Timothy didn't have to contend with television, radio, the Internet, and so forth, but he lived in a pagan culture, and he too was bombarded by the mindset of the surrounding pagan culture. Many of the Christians in the Ephesian church were new converts from paganism.

So Paul was deeply concerned that Timothy, the people of the Ephesian church, and all Christians (including you and me) learn how to think Christianly. That's the essence of his message in the next three verses of his letter. He writes:

> But as for you, continue in what you have learned and have become convinced of, because you know those from whom you learned it, and how from infancy you have known the holy Scriptures, which are able to make you wise for salvation through faith in Christ Jesus. All Scripture is God-breathed and is useful for teaching, rebuking, correcting and training in righteousness. (2 Timothy 3:14–16)

How do we learn to think Christianly? Paul begins, naturally enough, with the Word of God. He tells us that we are to saturate our thinking with the thoughts of God, and those thoughts are found in the Bible. As John Wesley wrote in the preface to his *Standard Sermons:*

> I am a creature of a day, passing through life as an arrow through the air. I am a spirit come from God, and returning to God: just hovering over the great gulf; till, a few moments hence, I am no more seen; I drop into an unchangeable eternity! I want to know one thing: the way to heaven;

how to land safe on that happy shore. God himself has condescended to teach the way; for this very end he came from heaven. He hath written it down in a book. O give me that book! At any price, give me the book of God!

These words summarize the Christian view of the Scriptures. The Bible is the book that points the way to God, that reveals the mind of God, and enables us to think God's thoughts after Him.

The ultimate realist

When Paul wrote his letters to Timothy, the Scriptures consisted of the Old Testament and a few circulating documents that have since become part of the New Testament. The gospels of Matthew and Mark might have been available to the churches at that time. Most of the letters of Paul were being copied and shared from church to church. Timothy was with Paul when the apostle wrote some of those letters, and he probably preserved copies of them for his own reading.

It's interesting to note that the apostle Peter, during Paul's lifetime, referred to Paul's letters as Scripture. He wrote:

Bear in mind that our Lord's patience means salvation, just as our dear brother Paul also wrote you with the wisdom that God gave him. He writes the same way in all his letters, speaking in them of these matters. His letters contain some things that are hard to understand, which ignorant and unstable people distort, as they do the other Scriptures, to their own destruction. (2 Peter 3:15–16)

So Paul commended the books of the Old Testament and the apostolic writings of the New Testament to Timothy as God's own Word. The Scriptures, Paul said, would make Timothy wise for salvation through faith in Jesus Christ. In other words, by bathing his mind in the Scriptures, Timothy would learn to see reality from God's point of view. He would learn to think Christianly.

Of course, to become wise through the Scriptures would require continual reading and rereading. You cannot learn all that God has to say to you in His Word in a single reading. We all need repeated, daily exposure to the Word of God.

One reason we need to expose ourselves to God's Word again and again is that we are relentlessly being assaulted by the false values of this dying world. Our society is ruled by Satan, the god of this world, and it is constantly trying to squeeze us into its mold. The truth of the Bible saws across the grain of the so-called truths of this world. If we do not continually wash our minds in the truth of God's Word, we will be brainwashed by the lies that this world passes off as truth.

Because God created reality, He is the ultimate realist. He sees the end from the beginning. He sees all of time and all of space at a glance. In the Bible, God gives us His utterly accurate perspective on ourselves, on life, on society, on morals and ethics, and on spiritual reality.

Transformed thinking

The Bible reveals to us what Paul calls "God's secret wisdom, a wisdom that has been hidden and that God destined for our glory before time began." The apostle adds that the wise and powerful people of our own age cannot understand God's secret wisdom, for if they had, "they would not have crucified the Lord of glory" (see 1 Corinthians 2:7–8). Because the wisest rulers of our world do not understand what is in God's Word, they make horrible errors in judgment. They even crucified the most righteous man who ever lived.

This is why it's so important to understand the Bible. If we go to God's Word and seek out His wisdom, our lives and thinking will be drastically altered. We cannot read this book without being changed. In its pages, we learn to think differently about ourselves and others. It transforms our view of our relationships with spouse, children, parents, siblings, and extended family. It changes our view of relationships in the workplace, the neighborhood, and the church. It changes our values and goals.

We see the transformational power of God's Word in the story of mutiny aboard the H.M.S. *Bounty* in April 1789. That historical incident has been the subject of several major motion pictures, but the movies don't tell the whole story. A group of British sailors, led by master's mate Fletcher Christian, mutinied and seized control of a ship that was used to transport breadfruit plants, a cheap source of food for slaves. The mutineers cast the captain and eighteen other men adrift in a small boat, then sailed to Pitcairn Island in the South Pacific.

The mutineers burned and sank the *Bounty* in the bay and started building a community on the island, where there were food, water, and Polynesian brides for the men. Fletcher Christian was the leader of the community, and the British mutineers treated the Polynesians as servants. One of the mutineers constructed a crude distillery and began brewing whiskey. Soon, the mutineers were drinking all the time, fighting, and murdering one another.

Then one of the mutineers, Alexander Smith, found a Bible in a trunk he had salvaged before the *Bounty* was scuttled. As he read the Bible, he gave his life to the Lord. Immediately, his conduct was transformed. He taught the Scriptures to others on the island, and the entire society at Pitcairn quickly changed.

In 1808, the American sailing ship *Topaz* reached Pitcairn Island. Though Alexander Smith had died by that time, he had left behind a peaceful and thriving Christian community on Pitcairn. There were about fifty islanders living together in peace and harmony, all of them Christians. There was no crime or drunkenness. The island was a Christian utopia.

That's the transforming power of the Bible. No other book in human history has ever achieved such results—not the Hindu *Vedas,* not the Buddhist *Sutras,* not the Norse *Eddas.* Not the *Kitáb-i-Aqdas* of the Bahá'í faith, not the Islamic *Qu'ran,* not the New Age *Urantia Book.* Not *Dianetics* of the Scientologists, not the *Tao Te Ching* of the Taoists, not the *Book of Mormon.* Of all the so-called sacred texts of the various religions, only the Bible has transformed lives and changed entire societies. Why? What sets this one book apart from all the rest?

The Bible doesn't just change our thinking. It enables us to live realistically, to distinguish reality from illusion, and to correct false thinking. The truth of the Bible leads to life, not death. Anyone who builds his or her life on its message becomes immeasurably enriched and strengthened. As the book of Proverbs tells us:

> My son, preserve sound judgment and discernment,
>> do not let them out of your sight;
> they will be life for you,
>> an ornament to grace your neck.
> Then you will go on your way in safety,
>> and your foot will not stumble;
> when you lie down, you will not be afraid;
>> when you lie down, your sleep will be sweet.
> Have no fear of sudden disaster
>> or of the ruin that overtakes the wicked,
> for the LORD will be your confidence
>> and will keep your foot from being snared. (Proverbs 3:21–26)

While the Scriptures are powerful, they are not magical. This book consists merely of paper, ink, and the cover that binds it. Your Bible will not change your life by sitting on your coffee table or nightstand. You must read it, study it, meditate on it, and memorize it in order for its truths to permeate your life.

Let me offer a simple suggestion: Turn off the television. Television is the biggest time waster ever devised by the mind of man. Today, most of us have cable or satellite television with two hundred or more channels to watch—and if we are honest we have to confess that there is rarely anything worth watching. While we vegetate in our easy chair, remote control in hand, there sits the most amazing book ever written, the revelation of God's own mind—unopened, unread, and unused.

When this life is over and we enter the life to come, we will not remember a single television program we have watched. But heaven is constructed on the precepts contained in God's Word. If we have fed our souls on the Bible, we'll be glad for all eternity.

A God-breathed book

The Bible changes lives. Where did a mere book, made of ink on paper, acquire such transformational power? Paul answers this question: "All Scripture is God-breathed and is useful for teaching, rebuking, correcting and training in righteousness, so that the man of God may be thoroughly equipped for every good work" (2 Timothy 3:16–17).

This is a good translation of Paul's meaning. Some translations render that opening phrase, "All Scripture is inspired by God." The word *inspired* comes from the Latin word *spiro,* meaning "to breathe." But the Bible was not *in-spired* (breathed in), it was *out-spired* (breathed out from God.). It was, as the NIV says, "God-breathed." The apostle Peter puts it this way: "For prophecy never had its origin in the will of man, but men spoke from God as they were carried along by the Holy Spirit" (2 Peter 1:21).

Genesis tells us that God created the first man, Adam, by heaping up a pile of dirt and breathing into it the spirit of life, and man became a living being. The wonder of the Bible is what God did with the words contained in it. He expressed His mind, His perspective on reality, through human beings, who wrote down His thoughts in this book.

Many people struggle with the concept of the inspiration of Scripture. "We know how the Bible was written," they say. "Ordinary, fallible human beings just like us wrote down their ideas about God, and their words are no more trustworthy than our own."

But Paul says that just as God breathed His breath into the dust of the ground and it became a living human being, he also breathed His breath into the words of men who wrote according to the leading of the Holy Spirit. So the words of Scripture have a unique quality: They come from the mouth of God.

Paul tells us that the words of Scripture accomplish four purposes in the life of the person who reads and believes them.

First, those words teach. All Scripture, Paul says, is "useful for teaching." The Bible instructs our minds about things no one but God understands. It tells us the truth about ourselves and about our world from a perspective that is unique to God.

The Bible contains the truth everyone wants to know about life and death. Every so often, we see magazine articles with titles like "New Evidence for Life after Death" or "Does Heaven Exist?" People hunger for knowledge about what lies beyond this life. They wonder, "Is this life all there is? Do we live for a few short decades, then disappear forever? Or is there more to come?"

The Scriptures speak of the One who came back from the grave and told us what is beyond. He demonstrated, in ways that cannot be denied or explained away, that He has conquered death. So God's Word is a reliable guide to realms of reality we could never know about from our own experience.

What are angels? What are demons? Why do humans want to do good but can't help doing evil? Why are human beings constantly in conflict, trying to bomb each other out of existence? Why can't we make human beings behave with better education or legislation? The answers to all of those questions are found in the Bible, God's instruction book, which is useful for teaching.

Next, Paul says that the Bible is useful for rebuking. A synonym for "rebuking" would be "conviction." If you have been a Christian for any length of time, you've probably had the experience of reading the Bible and becoming aware that something in your life needed changing. Perhaps it was some habit or relationship or way of treating other people that never seemed wrong before, but suddenly you knew you had to change your way of life. That is conviction. The Bible has a tremendous ability to rebuke our sins and confront the areas of wrongdoing in our lives.

The Bible is also a powerful instrument for correcting, for moving us off of the wrong path and onto the path that leads to life. The Bible is like a roadmap that displays all the potential pathways of our lives. By reading this roadmap, we can find the pathways that lead to blessing and avoid those that lead to destruction.

Finally, the Bible is for training in righteousness. This phrase suggests that the Bible has the power to fine-tune our lives. God's Word coaches us, empowers us, motivates us, and enables us to achieve more for God than we ever thought possible. The ultimate goal of God's Word in our lives is "so that the man of God may be thoroughly equipped for every good work."

I have been studying the stories and principles of this book for decades, and I never opened my Bible without a sense of excitement and expectation. I know I will find some new and challenging truths in its pages. That's why this book never gets old. This God-breathed book has the power to change lives, make broken people whole, and transform a society. It will steady you through any time of crisis. It will teach you how to think Christianly.

"The book that understands me"

Dr. Emile Caillet was for many years a professor at Princeton Seminary. He fought in the French army in World War I, and the terrible suffering and devastation of war confirmed his belief that religion offered no hope for the human soul. As a result, he became a militant atheist.

Caillet longed for a source of solace in times of trouble, so he began compiling a notebook that he called "The Book That Would Understand Me." He wrote down insights, ideas, and quotations in the book and kept it with him at all times. One day, while going through a time of discouragement, he sat down and read through the book he had compiled. His heart sank. Everything he read seemed empty and meaningless. He realized that since the book came completely from himself, it had no power to minister to his needs.

At around the same time, Caillet's wife took a walk past a quaint stone church. She saw an old man sitting at a table in the church courtyard, and she asked him how old the church building was. He told her that it was built centuries earlier by the Huguenots, the French Protestants.

She chatted with the old man for a while, and it occurred to her to ask, "Do you have any Bibles in the French language?"

The old man picked up a Bible from the table. "You may keep this," he said.

She took the Bible home but hid it from her husband. He had ordered that God never be mentioned in their house. After a few days, however, she went to her husband and confessed that she had brought a Bible into the house.

"Give it to me," Emile Caillet said. "Let me read it."

He opened the Bible and began reading the Gospels. He became fascinated with the story and teachings of Jesus. Then he read several more books of the Old and New Testaments. Finally, he set the Bible down and bowed his head.

"At last," he said, "I have found the book that understands me." And he opened his heart and invited Jesus to become his Lord and Savior.

Eventually Caillet became a university professor. He talked and wrote on subjects ranging from French literature to Christian theology. One of his most famous statements is this often-quoted line: "The Bible is not only a book which I can understand; it is also a book which understands me."

That is the testimony of millions of Christians down through the ages. Again and again, lives and families and cultures have been transformed by the message of God's Word. This is a book anyone can understand. But more importantly it is a book that understands us all. It is a God-breathed book that instructs the mind, touches the heart, enlivens the spirit, and leads us to salvation and eternal life with God.

CHAPTER 31

The Majesty of Ministry

2 Timothy 4:1–4

We have reached the heart of Paul's message to Timothy. Sitting in his dark and lonely cell, the apostle knows that the moment of his martyrdom is near. So Paul addresses these heartfelt and solemn words to his spiritual son:

> In the presence of God and of Christ Jesus, who will judge the living and the dead, and in view of his appearing and his kingdom, I give you this charge: Preach the Word; be prepared in season and out of season; correct, rebuke and encourage—with great patience and careful instruction. For the time will come when men will not put up with sound doctrine. Instead, to suit their own desires, they will gather around them a great number of teachers to say what their itching ears want to hear. They will turn their ears away from the truth and turn aside to myths (2 Timothy 4:1–4).

Though Paul wrote these words nearly two thousand years ago, no other passage in Scripture describes more accurately the day in which we live. In these words, the apostle underscores the importance of Timothy's calling. Paul flings back the boundaries of time and space, revealing to Timothy and to us the unseen realities that surround us. "In the presence of God and of Christ Jesus, who will judge the living and the dead," he says, reminding Timothy of the eternal importance of his ministry in Ephesus.

When we undergo pressure and opposition in our ministry, it's helpful and encouraging to remember that we are engaged in important work. It's easy to become discouraged and feel our efforts are wasted, especially when our obstacles and problems never seem to end. So Paul reminds Timothy that his work has eternal significance.

Timothy was surrounded by unbelief, false religion, and immorality. Sexual perversion was accepted as a way of life in Ephesus, just as in our day. Those who practiced the worst forms of depravity were applauded and celebrated. Meanwhile, those who upheld morality and righteousness were ridiculed and censured for intolerance. At times, Timothy must have felt he was making no headway against the tide of evil.

So Paul encourages Timothy and us with the reminder that God, the Creator of the universe, and His Son, the Lord Jesus Christ, are witnesses to our labors. Indeed, Paul tells us that we believers are a "spectacle" to the whole universe. The angels of heaven are watching what we do here on earth: "We have been made a spectacle to the whole universe, to angels as well as to men" (1 Corinthians 4:9b). And the writer to the Hebrews reminds us that we are surrounded by "a great cloud of witnesses" (see Hebrews 12:1).

From our limited, earthbound perspective, we often feel alone and abandoned. But Paul tells us that not only does God watch and care intensely about our ministry, but all of heaven watches, both angels and human beings. We are not alone. Our ministry for God has eternal significance, and a great cloud of witnesses cheers us on.

The majesty of ministry

Next, Paul charges Timothy not only in the presence of God the Father and Jesus the Son but also "in view of his appearing and his kingdom." Many Bible commentators interpret this phrase "in view of his appearing" to be a reference to the second coming of Christ. The Greek word that is translated "appearing" is *epiphania,* from which we get the English word *epiphany.* This word is often used in reference to the second coming of Christ. Also, Paul's use of the phrase "who will judge the living and the dead" in this same verse would seem to lend credence to that view.

But I am convinced that the phrase "in view of his appearing" refers to the first coming of Jesus Christ. The usage here is the same as when Paul wrote earlier in this letter that God's grace "has now been revealed through the appearing of our Savior, Christ Jesus, who has destroyed death and has brought life and immortality to light through the gospel" (see 2 Timothy 1:10).

When Paul says to Timothy "in view of his appearing," he is pointing Timothy back to the first appearance of Jesus, who, by His death and resurrection, brought us everlasting life. With His first appearance, Jesus gave us the gospel and commissioned us to spread the kingdom of God throughout the earth. By His witness and His ministry in Ephesus, Timothy is involved in the advance of the greatest work God has ever done.

This understanding of Paul's words puts Timothy's ministry and ours into a rightful perspective. When we witness for Christ through our words and example, we are engaged in a work that is infinitely more important than any war ever waged, any social program ever launched, any achievement ever claimed by a king, president, or dictator.

This is what I call "the majesty of ministry." The world may think that the church is irrelevant, that the gospel is out of touch with social realities, that Christians are a pack of eccentrics who believe ancient myths. But Paul wants us to know that our ministry and witness are eternally significant.

Jesus taught us to pray, "Your kingdom come, your will be done on earth as it is in heaven" (Matthew 6:10). When we conduct our lives as Christians, when we witness to others of what Jesus Christ has done in our lives, we allow God to use us as the answer to that prayer. We become His instruments for advancing the kingdom of God. The will of God is done on earth as in heaven through us. There is no higher calling than that.

After Lyndon Johnson was elected president in 1964, he approached evangelist Billy Graham and asked him what role he would like to have in a Johnson White House. Dr. Graham replied, "Sir, I believe that Jesus Christ has called me to preach the gospel. To me that's the highest calling any man could have on earth."

Dr. Graham understood what Paul was saying to Timothy: <u>As believers, we are called to proclaim the gospel of Jesus Christ in our generation</u>. There is no higher calling than that. Anything else, even a position in the White House, would be a step down.

That is the majesty of the ministry Jesus Christ has given us.

Preach the Word

Next, Paul reminds Timothy of the most essential element of our Christian witness in a dying world: "Preach the Word; be prepared in season and out of season; correct, rebuke and encourage—with great patience and careful instruction" (2 Timothy 4:2).

What do you think of when you see that phrase "preach the Word"? You probably think Paul is talking only to preachers and evangelists. But in Paul's day, there were no pulpits, no church buildings with rows of pews all facing a platform. There was no distinction between clergy and laity, as we unfortunately have today. When Paul wrote those words, any Christian reading his words would have thought, "Paul is speaking to me." Every believer is called to preach the Word.

Personally, I don't like pulpits. I don't like standing behind a wooden barrier when I teach God's Word to other people. I agree with Charles Haddon Spurgeon's designation of a pulpit as a "coward's castle."

I also don't like standing on a platform in front of a congregation. I realize that the purpose of the platform is to make it possible for everyone to see and hear. But there's a subtle psychological effect of platforms: They elevate the pastor three or four feet above the heads of the congregation. The platform makes it seem as if the pastor is more important than the people. Nothing could be further from the truth.

In the Scriptures, the person with the gifts of a pastor-teacher is no more important than any other individual in the church. The pastor's role is to equip everyone else in the church to do the ministry of the church. Everyone in the church is a minister. To view the pastor as the minister and all the other people as mere spectators of the ministry is alien to everything the New Testament tells us about the church.

So when Paul says, "preach the Word," he is talking to you and me and to everyone in the church. Every believer has the privilege and responsibility of making God's truth known to the world. You can preach the Word over a cup of coffee in your neighbor's breakfast nook or in the lunchroom at your office. You can preach that Word in your carpool on the way to work. You can preach the Word on the golf course or during a backyard barbecue party.

You don't have to deliver a sermon. All you have to do is gently, naturally share the story of what God has done in your life. You don't have to deliver lofty theological treatises. Just speak from your heart and your experience. People are hungry for truth. Pray for opportunities to speak the truth, and God will open doors.

Remember, the gospel of Jesus Christ is good news. Most people are wallowing in a swamp of bad news, and they will clutch at any good news you have to share. So don't be ashamed of the good news of Jesus Christ. If you had the cure for cancer, you would share it with your cancer-stricken friends. You have the cure for sin and guilt. Why keep that good news to yourself?

In season and out of season

Next, Paul tells us how to go about proclaiming God's truth. He writes, "Be prepared in season and out of season." In other words, be ready at all times to share God's truth with others. Don't be reticent or bashful. Speak it boldly! Share it eagerly! Be always ready and prepared to be God's witness for the truth.

Some people have mistakenly taken this passage to mean that you should push the gospel onto people whether they are willing to listen or not. In other words, some Christians take this passage as a license to be obnoxious. As John R. W. Stott has wisely said, "This is not a biblical warrant for rudeness, but a biblical appeal against laziness." In other words, share the gospel whether you feel like doing so or not. But don't defame and demean the gospel by treating people with disrespect.

Next, Paul says that, when sharing the good news of Jesus Christ, we should use a variety of approaches. "Correct, rebuke and encourage—with great patience and careful instruction," he says. These words reflect three different approaches that we can use in sharing the gospel.

How do we correct others while preaching the Word? To correct someone is to replace their misimpressions with the truth. We use reason and evidence to move someone from false belief to true belief. They may not be immediately convinced, because people don't like to be proved wrong. So be gentle and gracious, and in time the people corrected may come around to a recognition of the truth.

The intellectual approach, which appeals to logic and evidence, is especially well-suited to people who have doubts and questions that need to be answered. We should all become experts at the evidence for the gospel. Study books like Josh McDowell's *Evidence That Demands a Verdict* and Lee Strobel's *The Case for Christ*. Learn to articulate sound, logical reasons for your faith.

Then, Paul says we must rebuke as an aspect of preaching the Word. Sometimes we encounter people who have fallen into sin. So we need to appeal to that person's conscience and growing awareness that sin is destroying his life and the lives of others. Sin demolishes and dehumanizes those who are involved in it. When you show people the destructive effects of sin in their lives, you preach the Word in a powerful way. You point people to their need of a Savior. You awaken in them a hunger for transformation.

Finally, the apostle says, "Encourage—with great patience and careful instruction." The gospel is a great encouragement to people. It offers not only hope of eternal life in heaven but also strength for this life.

We are not merely to pound our Bibles and demand that people believe it. We are to preach the Word with gentleness, great patience, and careful instruction. Our message must be tailored to each hearer. Even though the gospel itself is for all people, our presentation of the gospel is not a one-size-fits-all proposition. We need to share our testimony with patience and love for the individual.

We should not expect to close the sale every time we talk to someone about the gospel. Don't use manipulation or pressure tactics. Don't abandon someone who doesn't immediately respond to the gospel.

Some people may need to hear the gospel presented numerous times. You may need to spend weeks or months in prayer for that person. You may need to spend many hours, conversing over coffee, answering question after question, in order for that person to recognize the reality of Christ. So when you encourage other people in the gospel, do so with great patience and careful instruction.

People with "itching ears"

At the beginning of 2 Timothy 3, Paul writes of terrible conditions that would prevail in the church. He says that people in the church would become lovers of self, lovers of money, and lovers of pleasure rather than lovers of God. He says that people in the church would have a form of religion but deny the power thereof. As we look around at the church today, we see the fulfillment of Paul's warning.

Now we come to a section where Paul describes a corresponding condition in the world at large. The basis of this condition is the world's fundamental hatred of the truth. Paul writes:

> For the time will come when men will not put up with sound doctrine. Instead, to suit their own desires, they will gather around them a great number of teachers to say what their itching ears want to hear. They will turn their ears away from the truth and turn aside to myths. (2 Timothy 4:3–4)

Surely that is descriptive of our own day. It indicates a time when the general population will forsake what was once called a Christian consensus, a general agreement that Western society is based on Christian principles. We have largely abandoned the Christian consensus in the United States and throughout Western civilization. Paul speaks of this condition when he writes, "For the time will come when men will not put up with sound doctrine."

He refers to sound Christian teaching that leads to wholeness in the spirit, soul, and body—teaching that enables human beings to live at peace with themselves, with God, and with one another. Paul says that human beings will turn away from sound Christian teaching and refuse to listen to the truth.

To accept this truth we must admit our human weakness, and people do not willingly admit they are weak. So they turn away from the truth of the gospel and the Christian consensus that was once the basis of our society. They hate the truth, and they turn away from it in rage and disgust.

Paul adds, "Instead, to suit their own desires, they will gather around them a great number of teachers to say what their itching ears want to hear." Since they will not listen to the truth of God's Word, Paul says, they turn to other teachings that they find more pleasant and agreeable. They seek out teachings that scratch where their ears itch. The phrase "itching ears" refers to a desire to have one's personal prejudices and preferences affirmed—an unwillingness to hear anything that contradict one's preconceived notions.

Truth versus myths

Paul adds that people "will turn their ears away from the truth and turn aside to myths." Look at the religion shelves at your local bookstore or turn on a television talk show, and you will likely see a parade of New Age teachers who have tailored their message to please their audience. These teachers become obscenely rich selling their feel-good myths because it is easier to sell attractive lies for money than it is to give away God's truth for free.

I don't know all the myths that were taught in Timothy's day, but these false gospels have appeared again and again in the course of human history. There are many such myths abroad in our culture.

Take, for example, the myth of reincarnation. Many people, even Christians, believe this lie, which has no basis in Scripture, logic, or fact. There is no empirical evidence that supports the idea that people die, then come back to earth to live another life, and another, and another, continually recycling their souls. This is a wishful myth that says, "If at first you don't succeed, die, die again!"

Or take the myth of humanism, which says that humanity is the measure of all things. Our destiny is in our own hands, and we can solve all of our own problems without guidance from God and His Word. All we need is a more enlightened educational process producing a more enlightened population, willing to follow the right enlightened leaders, and we will embark upon a brave new utopia. The myth of humanism is the underlying assumption of much that is proclaimed in academia, the media, and our political establishment. This myth is leading our society to ruin.

Or take the myth of sexual liberation. Biblical morality, some say, is repressive and makes people sexually and psychologically unhealthy. Every sexual proclivity should be approved, applauded, and accepted, no matter how deviant. This is an outright denial of what God has taught us about our humanity. The more we follow such myths, the more devastation we are seeing in the lives of individuals, families, and communities.

So it is urgent that we proclaim the truth of Jesus Christ. And we must do so gently, patiently, and lovingly. God has not called us to organize demonstrations and chant mindless slogans. He has not called us to wage war against the enemies of truth. He calls us to love our enemies with the love of Jesus Christ. He calls us to urgently speak his truth, in season and out of season, with great patience and careful instruction.

All of heaven is watching. God's eternal program of salvation is being carried out, step by step and day by day, through your life and mine. Do not let anybody tell you that your life and work as a Christian does not count. There is no more important work you could do than to preach the Word in your neighborhood, over your back fence, in your workplace, on your campus, on your military base, wherever God has placed you.

Carry out your work with boldness, confidence, and joy. You have the most important job in the world!

CHAPTER 32

Passing the Torch

2 Timothy 4:5–8

The passing of the Olympic torch has been a thrilling part of the opening ceremonies of the Olympic Games since the 1928 Summer Olympics in Amsterdam. The torch is first lit at the site of the original Olympic Games in Greece. Athletes keep the fire burning and pass the torch from one runner to the next until the final runner enters the current Olympic stadium. As the crowd cheers, the runner carries the torch to the cauldron and lights the Olympic flame that will burn throughout the games.

It's a great honor and responsibility to pass the torch. The torch must be held high for all to see. It cannot be fumbled or dropped, because it might go out. One runner must pass the torch carefully to the next runner to prevent it from being extinguished.

In this section of Paul's second letter to Timothy, we see the old apostle passing the torch to the young pastor. The torch of God's truth is being handed from man to man, from generation to generation. As Paul told Timothy earlier in this letter, "And the things you have heard me say in the presence of many witnesses entrust to reliable men who will also be qualified to teach others" (2 Timothy 2:2).

The torch of God's truth must not only be passed along from hand to hand, but it must be guarded and kept from being extinguished. As Paul also said to Timothy, "Guard the good deposit that was entrusted to you—guard it with the help of the Holy Spirit who lives in us" (2 Timothy 1:14). Paul charges Timothy—and us—to pass the torch of the gospel from generation to generation and to guard it faithfully so that God's truth is neither distorted nor perverted.

Keep your head

As Paul nears the end of this letter, he gives some final instructions to his son in the faith. He knows his time on earth is nearly over and the future of the gospel belongs to the young. So he writes, "But you, keep your head in all situations, endure hardship, do the work of an evangelist, discharge all the duties of your ministry" (2 Timothy 4:5).

This verse is a summary of many things Paul has taught Timothy over the course of their mentoring relationship. In these phrases, Paul gathers up all that he expects Timothy to do as a minister of the gospel. Paul begins this section by saying, "Keep your head in all situations." In other words, remain steady, calm, and consistent. Don't bounce around like a ping-pong ball. Don't soar one day and sink the next. Be consistent in your Christian commitment.

Steadiness comes from a firm foundation. The apostle exhorts Timothy to rest upon a foundation that will enable him to withstand the pressures and conflicting forces that oppose him on a daily basis. As Paul earlier told Timothy, "Be strong in the grace that is in Christ Jesus" (see 2 Timothy 2:1).

What is the foundation of your life? Does an awareness of God's gracious involvement in your life make you strong and steady for the battles of life? Are you saturating your thoughts with God's thoughts, drawn from His Word, so that you can think Christianly about life? That's the foundation that will enable us to keep our heads in all situations.

Next, Paul says, "endure hardship." This theme is woven throughout this letter. Paul frequently talks about the trials of the Christian life. For example, he earlier told Timothy, "Endure hardship with us like a good soldier of Christ Jesus" (2 Timothy 2:3). There is an old hymn, written by Isaac Watts (1674–1748), which speaks to this issue:

Am I a soldier of the cross,
    a follower of the Lamb?
And shall I fear to own his cause
    or blush to speak his name?

Must I be carried to the skies
    on flowery beds of ease,
While others fought to win the prize
    and sailed through bloody seas?

Everyone who seeks to live a godly life in Jesus Christ will suffer persecution. Godly Christians don't merely risk persecution. They invite persecution. When you speak God's truth, the world will try to silence you. So when you are persecuted, endure hardship like a good soldier of Jesus Christ. Then rejoice that God has found you worthy to suffer for His cause. As the hymn goes on to say:

Sure I must fight, if I would reign;
    increase my courage, Lord;
I'll bear the toil, endure the pain,
    supported by thy Word.

That's the Christian life. Toil and pain are not extraordinary circumstances. Hardship is the essence of a life lived for Jesus Christ.

The work of an evangelist

Next, Paul says to Timothy, "Do the work of an evangelist."

I used to think that Paul was identifying Timothy's primary spiritual gift. I have had to change my mind about that. A person with the gift of an evangelist is one who has a special gift for speaking to non-Christians and leading them to Christ. But I have found no other indication in any of Paul's letters that Timothy had this gift. On the contrary, he was a shy young man, inclined to keep to himself. Paul had to encourage Timothy to mix with other people and become involved in public life. Timothy's introverted personality is inconsistent with the spiritual gift of an evangelist.

So it appears that Timothy had the gift of a pastor-teacher. That spiritual gift seems more fitting for a personality like his. Since that is so, why does Paul tell Timothy, "Do the work of an evangelist"? He does so because all spiritual gifts must ultimately be directed to the world as well as to the church. The work of the church is to reach the world with the gospel. So even though Timothy may not have the gifts of an evangelist, he is to do evangelistic work. He is to proclaim God's truth at every opportunity.

Next, Paul says, "Discharge all the duties of your ministry." In other words, do not quit until you have fully achieved your mission. Persevere until you have accomplished all that God has given you to do. When your work is done and the Lord takes you home, you will have plenty of time to rest. Until then, fulfill your ministry. Discharge your duties faithfully.

You may say, "I'm not a pastor, an evangelist, or a Bible teacher. What is my ministry? What are the duties I'm supposed to discharge to the end?' Answer: Your ministry is to live as a Christian, walk as a Christian, talk as a Christian, and represent Christ wherever you are, whatever you do. That's your ministry.

Paul displayed the attitude we all should have when he prayed with the Ephesian elders and said, "I consider my life worth nothing to me, if only I may finish the race and complete the task the Lord Jesus has given me—the task of testifying to the gospel of God's grace" (see Acts 20:24). Paul spoke those words years before 2 Timothy was written. He was on his way to Jerusalem, where he would be arrested, imprisoned, and taken to Rome. He expected to die. As it turned out, it was many more years before he was again arrested in Asia Minor and taken to Rome to be executed.

But Paul always had a sense that his life was a fast-burning candle, giving off a brilliant but temporary light. Here we see the true test of authentic Christian commitment. Many people profess Christ for a while, but they fall away in time. Those who persevere and endure to the end have demonstrated that they belonged to Jesus Christ all along.

A drink offering

Having urged Timothy to faithfully discharge all the duties of his ministry, Paul now goes on to say, in effect, "You must take my place." He writes, "For I am already being poured out like a drink offering, and the time has come for my departure" (2 Timothy 4:6).

Here Paul implies that he is passing the torch to this younger man, and in a real sense, to succeeding generations of Christians. This doesn't mean Timothy will replace Paul as an apostle. The Word of God is being written down and the New Testament is rapidly taking the place of the apostles in the world. But Paul does expect Timothy to carry on the ministry of preaching the Word and planting churches.

The great apostle uses two interesting phrases to describe his outlook on death. He says, first, "I am already being poured out like a drink offering." In other words, he is already in the process of being sacrificed. Second, he says, "The time has come for my departure." Let's take a closer look at each of these statements.

First, Paul tells us that he sees the minutes and seconds of his life being poured out like wine from a cup, like a ritual pouring of a drink offering to God. He employs an image that was common in Judaism, the image of wine being poured out as a holy sacrifice. In the Old Testament, we read of this example: "Jacob set up a stone pillar at the place where God had talked with him, and he poured out a drink offering on it; he also poured oil on it" (Genesis 35:14).

And the Old Testament prophet Isaiah used the metaphor of a drink offering when he prophesied regarding the sacrificial death of the Lord Jesus Christ: "He poured out his life unto death" (see Isaiah 53:12).

The drink offering was made during the Jewish feasts at the termination of the great Day of Atonement. At the end of all the offerings, wine was poured out upon the altar—a drink offering. This is how Paul sees himself. He knows he will soon be beheaded, for that was the Roman method of execution for citizens of the empire. Other criminals might be crucified, but a Roman citizen was at least spared the unimaginable torture of crucifixion. In a real sense, Paul's metaphor is graphic. His words paint a vivid picture of what will happen when the executioner swings his sword and Paul's lifeblood is spilled upon the ground. Paul has no regrets. He does not view his execution as a disaster to be feared but as the completion of a life faithfully lived. His life is not being wasted. It is being gloriously sacrificed.

Did Paul experience any dread of his approaching execution? I don't believe so. It seems he viewed his death with a sense of expectation and thankfulness that God could use him until the last moment of his life. Just as Paul offered his entire post-conversion life to God, he now offers his death to the Lord as a sacrifice.

Next, Paul says, "The time has come for my departure." Here, Paul uses the Greek word *analusis,* a term soldiers used when they pulled up their tent stakes to leave one encampment and move on to the next. This word is also used in Greek literature when a ship is said to loose its moorings and set out to sea.

This is the most beautiful figure of speech the apostle could employ: "The time of my loosing has come." He will be set free from earthly ties to sail out on a new adventure. As he wrote to the Christians in Philippi, "I am torn between the two: I desire to depart and be with Christ, which is better by far" (Philippians 1:23).

What a wonderful view of death this is! There is no fear or dread in these words, no sense of regret. There is only a sense of adventure and expectation.

The good fight

Paul goes on to use three phrases that sum up his life's accomplishments—two sports metaphors and a simple declaration of fact.

> I have fought the good fight, I have finished the race, I have kept the faith. Now there is in store for me the crown of righteousness, which the Lord, the righteous Judge, will award to me on that day—and not only to me, but also to all who have longed for his appearing. (2 Timothy 4:7–8)

These are wonderful, triumphant words. I can't help reading these words without a sense of excitement and expectation of the joy that awaits us in heaven. What would you say about your life if you were to sum it up in a few phrases?

First, Paul says, "I have fought the good fight." Notice, he did not say, "I have fought a good fight," as he is sometimes misquoted. He is not patting himself on the back. He's not boasting, "I've done a great job, I've really battled like a champ." That's not what he's saying.

Paul is saying, "I have fought the good fight, the right fight, the significant fight, the fight that truly matters." That's a huge difference! What battle is Paul talking about? He tells us in his letter to the Ephesians: "For our struggle is not against flesh and blood, but against the rulers, against the authorities, against the powers of this dark world and against the spiritual forces of evil in the heavenly realms" (Ephesians 6:12).

That's where the battle is. We are not at war against flesh and blood but against spiritual forces of evil. Paul has been persecuted, stoned, beaten, flogged, and more, but even though human beings inflicted all of this pain on him, he knew all along that the real enemy was an invisible enemy, a spiritual enemy. He has fought that battle—and he has finished his fight.

I hope I can say that at the end of my fight. I pray that God will enable me to say, at the end of my life's battles, "I have fought the good fight. I have fought the right fight. I have battled the right enemies."

Next, Paul says, "I have finished the race." This is a common metaphor in Paul's writings. In his letter to the Philippians, he writes, "Forgetting what is behind and straining toward what is ahead, I press on toward the goal to win the prize for which God has called me heavenward in Christ Jesus" (Philippians 3:13b–14).

The race Paul speaks of, of course, is the Christian life. This race is not a sprint. It's a marathon. The race of this life is lived moment by moment, just as a marathon is run step by step. The question we must daily ask ourselves is whether we live in the flesh or in the Spirit, whether we run this race in our own power or in the power that comes from Jesus Christ alone.

Paul said he pressed on toward the goal to win the prize. What is the goal? It's the end of the race, the death of the believer. Most human beings would dread reaching that finish line, but not the believer. When we as Christians reach the finish line, we win the prize for which God has called us heavenward in Jesus Christ. That's why Paul says to Timothy, "I have finished the race." Paul is not dismayed by the approach of death. That's the finish line. He has reached his goal. This is his moment of triumph!

What is the prize he speaks of? It's his new body, the glory that awaits him in eternity. Paul has not run this race in vain. He has not simply been marking time, waiting to collect Social Security, planning a Caribbean cruise. No, he has been fighting the good fight and running a race. Soon he will collect the prize that awaits him.

We noted earlier that Paul sums up his life in three phrases—two sports metaphors and a simple declaration of fact. The sports metaphors are "I have fought the good fight," and, "I have finished the race." Now comes the statement of fact: "I have kept the faith." Paul is saying he has safeguarded the entire body of truth contained in the gospel, what he calls "God's secret wisdom, a wisdom that has been hidden and that God destined for our glory before time began" (1 Corinthians 2:7b).

Here, as he is on the verge of stepping out of this life and into the heavenly realm, he says that he has kept the faith. He has not lost any of the deposit of truth that God has entrusted to him. He has guarded the faith as a treasure, and now he hands that treasure over to his spiritual son, Timothy.

Paul's expectation

The apostle knows that death is just a doorway to the next great adventure. He now describes four aspects of the great eternal adventure that awaits him: "Now there is in store for me the crown of righteousness, which the Lord, the righteous Judge, will award to me on that day—and not only to me, but also to all who have longed for his appearing" (2 Timothy 4:8).

The first aspect of the life to come is "the crown of righteousness." Please understand, Paul has already been made righteous before God. He has received the gift of righteousness that comes through faith in Jesus Christ. God makes us righteous at the beginning of our Christian journey, not at the end of our Christian life. So Paul is not waiting to be made righteous. He is waiting for the crown, the heavenly manifestation of glory that accompanies the righteousness he has already received.

He refers to this same heavenly manifestation of glory in his second letter to the Corinthians. I love the way this is translated in the King James Version: "For our light affliction, which is but for a moment, worketh for us a far more exceeding and eternal weight of glory" (2 Corinthians 4:17). For Paul, heavenly glory was something tangible, something with weight and substance. He looked forward to the crown that comes from possessing the righteousness of Jesus Christ.

Righteousness is glorious. God is a glorious being because He is a righteous being. In this present life, the glory of that righteousness is hidden from view. It is invisible. We have God's righteousness hidden within us, but the glory is not visible. That is why John can say, "Dear friends, now we are children of God, and what we will be has not yet been made known. But we know that when he appears, we shall be like him, for we shall see him as he is" (1 John 3:2).

Why did Paul view the crown of righteousness to be something of substance, a "weight of glory"? Because that crown that awaits us is the resurrected body. We shall have bodies like the Lord's body, for we shall see Him as He is.

This seems unbelievable, indescribable. Imagine what it will mean to have a new body, totally responsive to your spirit, able to do anything at the speed of thought! You'll be able to do things you always dreamed of—even sing with a voice that will make the heavens ring.

Paul tells Timothy that "the Lord, the righteous Judge," will award him the crown of righteousness "on that day." That is what Paul has been looking forward to throughout his post-conversion life. Even now, as he awaits execution, he looks beyond his forthcoming appearance before Nero, the unrighteous judge, to his appearance before the righteous Judge of the universe, who will hand him his reward. God will give Paul the crown of glory, a new and glorified body, because Paul has been made righteous by faith in Jesus Christ.

What does Paul mean when he says that this appearance before the Lord will occur "on that day"? This is an indefinite and vague expression that we find throughout Scripture, a reference to a far-off supreme event. It is the day when all that is now invisible to the human race will be made visible. It is the day when time gives way to eternity. It is the day toward which God is moving all of creation.

Though Paul looks forward to that day with an intensely personal longing, it is a day that he will joyfully share with millions of other believers. He says that he will receive the crown of righteousness from the Lord, the righteous Judge, and not only will he receive that crown, but also "all who have longed for his appearing." Many commentators believe that this is a reference to the second coming of Jesus Christ. I used to think so myself.

However, I now believe that this is a reference to the Lord's first appearing. It is consistent with Paul's words in 2 Timothy 1:10, where he said that the grace of the Lord "has now been revealed through the appearing of our Savior, Christ Jesus, who has destroyed death and has brought life and immortality to light through the gospel." This is clearly a reference to the Lord's first appearance, not His second coming. And that, I'm convinced, is why Paul uses the past tense: "all who have longed for his appearing." If this were a reference to the Lord"s second coming, he would have said, "all who long for his appearing" (present tense).

Is this an important distinction? I believe it is. Paul is speaking here of all who love the Lord Jesus Christ, who are moved by the story of His ministry among broken people, who are touched and convicted by His Sermon on the Mount, who are heartbroken by the story of His suffering and death on the cross and thrilled by the realization that His tomb now stands empty.

Do you love His appearing? If you are truly a Christian, I'm sure your heart responds yes. You love the story of Jesus, and you never tire of hearing it. You love the words He spoke. You love the compassion He showed to the woman caught in adultery. You love the wisdom He showed to the woman at the well. You love the truth He revealed to Nicodemus. You love the hurt in His eyes when He watched the rich young ruler walk away sorrowing. You love His story.

If you truly know him, the lines of this old song express the feelings of your heart:

Tell me the old, old story
      of unseen things above,
Of Jesus and His glory,
      of Jesus and His love.

Tell me the story simply,
      as to a little child;
For I am weak and weary,
      and helpless and defiled.

If those words express the feelings of your heart, then there is nothing you love better than the story of the Lord's appearing. You love that story because He has lifted your load of guilt and He has healed you of hurt and shame. And the time is coming—a time Paul refers to as "that day"—when all of God's people will receive the crown of glory, a resurrection body. The weight of glory will be ours for ever and ever. We will all be conformed to the perfect image of Jesus, because we will see Him as He is.

That was Paul's expectation. That was his joy. May it be our joy as well.

CHAPTER 33

The End of the Road

2 Timothy 4:9–22

The noted preacher Dr. Clarence McCartney, pastor of the First Presbyterian Church of Pittsburgh, Pennsylvania, used to preach a sermon on the closing verses of 2 Timothy 4. That sermon was so moving that his congregation requested that he preach it annually, and he did so for nearly four decades. Entitled "Come Before Winter," it was one of the most famous and oft-reprinted sermons of the early twentieth century.

Why did that sermon tug at the heart of everyone who heard it? Dr. McCartney had a gift for revealing the throbbing human heart of the apostle Paul. When he finished preaching, you knew the apostle Paul not as some distant saint from a bygone era but as a friend, a beloved Christian brother languishing alone in prison. You ached for him and felt the dear old apostle's pain.

One of the best ways to truly get to know the apostle Paul is to start with the book of Romans and read all thirteen of his letters straight through. You will discover not only the amazing depths of his brilliant theological mind but also the human soul of this great apostle. You will feel his great passion for God and his great compassion for lost people. You'll discover what makes him angry and what makes him weep. You'll learn to appreciate this great man of God in amazing new ways.

The impact Paul left on this earth is second only to that of the Lord Jesus. It's not surprising that cities from St. Paul, Minnesota, to São Paulo, Brazil, are named in his honor, as are innumerable churches, schools, and benevolent societies.

Like Paul's beloved Lord, Paul himself never ruled a nation or led an army. And like his Lord, Paul was (from an earthly perspective) just another itinerant preacher who ended up being executed as a troublemaker by the Roman Empire. This man has left his imprint on millions of lives down through the centuries and all across the globe. But here, in 2 Timothy 4, we find him sitting alone in a cold, dark dungeon in Rome, facing the end of his life.

Despite his bleak circumstances, Paul is full of faith in his Lord. He has no regrets about the past. He knows he has fought the good fight and finished his race. Above all, he has kept the faith. He looks forward to being united in eternity with the Lord he has served so faithfully. His thoughts are captured in these lines by Charles Wesley:

Bold I approach the eternal throne,
and claim the crown, through Christ my own.

The lonely apostle

Paul is exultant and expectant at the thought of being home at last with the Lord Jesus. Yet he also feels alone and abandoned. His hurt and rejection come through clearly in these final verses. Paul writes:

Do your best to come to me quickly, for Demas, because he loved this world, has deserted me and has gone to Thessalonica. Crescens has gone to Galatia, and Titus to Dalmatia. Only Luke is with me. Get Mark and bring him with you, because he is helpful to me in my ministry. I sent Tychicus to Ephesus. When you come, bring the cloak that I left with Carpus at Troas, and my scrolls, especially the parchments. (2 Timothy 4:9–13)

Notice how many times Paul appeals to his young friend Timothy to come to him before his execution. In these few lines, Paul repeats his appeal three times: "Do your best to come to me quickly... Get Mark and bring him with you... When you come, bring the cloak." Later, in verse 21, Paul will repeat his appeal yet again: "Do your best to get here before winter."

Paul clearly wishes for Timothy to leave Ephesus and come to Rome, not by ship across the Mediterranean, but by overland route. This would take him north from Ephesus across the Hellespont into Macedonia. Then he would take the Egnatian Road, the great Roman highway, across the Greek peninsula down to the eastern shores of the Adriatic Sea. Then Timothy would journey a short distance across to the heel of the boot of Italy and across the Italian mountains to Rome.

Because Timothy's journey would involve two water crossings, and the storms of winter would make such crossings dangerous and difficult, Paul wanted Timothy to come before the winter weather set in. In this passage, Paul gives Timothy several reasons for the urgency of his request.

One reason was that Demas, a man who had been Paul's longtime fellow worker, had forsaken him. With obvious pain, Paul explains the reasons for the defection of Demas. Paul's former partner in ministry defected "because he loved this world."

Paul says that Demas has gone to Thessalonica, a Greek seaport city and a prosperous center of commerce, culture, and worldly pleasures. Perhaps it was the hometown of Demas. Having tired of the harsh rigors of missionary life, he wanted to return to the familiar surroundings of home. In any case, he had been lured away from the apostle's side by love for the things of this present age.

Paul's heartbreak over the defection of Demas is palpable. I can testify from experience that nothing hurts more than seeing a trusted friend and partner turn his back on you and walk away. Paul not only felt abandoned by Demas, but also he felt personally rejected. He also felt the pain of knowing that Demas had departed from fellowship with the Lord and returned to the emptiness of the world.

Demas stands for those Christian believers who have begun well, whose faith seemed strong and promising, but who eventually drifted from faith, preferring the empty pleasures of the world. They lose their Christian testimony, they fall away from Christian fellowship, and nothing further is heard from them. Paul was heartbroken over the defection of Demas, and he writes these words with tremendous pain and loss.

Next, Paul speaks of Crescens, who has gone to Galatia. Crescens has not defected. Paul has sent him on a mission to the Galatians. This indicates that Crescens was probably a trustworthy servant of Christ and friend of Paul. The apostle trusted him to help the Galatians resolve their struggles and problems.

Then Paul speaks of Titus, a familiar name. We will learn more about Titus in the next chapter. He is another young man, like Timothy, whom Paul calls "my own son." Though Titus is not mentioned by name in the book of Acts, we know that Titus was a Gentile whom Paul apparently led to the Lord in Antioch of Syria, early in his missionary travels with Barnabas. Titus became a test case when the council at Jerusalem met to decide the question of whether Gentile Christians should be circumcised according to the law of Moses. The council decided that the Jewish law should not be imposed on Gentile Christians like Titus.

Titus was Paul's trustworthy partner in ministry, and Paul knew he could rely on Titus to encourage congregations, bring peace out of conflict, and collect offerings for believers who were in need. Paul had sent Titus to the churches in Dalmatia (modern Croatia) to strengthen the churches there.

"When you come…"

Paul writes, "Only Luke is with me." Only one man remains at the apostle's side: faithful Luke, the beloved physician. Luke may well have stayed with Paul because of Paul's mysterious ailment, his "thorn in the flesh" (see 2 Corinthians 12:7–10).

Bible commentator William Barclay tells us it was a Roman custom that when a citizen went to Rome for trial, he was permitted to take two slaves with them. It may well be that in order to travel with Paul and minister to the apostle's physical needs, Luke may have had to volunteer to be Paul's slave. This might explain why Luke remained with Paul to the end of his life, and it tells us a great deal about the faithful heart of Luke.

Paul goes on to say, "Get Mark and bring him with you, because he is helpful to me in my ministry." Mark is a familiar name in the New Testament. He is also known as John Mark and was a companion of the apostle Peter. He accompanied Paul and Barnabas on the first missionary journey and was a kinsman of Barnabas (see Colossians 4:10). John Mark's mother was a wealthy woman and a prominent member of the church in Jerusalem. Her spacious home was a meeting place for the Christian brothers (see Acts 12:12–17).

Paul and Barnabas became involved in a dispute over whether or not they should take John Mark with them on the second missionary journey. Paul felt that Mark had proven unreliable when he quit during the previous journey. John Mark undoubtedly grew in character and toughness as a result of his earlier failure. Paul had changed his opinion of John Mark by the time he wrote 2 Timothy, because he writes, "Get Mark and bring him with you, because he is helpful to me in my ministry." It is a tribute to Paul that he found the grace to forgive Mark's earlier failure and restore him to ministry.

The apostle says, "I sent Tychicus to Ephesus." Tychicus went to Ephesus as Timothy's replacement, allowing Timothy to come to Rome. We know Tychicus as Paul's faithful ministry partner and the bearer of the letters to the Colossians and the Ephesians.

Paul also instructs Timothy, "When you come, bring the cloak that I left with Carpus at Troas, and my scrolls, especially the parchments." Why had Paul left these valuable personal effects at the home of a friend in Troas? Paul was probably rearrested by the Roman authorities in Troas. His arrest took place so quickly and unexpectedly that he had no time to return to the home of Carpus for his belongings.

Timothy was probably present at Paul's arrest, as suggested by Paul's words in 2 Timothy 1:4: "Recalling your tears, I long to see you, so that I may be filled with joy." This is probably a reference to their tearful parting when Paul was arrested. So now Paul asks Timothy to go to Troas and pick up his cloak and books.

Those books were copies of the Scriptures and may have included the gospels of Mark and Matthew, which were probably circulated by that time. Paul's emphasis on the parchments indicated that they were probably copies of the Old Testament Scriptures. Parchment is an especially durable form of writing material made from the dried skin of sheep or goats, and therefore especially suitable for valuable manuscripts. He wanted those books to comfort him as he faced his coming execution.

Delivered from the lion's mouth

Next, Paul offers Timothy a personal word of warning: "Alexander the metalworker did me a great deal of harm. The Lord will repay him for what he has done. You too should be on your guard against him, because he strongly opposed our message" (2 Timothy 4:14–15).

It may well be that Alexander the metalworker was the one who betrayed Paul into the hands of the Romans. This man, Paul says, "did me a great deal of harm." This is a phrase often found in Greek literature to describe the actions of a traitor or informer. At the very least, we know that Alexander opposed Paul's message of salvation by grace through faith in Jesus Christ.

This is probably the same Alexander we encountered in 1 Timothy 1:20, when Paul referred to Hymenaeus and Alexander, "whom I have handed over to Satan to be taught not to blaspheme." Alexander's motive for betraying Paul to the Roman authorities may have been simple revenge. So Paul now warns Timothy, "Watch out for Alexander. He did me great harm, and he will harm you too, if he gets the chance."

But Paul does not urge Timothy to take any action against Alexander. He entrusts himself to the righteous Judge: "The Lord will repay him for what he has done." As Paul wrote in his letter to the Romans, the Lord has said, "It is mine to avenge; I will repay" (see Romans 12:19). This is how we should always respond when mistreated.

Next, Paul reports to Timothy on the conditions he is enduring in Rome:

> At my first defense, no one came to my support, but everyone deserted me. May it not be held against them. But the Lord stood at my side and gave me strength, so that through me the message might be fully proclaimed and all the Gentiles might hear it. And I was delivered from the lion's mouth. The Lord will rescue me from every evil attack and will

bring me safely to his heavenly kingdom. To him be glory for ever and ever. Amen. (2 Timothy 4:16–18)

These are heartbreaking words. When Paul was brought up for his arraignment, no one stood with him. Everyone forsook him. On one level, this is understandable. These were dangerous times in Rome. Emperor Nero was noted for his vindictiveness and irrationality. Anyone who sided with Paul would be viewed as an enemy of the emperor. Nero's assassins were everywhere, ready to slit a throat at Nero's word.

So the apostle had to face his accusers alone. Though Paul is saddened, he is not bitter. In fact, he says, "May it not be held against them." Though Paul was alone in a human sense, he was not abandoned. "The Lord stood at my side," he writes, "and gave me strength." The presence of Jesus, Paul says, produced two profound effects in his life.

First, Paul says that the Lord's presence gave him the strength to testify, so that his message might be proclaimed to the Gentiles. Even though he was in chains and on trial for his life, Paul faithfully preached the Word, in season and out of season.

Second, Paul says that the Lord delivered him "from the lion's mouth." This does not mean that Paul thought that he was literally going to be thrown to the lions in the Roman Coliseum. Although Christians were thrown to the lions in later years, this form of persecution was not in use during Paul's day. Furthermore, as a Roman citizen, the law required that he be executed humanely, not by torture. So "the lion's mouth" was a figurative term.

The lion Paul spoke of was probably a reference to Satan, the lying demon who was truly behind the false charges against Paul. Undoubtedly, Paul felt that Satan was the one who weakened the courage of the Christians who abandoned him. Paul gave the Lord Jesus Christ the credit for delivering him from the jaws of the lion. Even though he was in chains and threatened with beheading, Paul felt safe in the sheltering hands of his Lord. So he concluded, "The Lord will rescue me from every evil attack and will bring me safely to his heavenly kingdom. To him be glory for ever and ever. Amen."

Final greetings

Paul closes his final letter with a series of greetings to brothers and sisters in the faith whom Paul knows he will probably not see again in this life. He writes, "Greet Priscilla and Aquila and the household of Onesiphorus. Erastus stayed in Corinth, and I left Trophimus sick in Miletus. Do your best to get here before winter. Eubulus greets you, and so do Pudens, Linus, Claudia and all the brothers" (2 Timothy 4:19–21).

We have seen some of these names before. Priscilla and Aquila were the Jewish couple, tentmakers like himself, whom Paul had met in Corinth. Every time they appear in Scripture, a church is meeting in their home. They had a church in Corinth; then they moved with Paul to Ephesus and had a church in their home there; they went to Rome, and, in Paul's letter to the Romans, he refers to the church in their home there. Now they are apparently in Ephesus and undoubtedly hosting a church there.

Paul also greets the family of Onesiphorus, who had ministered to him while he was a prisoner in Rome. Now, apparently, Onesiphorus is still away from his family. Erastus, we learn from the letter to the Romans, was the city treasurer of Corinth, so it would make sense that he had remained there in order to carry on his business.

"I left Trophimus sick in Miletus," Paul says. This is a fascinating statement. As we have mentioned elsewhere in this book, there are many preachers and faith healers today who claim that if a Christian is ever sick, it is because of hidden sin or lack of faith. If that is so, then why did Paul leave his friend Trophimus sick in Miletus? Did Trophimus lack faith? Did he have hidden sin? Why didn't Paul heal him?

Trophimus, you may recall, was the man accused of unlawfully entering the temple in Jerusalem with Paul. That false accusation precipitated a riot, causing Paul to be arrested in Jerusalem. That arrest ultimately led to Paul's first journey to Rome and his first imprisonment there, as recorded in Acts.

Paul also mentions someone named Eubulus, of whom we know nothing. Then Paul mentions three more names that are intriguing: Pudens, Linus, and Claudia. They are Roman Christians who greet the brothers in Ephesus.

Linus is likely Paul's successor as leader of the church in Rome. The early church father Irenaeus mentions a man named Linus who was the bishop of Rome and was probably this same man.

Many Bible scholars consider Pudens and Claudia to be husband and wife. Pudens is a male name, Claudia a female name. It was sometimes the custom to list the names of family members in this order: father, child, mother. So Pudens and Claudia may well have been the parents of Linus. The Roman historian Tacitus mentions a Roman nobleman named Pudens who had married a princess, the daughter of the British king Tiberius Claudius Cogidubnus (the daughter might well be named Claudia after Claudius). In the city of

Chichester, England, a plaque has been found bearing the name of this king and of his son-in-law, Pudens. So there appears to be secular confirmation of the view that Pudens and Claudia were Roman Christians and parents of Linus.

This evidence suggests that Claudia came to Rome from Britain and married Pudens. At some point, they became Christians, and their son Linus also converted to Christianity. So these closing lines of Paul's final letter suggest a connection with British Christianity. The British Christians eventually settled in America, establishing American Christianity. This is a fascinating thread to follow as we trace the progress of the gospel down through history and across the globe.

Did Timothy reach Rome in time for one last reunion with Paul? We don't know. I like to think he did, and there is some historical evidence to suggest that the apostle Paul was not beheaded until the spring of the year 68. This letter was probably written in the late summer or fall of 67. If Timothy did indeed "come before winter," as Paul urged him to, then Timothy may well have spent several months with his beloved father in the faith. This visit would have been a great comfort to Paul in the final weeks of his life.

It's hard to imagine Timothy saying no to the apostle's pleadings. I feel sure that Timothy, upon reading those words, would have done everything within his power to rush to Paul's side. If Timothy had missed his opportunity to see Paul one last time and comfort him in his final days, it's hard to imagine how he could have lived with himself.

And there is a lesson here for us all: When God calls you to do something, don't hesitate. Do it. When God calls you to minister to someone's need, don't procrastinate. Do it. You never know if you will get another chance to answer that call.

There is a story told about three demons who were assigned to earth to cause trouble for Christians. They had a meeting with Satan, the lord of the demons, to discuss their strategy of attack. Satan asked all three demons how they planned to proceed against their human victims.

The first demon said, "I will tempt them to atheism. I will tell the humans that there is no God."

Satan said, "We have tried that strategy, and it is not very effective. Deep down, the miserable humans know God exists."

The second demon said, "I will whisper to them that there is no evil, no sin, no Satan, and no hell. I will urge them to throw off moral restraints and live as they please."

Satan said, "We have tried that, too. But just when they start to believe that there is no evil, they notice the evil in the world all around them—the wars, crime, terrorism, child abuse, and so forth. Any other ideas?"

The third demon said, "I will tell them there is no hurry."

Satan laughed. "Brilliant," he said. "Go, tell them there is no hurry, and they will belong to us."

This is only a fable, but there is a great deal of truth in those words. The world is growing darker. Our mission is urgent. Human need is great. We have no time to waste, no time to lose. Don't hesitate, don't procrastinate. If God calls you to act for Him, do it, and do it *now*.

Our road goes on

A day came when Paul appeared once more before Nero, and he was condemned to death. The sentence was probably carried out without delay. Paul was led in chains along the Via Ostiensis (the Ostian Way), outside of Rome. At a place called Aquae Salviae, the Roman guards placed Paul's head on the executioner's block. The sword flashed in the sun—

And Paul was instantly transported into the presence of the Lord.

This was a triumphant conclusion to a marvelous life!

The world owes so much to this mighty apostle who spread the love of Jesus Christ from city to city, from continent to continent. He instructed us and modeled for us what it means to follow Christ. Paul's last recorded words are simple yet profound: "The Lord be with your spirit. Grace be with you" (2 Timothy 4:22).

The presence of the Lord, His Spirit with our spirit, is the foundation of the Christian life. His presence is the daily supply we need to encourage us and strengthen us. "Grace be with you" is the message that sustains us in these dark and dangerous days. It is the grace of our Lord that empowers us to stand for God's truth against the pressures and opposition we face.

Paul has come to the end of his road. He has fought the good fight, he has finished his race, he has kept the faith.

Your road and mine still go on. Our fight continues. Our race is still unfinished. But Paul has shown us the way. We follow in his footsteps and in the footsteps of our Lord. As we go, the Lord is with us. His Spirit whispers comfort to your spirit and mine. His grace sustains us every step of the way.

The Lord be with your spirit, my friend. Grace be with you.

Part III

Fighting Falsehood
with Truth

Titus

CHAPTER 34

Grace for Liars, Brutes, and Lazy Gluttons

Titus 1

The Communist government of East Germany began building the Berlin Wall, separating East Berlin from West Berlin, on August 13, 1961. That wall would stand for twenty-eight years, until a wave of pro-democracy reforms swept the Iron Curtain away in 1989. As the people of Berlin watched the wall being built, they had no way of knowing if it would stand for decades or centuries.

One man who watched the wall being built was an evangelical Lutheran theologian, Dr. Paul Toaspern. He lived in free West Berlin, but as the Communists began erecting the concrete wall, he realized that many of his fellow Germans were about to be imprisoned by Marxist-Leninist tyranny. He had already spent years under the jackboot of Hitler and the Nazis, and he knew that the Communists were every bit as cruel and anti-Christian as the Nazis.

Dr. Toaspern could have easily remained safe and free in West Berlin. But he felt God calling him to do something most people would consider incredibly brave or foolish. While thousands of refugees fled from East Berlin to the West, Paul Toaspern gathered up his wife and children and took them into East Berlin to begin a new life under Communist rule.

Why did he do it? Paul Toaspern knew that the Christian church in East Berlin would need strong leaders who could teach the Scriptures and were willing to risk arrest and imprisonment to boldly proclaim the gospel behind the Iron Curtain. He became one of the most outspoken evangelists and leaders in the East German church.

It was a difficult existence, not only for Paul Toaspern but also for his family. As his children grew up, they were denied higher education. The state would not allow students to enter the university unless they joined the Young Communist League.

Paul Toaspern was not allowed to leave East Berlin to visit his parents in West Germany, nor could he telephone or write to them. So he arranged to go to the wall on a regular basis. He would shout over the wall to friends on the free side. They would act as messengers, carrying news back and forth between Paul and his parents. His parents both died before the wall came down.

After the reunification of Germany, Paul Toaspern was free once more. Both he and his family paid a high price to answer God's call to East Berlin. But he fulfilled his mission, he strengthened and encouraged the Christian church in East Berlin, and the church was sustained and established in that city in large part because of his courage and commitment.

When I think of his story, I'm reminded of Titus, a young man who was led to Christ and discipled by the apostle Paul. Titus was called by God and commissioned by Paul to go to a difficult place and minister under oppressive conditions among a difficult people. But he went in obedience to his calling. He fulfilled his mission, and he strengthened and encouraged the church in Crete.

The verse that summarizes the theme of Paul's letter to this young church leader is Titus 1:5, where the apostle writes, "The reason I left you in Crete was that you might straighten out what was left unfinished and appoint elders in every town, as I directed you" (Titus 1:5). Paul has given Titus an important and challenging task: Straighten out what was left unfinished in Crete, and appoint leaders so that the church in Crete will be strengthened and established. As we shall see, Paul's counsel to Titus is just as applicable and practical for us today as it was two thousand years ago.

Paul's son in the faith

Paul's letter to Titus was probably written in A.D. 66, between the writing of 1 Timothy and 2 Timothy. Historians believe Paul wrote this letter after his release from his first house arrest in Rome and before his second arrest in Troas. Paul wrote it from either Macedonia or Ephesus, and a messenger took it to Titus, who was ministering on the island of Crete.

All three of the pastoral letters of Paul, the two letters to Timothy and the letter to Titus, demonstrate similar themes and intent on the part of Paul. In all three letters, Paul instructs Timothy and Titus in four basic issues: appointing leaders (elders) in the church; teaching those leaders to guard the faith; teaching the congregation sound doctrine; and remaining on guard against false teachers. Paul told Timothy to carry out these four tasks in Ephesus; he charged Titus to do the same in Crete.

The church in Crete was probably begun by Paul and Titus after Paul's first imprisonment in Rome. You may recall that he had expressed the desire to go to Spain (see Romans 15:24, 28), and many scholars feel that after his journey to Spain, he and Titus went to the island of Crete and founded the church there.

Paul opens his letter to Titus with this greeting:

Paul, a servant of God and an apostle of Jesus Christ for the faith of God's elect and the knowledge of the truth that leads to godliness—a faith and knowledge resting on the hope of eternal life, which God, who does not lie, promised before the beginning of time, and at his appointed season he brought his word to light through the preaching entrusted to me by the command of God our Savior,

To Titus, my true son in our common faith:

Grace and peace from God the Father and Christ Jesus our Savior. (Titus 1:1–4)

Paul begins with his credentials. He is a servant, a slave of God; and his life is not his own because he is owned, body and soul, by God. He is also "an apostle of Jesus Christ," which means that he is a messenger on behalf of the Son of God. By setting forth his own credentials, Paul supplies credentials to Titus. If anyone questions the authority of Titus to appoint elders in Crete, Titus can present this letter and say, "Here is my authority. I have been charged by the apostle Paul himself to undertake this task."

Next, Paul speaks of his purpose. He is an apostle on behalf of the Christian faith and the truth that leads to godliness and the hope of eternal life. Paul was chosen to be an apostle in order to take the gospel to those who were chosen ("God's elect") to receive the hope of eternal life. To know that God has chosen us even before we chose Him should fill our hearts with awe, gratitude, and love for Him.

Paul addresses this letter "to Titus, my true son in our common faith." Titus was one of the young men who accompanied the apostle Paul on several of his missionary journeys. Paul had met Titus in the city of Antioch of Syria, and there he had led Titus to Christ. Paul had mentored and discipled Titus, and they had a father-son relationship. In another letter, Paul refers to Titus as "my partner and fellow worker among you" (see 2 Corinthians 8:23). Paul had designated Titus and Timothy as his representatives to the churches. Both of these young men were involved in collecting offerings for the church in Jerusalem during the famine there.

The uncircumcised disciple

There is an interesting distinction between Titus and Timothy that many people find confusing. Paul led both of these young men to the Lord, he took them both on his travels, he discipled them both and recruited them both into missionary and church ministry. Acts 16 tells us that Paul made a point of having Timothy circumcised according to the Old Testament tradition, yet, as Paul relates in Galatians 2:1–6, he refused to have Titus circumcised. Why did Paul treat Titus and Timothy differently?

The difference was that Timothy was Jewish; Titus was not. Technically, Timothy was half-Jewish; that is, he had a Greek father and a Jewish mother. The Hebrew people had a practical approach to matters of lineage: A person may not know who his father is, but he almost always knows who his mother is. So if a person had a Jewish mother, that person was considered fully a Jew. So it was with Timothy.

In Acts 16:3, we read, "Paul wanted to take [Timothy] along on the journey, so he circumcised him because of the Jews who lived in that area, for they all knew that his father was a Greek." Paul wanted Timothy to have credibility with the Jews as he worked among them and shared the gospel with them. So Paul had Timothy undergo the Jewish ritual of circumcision. In this way, Timothy identified himself with the Jewish people and the Jewish origins of the Christian faith.

In the case of Titus, however, we find a situation that seems similar on the surface. Paul and Barnabas, along with Titus, went to the council in Jerusalem to discuss Paul's revelation from God that he was to take the gospel to the Gentile world. Paul writes that "some false brothers had infiltrated our ranks to spy on the freedom we have in Christ Jesus and to make us slaves." In other words, some people claiming to be Christian converts from Judaism had entered the church and wanted to require Christians to observe the Jewish legalistic rules and rituals. They tried to force Titus to be circumcised, but Paul refused to allow it.

Why would Paul require Timothy to be circumcised and refuse to allow Titus to be circumcised? Here we find the key to understanding biblical principles in situations where customs and rituals are involved: We must always understand the underlying principle and act accordingly.

Paul had Timothy circumcised according to the Old Testament rituals in order to carry out the principle he explained in another letter: "I have become all things to all men so that by all possible means I might save some" (see 1 Corinthians 9:22). Paul had Timothy circumcised as part of a strategy to "become all things to all people" in order to reach the lost.

But Paul refused to have Titus circumcised. To do so would have meant giving in to the legalistic demands of false brothers. If he had yielded, Paul would have set a precedent that might have placed the Christian church under bondage to legalism. So Paul wisely resisted the pressure from the legalists.

In spite of the superficial similarities of the two situations, they were fundamentally different. By examining the underlying principles of these two situations, we gain insight into how we should apply biblical principles to the difficult choices in our own real-life situations.

Paul concludes his greeting with these words of blessing: "Grace and peace from God the Father and Christ Jesus our Savior." These are not empty words and should not be passed over lightly. Grace refers to that marvelous gift of God's unmerited blessing toward us, including His forgiveness and acceptance of us, purchased at the cost of the blood of Jesus. Peace refers to the reconciliation we have with God the Father through Jesus. Because He suffered and died, we have peace with God.

Straighten out the church

Next Paul states the theme of this letter in a single verse. He writes, "The reason I left you in Crete was that you might straighten out what was left unfinished and appoint elders in every town, as I directed you" (Titus 1:5).

In this letter, Paul gives us a fascinating insight into how the early church was governed and structured. As the apostle Paul went from place to place and established churches, he sent various men, such as Timothy and Titus, to serve as his apostolic delegates. They would represent Paul's apostolic authority and carry out tasks and solve problems in the churches.

Paul reminds Titus that his reason for leaving him in Crete was to establish the Christian church there ("straighten out what was left unfinished") and to make sure that every church in every town on the island of Crete had strong spiritual leadership ("appoint elders in every town"). Next, Paul sets forth the qualifications for those elders:

> An elder must be blameless, the husband of but one wife, a man whose children believe and are not open to the charge of being wild and disobedient. Since an overseer is entrusted with God's work, he must be blameless—not overbearing, not quick-tempered, not given to drunkenness,

293

not violent, not pursuing dishonest gain. Rather he must be hospitable, one who loves what is good, who is self-controlled, upright, holy and disciplined. He must hold firmly to the trustworthy message as it has been taught, so that he can encourage others by sound doctrine and refute those who oppose it. (Titus 1:6–9)

We have already looked at the qualifications for elders in detail when we examined 1 Timothy 3, so we shall not go into detail on that subject here. The qualifications Paul sets forth here are essentially the same as those he gave to Timothy for the elders of the church in Ephesus.

"Cretans are always liars"

Next, Paul writes about the specific challenges Titus faces in ministering among the people in Crete. These challenges center on the culture and character of the Cretan people. (Incidentally, the word *Cretan* is *not* related to *cretin,* an offensive term for a person afflicted with mental handicaps; the term *cretin* comes from the French *crétin* by way of an ancient Latin term, *christianus,* which was intended by the Romans as an insult to Christians.) In one of the most unusual passages in the New Testament, Paul quotes the Cretan philosopher Epimenides of Knossos, who lived about six centuries before Christ. Paul writes:

For there are many rebellious people, mere talkers and deceivers, especially those of the circumcision group. They must be silenced, because they are ruining whole households by teaching things they ought not to teach—and that for the sake of dishonest gain. Even one of their own prophets has said, "Cretans are always liars, evil brutes, lazy gluttons." This testimony is true. Therefore, rebuke them sharply, so that they will be sound in the faith and will pay no attention to Jewish myths or to the commands of those who reject the truth. (Titus 1:10–14)

Paul's message here is clear: Titus will encounter many challenges because the Cretans are a challenging people. He quotes a line from the poem "Cretica" by Epimenides: "Cretans are always liars, evil brutes, lazy gluttons." (This statement has become a famous problem in logic, the Epimenides paradox. The problem is this: If the Cretan Epimenides says "Cretans are always liars," then how can that statement be true, since Epimenides must be lying?)

Who are these Cretan people Paul warns about? The Cretans are descendents of the ancient tribes of Philistines—the same tribes who had troubled the Jewish people during the time of King Saul and King David. Some historians believe the Philistines to have been part of a great naval alliance called the Sea Peoples. These people were pirates and sea warriors from the Aegean islands who invaded the lands of Canaan and Egypt more than a thousand years before Christ.

So when Paul agrees with the Cretan Epimenides that these descendents of Philistine pirates were liars, evil brutes, and lazy gluttons, we would do well to believe him. As Paul emphasizes in this passage, "This testimony is true." Yet it is important to realize that even though Paul describes these people in such disparaging terms, the Cretans are clearly not beyond the reach of God's grace. God loves even liars, brutes, and lazy gluttons, and He gave His Son to die for them.

Paul's tough words regarding the Cretans are not meant to defame them. Rather, Paul is sharing some insights with his son in the faith, Titus, so that this young Christian leader will be able to serve the spiritual needs of the Cretans. Paul tells Titus to "rebuke them sharply" so that they will have a sound faith and not be swayed by foolish myths or the teachings of false prophets. He also warns Titus: "To the pure, all things are pure, but to those who are corrupted and do not believe, nothing is pure. In fact, both their minds and consciences are corrupted. They claim to know God, but by their actions they deny him. They are detestable, disobedient and unfit for doing anything good" (Titus 1:15–16).

Here, Paul refers to the difficulty of trying to build a community of people who would think Christianly amid a corrupt culture. There would be many people coming into the church who would claim to know and follow God, yet they would deny God by their conduct. Paul warns Titus against the kind of worldly Christian who talks the talk but will not walk the walk. Such people, Paul says, should not be trusted, for they are not genuine. They are, he says, "detestable, disobedient and unfit for doing anything good."

The church of Jesus Christ has a clear mission: invade the world. When the church is functioning as God intended it to function, the church advances and the world retreats. But when the church is dysfunctional, when the church is troubled, divided, and unhealthy, then we know that the world is invading the church instead of the church invading the world.

The gospel is a disturbing force. It unsettles and subverts society. Whenever the church is true to its message, it attacks the status quo. Christianity is a revolutionary force, but it can carry out its revolutionary mission only when

Christians live in obedience to God. Our minds must be pure and our consciences cleansed. If we claim to be revolutionaries for God but our thoughts and actions are aligned with this dying world, then we are disobedient and unfit to take part in the revolution.

Evil brutes, lazy gluttons

Paul warns Titus that the Cretans are "evil brutes, lazy gluttons." What is Titus supposed to do with such people? How is he supposed to minister to people who act like animals, snarling and griping at one another, people who engage in stupid controversies and quarrels? How is he supposed to deal with people who are so easy-going and pleasure-loving that they are not inclined toward spiritual things?

The apostle is not saying the Cretans are beyond hope. Later in this letter, Paul reminds Titus that the two of them were, at one time, no better than Cretans:

> At one time we too were foolish, disobedient, deceived and enslaved by all kinds of passions and pleasures. We lived in malice and envy, being hated and hating one another. But when the kindness and love of God our Savior appeared, he saved us, not because of righteous things we had done, but because of his mercy. (Titus 3:3–5a)

Apart from faith in Jesus Christ, we are all lost, foolish, disobedient, deceived, and enslaved by sins. We are all Cretans at heart. Only when the kindness and love of God breaks through, like the light of the sun breaking through the storm clouds, can we be transformed from liars, evil brutes, and lazy gluttons into people who are becoming more and more like Christ.

There must have been many times during Titus's ministry in Crete when he wondered, "What have I gotten myself into?" Here he was, stuck on an island populated by the descendents of Philistine pirates and cutthroats. His mission was to establish a Christian church among these people. At times, the task must have seemed daunting and even impossible.

But Paul wanted Titus to understand that the challenge of converting a Cretan was no worse than the challenge of transforming a hard-hearted, murderous persecutor like Saul of Tarsus or a pagan Greek like Titus. Titus had his work cut out for him. But God was up to the challenge. Titus was God's chosen instrument for reaching the Cretans with the good news of Jesus Christ.

Who are the Cretans in your life? Who are the challenging people you are tempted to dismiss as unreachable? Who are the liars, evil brutes, and lazy gluttons that you have written off as hopeless? Is God calling you now to attempt an impossible task, to reach an impossible person, to achieve an impossible goal for Him?

What are you waiting for?

CHAPTER 35

Ruled by the Truth

Titus 2–3

Dr. Steve Bilynskyj, pastor of Valley Covenant Church in Eugene, Oregon, has devised a simple yet profound means of illustrating how we determine what truth is. He has used this illustration when teaching confirmation classes in his church. He shows his students a jar filled with beans and asks them to guess the number of beans in the jar. He writes down their estimates on a large sheet of paper.

Then he asks his students to make a second list—this time, a list of their favorite songs. When both lists have been written, Dr. Bilynskyj reveals the actual number of beans in the jar.

Next, Dr. Bilynskyj indicates the list of favorite songs and says, "Now, which of these lists is the closest to being right?"

"There's no right answer!" the students reply. "Your favorite song is just a matter of personal taste."

"Oh?" says Dr. Bilynskyj. "Well, what about your faith? When you decide what you believe about God and eternity and the meaning of life, how do you determine what is true? Is it more like guessing the number of beans in a jar? Or is it more like choosing your favorite song?"

Invariably, most, if not all, of his students reply: Choosing your faith is more like choosing your favorite song. It's a matter of personal taste. In fact, Dr. Bilynskyj says that over the years, a purely subjective, personal-preference approach to truth (which he calls "favorite song theology") has become increasingly more prevalent among Christians.

"In our postmodern world," he says, "people are becoming less and less inclined to think of their religious convictions in terms of truth or falsehood. Even many evangelical leaders today say that an excessive focus on objective truth is a disservice to the gospel and the wrong way to speak to the current generation. And yet, if we lose our ability to speak to this generation in terms of factual truth, we will find it ever more difficult to proclaim our Lord, who called himself the way, the truth, and the life.

"This is not to say that the biblical notion of truth is limited to that which is scientifically and empirically quantified. Scripture reveals to us a much richer notion of truth than my simple jar of beans experiment might imply. Biblical truth is personal, life-changing, and relational—it transforms our relationships with God and with each other. But biblical truth also corresponds with facts and objective reality. The key to the apostolic proclamation was that Jesus did in fact rise from the dead and that His resurrection was in fact confirmed by many witnesses.

"So the right answer to the jar of beans or favorite song question might be, 'Both.' One's faith should be truthful and accurate with regard to objective facts (as the jar of beans illustrates), and one's faith should be personally moving, personally challenging, and personally transformational (as the favorite song list illustrates). The good news about the Good News is that it is true in both ways. Our challenge in this postmodern age is not to lose the importance of objective, factual, jar of beans truth."

Truth and sound doctrine

As we come to Titus 2, we see the apostle Paul now turn to the issue of objective biblical truth, which he calls "sound doctrine." Paul tells Titus, "You must teach what is in accord with sound doctrine" (Titus 2:1).

Don't let that word *doctrine* put you off; it simply means "teachings." Christian doctrines are the truths that are taught from the Christian Scriptures. Here, Paul underscores the need for sound biblical doctrine in the church. Paul understood that in order to change society, people need to be told the truth. They need to be led out of the darkness of their ignorance about God, the world, and their own nature.

While the Christian message is universal, Paul says that the process of teaching sound doctrine must be tailored to the needs of various groups within the church. Paul identifies five specific groups in the church. He urges Titus to teach each of these five groups according to sound biblical doctrine.

The apostle begins by addressing the needs of the first group, the older men: "Teach the older men to be temperate, worthy of respect, self-controlled, and sound in faith, in love and in endurance" (Titus 2:2).

Remember, Paul has already said that the people of Crete have been negatively influenced by their Philistine culture. In the ancient Mediterranean cultures, young people were expected to show respect to older men simply because they were old. But Paul says that the older men need to live in such a way that they are "worthy of respect." In effect, Paul says the older men must earn respect by demonstrating certain character qualities.

They are to be "temperate," or sober—not given to drunkenness. It's not surprising that these descendents of Philistine pirates would have a problem with alcohol. But Christians are expected to be filled with the Spirit, not drunk with wine.

Next, older men are to be "worthy of respect," or dignified. Their behavior should bring honor to God. And they are to be "self-controlled." This term in the Greek has the sense of being sensible, mature, and of sound mind.

Then, Paul says that older men are to be "sound in faith, in love and in endurance." Paul wants Titus to teach the older men to be spiritually strong, abounding in Christian love, and sound in their endurance and perseverance. If the older men in the church in Crete adopt these character traits, they will stand in stark contrast to the liars, evil brutes, and lazy gluttons of the surrounding culture.

Paul then turns his attention to the second group of people in the church of Crete, the older women.

> Likewise, teach the older women to be reverent in the way they live, not to be slanderers or addicted to much wine, but to teach what is good. Then they can train the younger women to love their husbands and children, to be self-controlled and pure, to be busy at home, to be kind, and to be subject to their husbands, so that no one will malign the word of God. (Titus 2:3–5)

Paul's message for the older women is not unlike his message for the older men. They need to exhibit a reverent way of life; in other words, they need to be role models of godliness and Christlikeness.

They are not to be "slanderers." In other words, they are not to gossip about other people. This is a serious problem in the church to this day. People do not take seriously God's condemnation of gossip. Many people say, "But it's not gossip if it's true!" For one thing, it doesn't matter if the gossip is true or not. If you tear down another person's reputation, even with accurate information, you are still doing what God hates. You are still gossiping against your brother or sister.

For another thing, we don't ever really know all the truth about another person. The gossip we spread may be the truth, or a half-truth, or a twisted truth, or a filthy lie. But God hates gossip and slander (see Proverbs 11:13; 16:28; Romans 1:29; 2 Corinthians 12:20), and so should we.

The older women are not to be addicted to wine but are to teach what is good. Here, Paul suggests that teaching takes place through both words and example. He wants the older women to be mentors to the younger women, teaching them how to be loving wives and mothers. In the brutish Cretan society, children were sometimes viewed as cheap labor rather than gifts from God; many Cretan mothers had to learn Christlike love for their children.

And in the lazy Cretan society, women sometimes had to be taught to be hardworking homemakers. They needed to learn such qualities as self-control, purity, kindness, and humility. Paul wants the women of Crete to understand that by demonstrating Christlike character, they will help to advance the gospel. Through their godly behavior, God and His Word will be honored and glorified.

Younger women, younger men, and slaves

Paul tells Titus that he should instruct the older women (the second group) to in turn teach and mentor the younger women (the third group). Paul does not tell Titus to instruct the younger women directly. I believe that Paul intentionally wishes to establish a boundary line, so that Titus, who is evidently a single young man, is not tempted toward any improper relationship with a younger woman. In fact, he doesn't want Titus to be vulnerable to a false accusation of such a relationship.

Next, Paul turns his attention to the fourth group, younger men. He writes:

> Similarly, encourage the young men to be self-controlled. In everything set them an example by doing what is good. In your teaching show integrity, seriousness and soundness of speech that cannot be condemned, so that those who oppose you may be ashamed because they have nothing bad to say about us. (Titus 2:6–8)

In these verses, it's clear that Paul views Titus as part of this fourth group. Paul's first word to Titus regarding this group is, "Encourage the young men to be self-controlled." And how should Titus encourage other young men to exercise self-control? "In everything set them an example by doing what is good." Titus is to be a role model for the other young men.

But Titus is not merely to teach by example. He must also speak the Word of God to the young men in the church. He must instruct them in sound doctrine. "In your teaching show integrity," Paul says, meaning that Titus's walk should match his talk.

Moreover, Titus's teaching should demonstrate "seriousness and soundness of speech that cannot be condemned." Paul knows that young men can be prone to coarse jesting and unsound speech. The apostle wants Titus to set an impeccable example before the other young men of his generation, so that no one would have any reason to complain about his words or behavior.

Next, Paul addresses the fifth group in the church of Crete, those who are living under the yoke of slavery: "Teach slaves to be subject to their masters in everything, to try to please them, not to talk back to them, and not to steal from them, but to show that they can be fully trusted, so that in every way they will make the teaching about God our Savior attractive" (Titus 2:9–10).

We already addressed this issue in detail when we studied 1 Timothy 6. So here, I will simply repeat that the principles Paul addresses to slaves apply equally well to employees. Even if you think your boss is an unreasonable tyrant, you should treat him or her with respect. As an employee, do your best to earn your pay, to please your employer, to show respect, to demonstrate honesty and integrity in all of your dealings, and to be trustworthy. If you do all of these things, then you will be a witness to your boss and your co-workers. You'll bring honor and credit to the gospel of Jesus Christ.

It's interesting that Paul felt it was important for slaves to understand doctrine and practice good Christian conduct. Paul didn't lower his expectations for anyone because he or she was in a disadvantaged position in life. He was confident that a slave could be just as effective a witness for Christ as a free man or woman.

Paul is not saying that slavery is a justifiable condition. Rather, Paul is saying that even though he is treated unjustly, a Christian slave represents Christ and reflects the image of God. By accepting Christ as Lord and Savior and living out his faith, the slave truly fulfills his humanity. The slave master and a tyrannical slaveholding society may try to rob the slave of his dignity, but the slave's true Lord is not the slave master but Jesus the Master. Knowing Christ is the true source of human worth and dignity.

Two appearings

Next, Paul gathers up all of these instructions to the five groups and places those instructions in the context of the central doctrines of Christianity—in particular, the doctrines of Christ's incarnation, the hope of salvation, and the second coming of Christ:

> For the grace of God that brings salvation has appeared to all men. It
> teaches us to say "No" to ungodliness and worldly passions, and to live

self-controlled, upright and godly lives in this present age, while we wait for the blessed hope—the glorious appearing of our great God and Savior, Jesus Christ, who gave himself for us to redeem us from all wickedness and to purify for himself a people that are his very own, eager to do what is good.

These, then, are the things you should teach. Encourage and rebuke with all authority. Do not let anyone despise you. (Titus 2:11–15)

Notice that there are two appearings in that passage. First, Paul says that "the grace of God that brings salvation has appeared to all men." Paul speaks of an event that has already occurred in history. The grace of God has appeared. This is a reference to the life and ministry of Jesus Christ. God's grace appeared when Jesus was born, when He ministered and taught and healed and raised the dead, when He suffered and died and rose again, and when He appeared to many believers after His resurrection. Through all of these wonderful events in the life of Jesus, the grace of God has appeared.

The second appearing is a future event: "We wait for the blessed hope— the glorious appearing of our great God and Savior, Jesus Christ." That appearing was a future event when Paul wrote these words, and it is still a future event as I write these words two thousand years later. These are prophetic words that will be fulfilled at some future date. This second appearing of Jesus Christ is our blessed hope.

It's interesting to notice the Greek words Paul uses to speak of these two appearings: *epiphaino* and *epiphaneia,* from which we get our English word *epiphany.* This word means a brilliant manifestation of light, a shining forth, as when the sun rises and illuminates the world. In fact, the *New English Bible* beautifully captures the majesty of the original language in these words: "For the grace of God has dawned upon the world with healing for all mankind."

A message of love and grace

Now, notice the distinction between these two appearings. The first was the appearing of the grace of our Lord Jesus. The second is the future appearing of His glory. His grace and his glory are two very different things. Since His first appearing, we have lived in the age of grace. Because of His first appearing, His grace is made available to us through faith. By grace, through the first appearing of the Lord Jesus, God reaches out to humanity.

During this age of grace, the first subject on God's agenda is not judgment but love. As Jesus told Nicodemus, "For God did not send his Son into the world to condemn the world, but to save the world through him" (John 3:17). We sometimes forget that the good news of Jesus Christ is, first of all, a message of love and grace.

I once attended a luncheon sponsored by Campus Crusade for Christ. At this event, several people stood and gave testimonials to the blessing of the ministry of Campus Crusade in their lives. One man startled us all by saying, "As a Christian, I've had a deep feeling of resentment against Campus Crusade for many years."

Hearing that, I wondered, *Resentment? How could any Christian resent a ministry that had been instrumental in bringing thousands of young people to Christ?* This man had captured my attention—and the attention of everyone in the room.

"The thing I resented," he continued, "was the Campus Crusade booklet called *The Four Spiritual Laws*. As you know, the laws are: (1) God loves you and has a wonderful plan for your life. (2) Humanity is sinful and separated from God. (3) Jesus Christ is God's only provision for our sin. (4) We must receive Jesus Christ as Lord and Savior in order to experience God's love and plan for our lives.

"Well, I read these four laws, and I thought, 'All Campus Crusade did was take the three points of our Southern Baptist Plan of Salvation and add one more point at the beginning! Then they print it up and call it *The Four Spiritual Laws*, like it's something they invented! They should have given credit to the Southern Baptists! So I felt resentful against Campus Crusade for years.

"Then one day it hit me: I had tried witnessing with the Plan of Salvation many times, but without much success. The three-point plan begins, 'You are a sinner, and if you acknowledge your sin, God will save you.' I would go to people and tell them they were sinners, but I could never get them to admit it!

"Three weeks ago, I decided to try *The Four Spiritual Laws* and see what happens. I started out with the first law: 'God loves you and has a wonderful plan for your life.' And in the past three weeks, using this approach, I have led four men to Christ. I know what made the difference: Instead of starting out with God's judgment, I started out with God's love."

This man made a profound discovery that we all need to understand: Ever since Jesus came, the first subject on God's agenda has been love. If we want to reach our generation for Christ, then our agenda must match His: We must start with the love and grace of Christ.

Though the first item on God's agenda is His gracious love, it's not the only item on His agenda. If human beings reject His love, then God must eventually move to the next subject on His agenda: judgment. And judgment, for those who reject His grace, results in condemnation. But for those who receive His grace, the result is salvation.

Paul writes, "For the grace of God that brings salvation has appeared to all men." We should not assume that salvation merely refers to life after death in heaven. Paul, in this passage, clearly tells us that salvation truly means a saved and effective way of life here and now. He adds that the grace of God, and the salvation it brings, "teaches us to say 'No' to ungodliness and worldly passions, and to live self-controlled, upright and godly lives in this present age, while we wait for the blessed hope."

Salvation is an altered allegiance. To be saved means that we renounce ungodliness and worldly passions. To be saved means that we live self-controlled and godly lives now, even while we wait for our eternal life with Christ to begin, either through His return or through our passage through death into glory.

During the fourth century, the heresy of Arianism arose within the church—a false teaching that denied the doctrine of the Trinity and asserted that Jesus Christ is not truly God. Emperor Flavius Julius Constantius (son of Constantine the Great, who had Christianized the Roman Empire) was won over to the Arian heresy and began persecuting orthodox believers. He had a special hatred for the faithful bishop of Alexandria, Egypt, a man named Athanasius.

The emperor demanded that Athanasius come before him and recant his belief that Jesus Christ is truly God—or risk execution. Standing before the emperor, Athanasius stoutly refused to surrender his faith in the deity of Christ. Exasperated, Emperor Constantius roared at him, "Stubborn old man! Don't you know that the whole world is against you?"

"Then, Sire," Athanasius calmly replied, "I am against the whole world."

The emperor backed down—and Athanasius lived to a ripe old age.

Sound doctrine sharpens the mind and emboldens the heart. When we are utterly convinced in our own souls that Jesus Christ is not only the Lord of our lives but also the Lord of the universe, we gain the courage to stand firm on our convictions, even if the whole world is against us.

Paul goes on to say that the grace of God teaches us to "live self-controlled, upright and godly lives in this present age." This salvation we have received by grace through faith in Jesus Christ changes the way we live.

A skeptic asked a Christian if he believed in miracles. "Absolutely," the Christian replied. "You mean," the skeptic said, "you believe Jesus could actually change water into wine?" The Christian, a former alcohol abuser, replied, "I certainly do. I've never seen Jesus change water into wine, but in our home He changed beer into furniture." Salvation changes the way we live. When our way of life changes, everything changes.

Paul goes on to say that Jesus "gave himself for us to redeem us from all wickedness and to purify for himself a people that are his very own, eager to do what is good." The key to this statement is the phrase "a people that are his very own." We, as the church, the body of Christ, are the Lord's own possession.

Here is a transcendent mystery embedded in the sound doctrines of our faith: that the God who became incarnate as a newborn baby in Bethlehem is also willing to become incarnate in your life and mine. The secret of a godly life is that God lives in our lives. Paul calls this "the mystery that has been kept hidden for ages and generations, but is now disclosed to the saints... which is Christ in you, the hope of glory" (see Colossians 1:26–27). That is why the Christian faith is not a mere religion, not an empty creed. It is the living Lord, present and active in our lives.

In conclusion

Next, Paul concludes his letter to Titus, showing us what a life looks like that is ruled by truth and sound Christian doctrine. He writes:

> Remind the people to be subject to rulers and authorities, to be obedient, to be ready to do whatever is good, to slander no one, to be peaceable and considerate, and to show true humility toward all men.
>
> At one time we too were foolish, disobedient, deceived and enslaved by all kinds of passions and pleasures. We lived in malice and envy, being hated and hating one another. But when the kindness and love of God our Savior appeared, he saved us, not because of righteous things we had done, but because of his mercy. He saved us through the washing of rebirth and renewal by the Holy Spirit, whom he poured out on us generously through Jesus Christ our Savior, so that, having been justified by His grace, we might become heirs having the hope of eternal life. This is a trustworthy saying. And I want you to stress these things, so that those who have trusted in God may be careful to devote themselves to doing what is good. These things are excellent and profitable for everyone. (Titus 3:1–8)

Paul wants Titus to remind his congregation to live peaceful lives, obedient and submissive to the authority of the government. The lives of the Cretan Christians should, Paul says, be characterized by good deeds, good speech (no slander or gossip), a gentle spirit, and considerate behavior toward everyone, without exception.

The apostle again identifies himself with the people of Crete. "At one time we too were foolish, disobedient, deceived and enslaved by all kinds of passions and pleasures," he says. "We lived in malice and envy, being hated and hating one another." Paul does not feel superior to the people of Crete because he, too, sinned greatly before his conversion to Christ. He is modeling a humble and repentant attitude to Titus—the attitude he wants Titus to display among the Cretans.

Paul lists eight sinful characteristics he has shared with the Cretans. He says that he, too, has been foolish, disobedient (in a hard-hearted sense), deceived by Satan, enslaved by lust, filled with malice (bitterness), envy, and hate. The kindness of God has saved him from all of those sinful tendencies, and God is faithful to save the Cretans from those sins as well.

And there is the issue of church peace and unity, which Paul underscores near the end of this letter:

> But avoid foolish controversies and genealogies and arguments and quarrels about the law, because these are unprofitable and useless. Warn a divisive person once, and then warn him a second time. After that, have nothing to do with him. You may be sure that such a man is warped and sinful; he is self-condemned. (Titus 3:9–11)

In other words, Paul wants Titus to teach the Cretan Christians to maintain their love for each other and their unity in the body of Christ. To do this, they must shun the behaviors that lead to factions and divisions, including foolish controversies and pointless arguments and nitpicking quarrels.

Moreover, Paul warns Titus against a certain kind of person who often worms his way into the church and causes division. Paul says that divisive people should be warned twice—and if they continue to serve up divisions, they are to be shunned by the congregation. In today's parlance, three strikes and you're out. People who persist in such sins, even after two warnings, are unwilling to change. They enjoy stirring up trouble. They condemn themselves by their stubborn and persistent sin.

With that, Paul has dealt with all the major issues that are likely to arise in the church in Crete. He has instructed Titus thoroughly in everything he needs to do to provide strong leadership, sound doctrinal teaching, and effective peacemaking in the Cretan church.

Paul's goodbye

Now Paul closes his letter with a personal note:

> As soon as I send Artemas or Tychicus to you, do your best to come to me at Nicopolis, because I have decided to winter there. Do everything you can to help Zenas the lawyer and Apollos on their way and see that they have everything they need. Our people must learn to devote themselves to doing what is good, in order that they may provide for daily necessities and not live unproductive lives. (Titus 3:12–14)

The identity of Artemas is uncertain, though ancient tradition holds that he was one of the seventy disciples whom Jesus sent out to minister in His name (see Luke 10), and he later became a traveling companion of the apostle Paul.

Tychicus was a faithful companion of Paul, mentioned in Acts and in four of Paul's letters. He was at Paul's side during both of his imprisonments in Rome. During Paul's second and final imprisonment, Paul mentions Tychicus to Timothy: "I sent Tychicus to Ephesus" (2 Timothy 4:12).

Paul urges Titus to provide help and hospitality to two travelers. One is Apollos, that mighty Bible scholar and preacher who was discipled by Priscilla and Aquila in Ephesus (see Acts 18). The other is Zenas the lawyer, of whom nothing else is said in Scripture. These two men will be passing through Crete as missionaries, and Paul wants Titus to help them in their ministry.

The apostle closes with these words: "Everyone with me sends you greetings. Greet those who love us in the faith. Grace be with you all" (Titus 3:15).

I believe there is far more to these words than meets the eye. This is more than just a sign-off at the end of one of Paul's many letters to churches and ministry partners in the ancient world. I believe this is Paul's message to you and me from the other side of that great impenetrable curtain called death.

Paul has passed through that curtain. He is there with his friends and loved ones, with the people who shared his risks and sufferings on the missionary road. Artemis and Tychicus are there with him, as are Zenas and Apollos, Priscilla and Aquila, Luke the physician and John Mark the evangelist, Barnabas and Silas, and Paul's two sons in the faith, Timothy and Titus.

Stephen is there as well—that first martyr who was stoned to death while a proud Pharisee named Saul of Tarsus stood by, giving his approval.

And above all, there is Jesus, Paul's beloved Lord and Savior, who died and gave himself for us all. By the grace of the Lord Jesus, Saul of Tarsus became Paul, the great apostle to the Gentiles. And by His grace, you and I are saved so that we can live to serve Him.

"Everyone with me sends you greetings," Paul now calls to us. "Greet those who love us in the faith." All of the great saints of the past call to us as well. They not only send their greetings but also cheer us on as we run this race that Paul has already completed—the race of the Christian life.

Finally, I end this book with Paul's closing words:

"Grace be with you all."

Notes

Chapter 6—The First Thing: Prayer

1. Jerry Cook with Stanley C. Baldwin, *Love, Acceptance, and Forgiveness: Equipping the Church to Be Truly Christian in a Non-Christian World* (Ventura, CA: Regal Books, 1979), pp. 69–70.

Chapter 11—The Great Mystery

1. C. S. Lewis, *Mere Christianity* (London: Collins, 1952), p. 54.

2. William Temple, *Readings in St. John's Gospel* (New York: Macmillan, 1952), p. 382.

Chapter 15—Caring for Widows

1. Dave Branon, "On Creaky Knees," *Our Daily Bread*, published by RBC International, November 1998 issue, entry for November 11, 1998.

Chapter 18—The Cost of Riches

1. Steve McVicker, "Billie Bob's (Mis)Fortune," *The Houston Press*, February 10, 2000, retrieved at http://www.houstonpress.com/2000-02-10/news/billie-bob-s-mis-fortune/; Deena Winter, "Financial Planners: Winning the Lottery Isn't Always a Dream," *The Lincoln Journal Star*, Saturday, February 25, 2006, retrieved at http://www.journalstar.com/articles/2006/02/25/special/doc4400ffe394163444263790.txt.

Note to the Reader

The publisher invites you to share your response to the message of this book by writing Discovery House Publishers, P.O. Box 3566, Grand Rapids, MI 49501, U.S.A. For information about other Discovery House books, music, videos, or DVDs, contact us at the same address or call 1-800-653-8333. Find us on the Internet at http://www.dhp.org/ or send e-mail to books@dhp.org.